To Bugsy

Happy Birthday

with love

from

"Bibba & U"

July·1973

DUVEEN

S. N. BEHRMAN

Little, Brown and Company
Boston and Toronto

The text of this book appeared originally as
a series of articles in *The New Yorker*, and was
first published in the United States of America in
book form in 1952 by Random House Inc., New York,
and simultaneously in Toronto, Canada, by
Random House of Canada, Limited.

The quotation from Bernard Berenson's
Sketch for a Self-Portrait are reprinted in
this volume by courtesy of Pantheon Books Inc.
The lyric from 'Blue Boy Blues' by Cole Porter on
page 151 is reprinted by courtesy of
Chappell & Co., London.

Library of Congress Catalog Card No. 78-183995
This edition first published in the United States
of America in 1972 by
Little, Brown and Company,
34 Beacon Street, Boston, Massachusetts 02106

This book was designed and produced by
George Rainbird Ltd,
Marble Arch House, 44 Edgware Road, London W.2
House Editor: Alison Cathie
Designer: Pauline Harrison
Indexer: Myra Clark

Text printed and bound by Jarrold & Sons Ltd, Norwich
Color printed by Westerham Press Ltd, Westerham, Kent

Printed in Great Britain

To William Shawn

Author's Note

The author wishes to thank the
following people for their extraordinary generosity
in sharing with him their recollections
of Joseph Duveen:

Bernard Berenson   Sam A. Lewisohn

Sir Cecil Beaton   Mrs Henry R. Luce

Sir Maurice Bowra   W. Somerset Maugham

Max Bruell   Elsa Maxwell

Lord Clark   Mr and Mrs Gilbert Miller

Count Alessandro Contini-Bonacossi   Mitchell Samuels

Lady Juliet Duff   Sir Osbert Sitwell

Edmund Duffy   Nate B. Spingold

Sir John Foster   Maurice Sterne

Dr Alfred M. Frankfurter   Mr and Mrs Edwin C. Vogel

Mrs William Randolph Hearst   John Walker

Alva Johnston   Felix Wildenstein

Louis S. Levy   Frank Wooster

Color Plates

Ghirlandaio: Francesco Sassetti and his Son Teodoro 17
Rembrandt: A Young Man Seated at a Table 18
Memmi: St John the Baptist 27
Franco-Flemish School: Profile Portrait of a Lady 28
Botticelli: Portrait of a Youth 29
Donatello: St John the Baptist 30
Lawrence: Pinkie 39
Romney: Mrs Davenport 40
Francia: Federigo Gonzaga 49
Benedetto da Maiano: The Virgin Annunciate 50
Dürer: The Virgin and Child with St Anne 51
Luca della Robbia: Madonna and Child 52
Mantegna: Judith and Holofernes 61
Raphael: The Small 'Cowper' Madonna 62
Van Dyck: Queen Henrietta Maria and her Dwarf 79
Ter Borch: Curiosity 80
Velásquez: The Infanta Maria Theresa 89
Verrocchio: Lorenzo de' Medici 90
After Raphael: Giuliano de' Medici, Duke of Nemours 91
Goya: Don Manuel Osorio de Zuñiga 92
Desiderio: The Young Christ with St John the Baptist 101
Holbein: Edward VI 102
Bulgarini: Nativity 119
Master of the Castello Nativity: Profile Portrait of a Lady 120
Sassetta and Assistant: The Meeting of St Anthony and St Paul 129
Giorgione: The Adoration of the Shepherds 130–131
Crivelli: Madonna and Child 132
Reynolds: Mrs Siddons as the Tragic Muse 141
Gainsborough: The Blue Boy 142
Reynolds: Lavinia, Countess Spencer and her son, Viscount Althorp 159
Hals: Balthasar Coymans 160
de Hooch: A Dutch Courtyard 177
van der Weyden: Portrait of a Lady 178
Filippo Lippi: Madonna and Child 187
Giotto: Madonna and Child 188
Daddi: Madonna and Child with Saints and Angels 189
Bellini: St Jerome Reading 190
Vermeer: The Smiling Girl 199
Rembrandt: Aristotle Contemplating the Bust of Homer 200

Contents

Chapter 1

ITINERARY 9

Chapter 2

A BEGINNING IN DELFT 45

Chapter 3

A BRISK MARKET IN IMMORTALITY 75

Chapter 4

B.B. 113

Chapter 5

THE BLUE BOY AND TWO LAVINIAS 143

Chapter 6

THE SILENT MEN 171

Catalogue of 500 masterpieces sold by Duveen 214
Acknowledgments for Illustrations 227
Index 229

Lord Duveen on his travels

Chapter I
ITINERARY

WHEN Joseph Duveen, the most spectacular art dealer of all time, travelled from one to another of his three galleries, in Paris, New York, and London, his business, including a certain amount of his stock-in-trade, travelled with him. His business was highly personal, and during his absence his establishments dozed. They jumped to attention only upon the kinetic arrival of the Master. Early in life, Duveen – who became Lord Duveen of Millbank before he died in 1939, at the age of sixty-nine – noticed that Europe had plenty of art and America had plenty of money, and his entire astonishing career was the product of that simple observation. Beginning in 1886, when he was seventeen, he was perpetually journeying between Europe, where he stocked up, and America, where he sold. In later years, his annual itinerary was relatively fixed: at the end of May, he would leave New York for London, where he spent June and July; then he would go to Paris for a week or two; from there he would go to Vittel, a health resort in the Vosges Mountains, where he took a three-week cure; from Vittel he would return to Paris for another fortnight; after that, he would go back to London; some time in September, he would set sail for New York, where he stayed through the winter and early spring.

Occasionally, Duveen departed from his routine to help out a valuable customer. If, say, he was in Paris and Andrew Mellon or Jules Bache was coming there, he would considerately remain a bit longer than usual, to assist Mellon or Bache with his education in art. Although, according to some authorities, especially those in his native England, Duveen's knowledge of art was conspicuously exceeded by his enthusiasm for it, he was regarded by most of his wealthy American clients as little less than omniscient. 'To the Caliph I may be dirt, but to dirt I am the Caliph!' says Hajj the beggar in Edward Knoblock's *Kismet*. Hajj's estimate of his social position approximated Duveen's standing as a scholar. To his major pupils, Duveen extended extra-curricular courtesies. He permitted Bache to store supplies of his favourite cigars in the vaults of the Duveen establishments in London and Paris. One day, as Bache was leaving his hotel in Paris for his boat train, he realized that he didn't have enough cigars to last him for the Atlantic crossing. He made a quick detour to Duveen's to replenish. Duveen was not in Paris, and Bache was greeted by Bertram Boggis, then Duveen's chief assistant and later one of the heads of the firm of Duveen Brothers. While Bache was waiting for the cigars to appear, Boggis showed him a Van Dyck and told him Duveen had earmarked it for him. Bache was so entranced with the picture that he bought it on the spot and almost forgot about the cigars; he finally went off to the train with both. There was no charge for storing the cigars, but the Van Dyck cost him two hundred and seventy-five thousand dollars.

Probably never before had a merchant brought to such exquisite perfection the large-minded art of casting bread upon the waters. There was almost nothing Duveen wouldn't do for his important clients. Immensely rich Americans, shy and suspicious of casual contacts because of their wealth, often didn't know where to go or what to do with themselves when they were abroad. Duveen provided entrée to the great country homes of the nobility; the coincidence that their noble owners often had ancestral portraits to sell did not deter Duveen. He also wangled hotel accommodation and passages on sold-out ships. He got his clients houses, or he provided architects to build them houses, and then saw to it that the architects planned the interiors with wall space that demanded plenty of pictures. He even selected brides or bridegrooms for some of his clients, and presided over the weddings with avuncular benevolence. These selections had to meet the same refined standard that governed his choice of houses for his clients – a potential receptivity to expensive art.

On immediate issues, Duveen was not a patient man. With choleric imperialism, he felt that the world must stop while he got what he wanted. He had a convulsive drive, a boundless and explosive fervour, especially for a picture he had just bought, and a reckless contempt for works of art handled by rival dealers. On one occasion, an extremely respectable High Church duke was considering a religious painting by an Old Master that Thomas Agnew & Sons, the distinguished English art firm, had offered him. He asked Duveen to look at it. 'Very nice, my dear fellow, very nice,' said Duveen. 'But I suppose you are aware that those cherubs are homosexual.' The painting went back to Agnew's. When, presently, through the tortuous channels of picture-dealing it came into Duveen's possession, the cherubs, by some miraculous Duveen therapy, were restored to sexual normality. Similarly, in New York, a millionaire collector who was so undisciplined that he was thinking of buying a sixteenth-century Italian painting from another dealer asked Duveen to his mansion on Fifth Avenue to look at it. The prospective buyer watched Duveen's face closely and saw his nostrils quiver. 'I sniff fresh paint,' said Duveen sorrowfully. His remarks about other people's pictures sometimes resulted in lawsuits that lasted for years, cost him hundreds of thousands of dollars, and brought to the courts of London, New York, or Paris international convocations of experts to thrash things out.

It was one of the crosses Duveen had to bear that the temperaments of the men he dealt with in the United States were the direct opposite of his own. The great American millionaires of the Duveen Era were slow-speaking and slow-thinking, cautious, secretive

– in Duveen's eyes, maddeningly deliberate. These other emperors, the emperors of oil and steel, of department stores and railroads and newspapers, of stocks and bonds, of utilities and banking houses, had trained themselves to talk slowly, pausing lengthily before each word and especially before each verb, in order to keep themselves from sliding over into the abyss of commitment. For a man like Duveen, who was congenitally unable to keep quiet, the necessity of dealing constantly with cryptic men like the elder J. P. Morgan and Henry Clay Frick and Mellon was ulcerating. He would read a letter from one of his important clients twenty times, pondering each evasively phrased sentence. 'What does he mean by that?' he would ask his secretary. 'Is he interested in the picture or isn't he?'

For a great many years, Duveen's secretary was an Englishman named H. W. Morgan. Some have said that Duveen hired him simply because his name was Morgan. It has even been suggested that Duveen made his secretary adopt the name, so that he could feel he was sending for Morgan instead of Morgan's sending for him. In any case, one of H. W. Morgan's duties was now and then to impersonate Mellon. The day before a scheduled interview with any of his important clients, Duveen would go to bed to map out the strategic possibilities. But before such an interview with Mellon, Duveen would, in addition to going to bed, rehearse with Morgan. Mellon was particularly hard to deal with, because he was supremely inscrutable. 'Now, Morgan, you are Mellon,' Duveen would say. 'Now you go out and come in.' Morgan would come in as Mellon, and Duveen would start peppering him with questions; Morgan would try to put himself into Mellon's inscrutable state of mind and answer without saying anything. The fact that Mellon's Pittsburgh speech was now doused in Cockney did not impair the illusion for Duveen.

Duveen sometimes came home from a talk with Mellon so upset by Mellon's doubts that he had to go back to bed, this time to ponder the veiled issues. There were never any doubts in his own mind. Each picture he had to sell, each tapestry, each piece of sculpture was the greatest since the last one and until the next one. How could these men dawdle, thwart their itch to own these magnificent works, because of a mere matter of price? They could replace the money many times over, but they were acquiring the irreplaceable when they bought, simply by paying Duveen's price for it, a Duveen. (When a Titian or a Raphael or a Donatello passed from Duveen into the hands of Joseph E. Widener or Benjamin Altman or Samuel H. Kress, it became a Widener or an Altman or a Kress, but until then it was a Duveen.) Still, Duveen learned to bear this cross, and even to manipulate it a bit. While coping with their doubts, he solidified his own convictions, and then charged them extra for the time and trouble he had taken doing it. Making his clients conscious that whereas he had unique access to great art, his outlets for it were multiple, he watched their doubts about the prices of the art evolving into more acute doubts about whether he would let them buy it.

Whenever Duveen was in Paris or Vittel, he received daily reports from his galleries in New York and London – précis of the Callers' Books, telling what customers or nibblers had come in, what pictures they had looked at and for how long, what they had said, and so on. From other sources he got reports on any major collections being offered for sale, and photographs of their treasures. There were also reports from his 'runners', the *francs-tireurs* he deployed all over Europe to hunt out noblemen on the verge of settling for solvency and a bit of loose change at the sacrifice of some of their family portraits. These reports might include the gossip of servants who had overheard the master saying to an important art dealer, as they savoured the bouquet of an after-dinner brandy, that he might – in certain circumstances, he just might – consider parting with the lovely titled Gainsborough lady smiling graciously down at them from over a mantel. Once Duveen had such a clue, he hastened to telescope the circumstances in which the Gainsborough owner just might. Often the dealer who had enjoyed the brandy did not find himself in a position to enjoy the emolument that went with handling the Gainsborough. In negotiating with the heads of noble families, Duveen usually won hands down over other dealers; the brashness and impetuosity of his attack simply bowled the dukes and barons over. He didn't waste his time and theirs on art patter (he reserved that for his American clients); he talked prices, and big prices. He would say, 'Greatest thing *I* ever saw! Will pay the biggest price *you* ever saw!' To this technique the dukes and barons responded warmly. They were familiar with it from their extensive experience in buying and selling horses.

In Paris, Duveen often got frantic letters from his comptroller in New York imploring him to stop buying. Duveen, who was never as elated by a sale as he was by a purchase, usually laid out over a million dollars on his annual trip abroad, and occasionally three or four times that sum. These immoderate disbursals of money paralleled the self-indulgence of Morgan. Frederick Lewis Allen, in his biography of Morgan, writes, 'As for his purchases of art, they were made on such a scale that an annual worry at 23 Wall Street at the year end, when the books of the firm were balanced, was whether Morgan's personal balance in New York would be large enough to meet the debit balances accumulated through the year as a result of his habit of paying for works of art with cheques drawn on the London or the Paris firm.' Each man, his bookkeeper thought, spent too much on art.

Duveen's finances were a puzzle to his friends, his clients, his associates, and other art dealers. In July 1930, when art dealers all over the world were gasping for money, he stupefied them by paying four and a half million dollars for the Gustave Dreyfus Collection. Bache, who was a close friend as well as a client, once said, 'I think I understand Joe pretty well – his purchases and his sales methods. But I confess I am quite in the dark about his financing.' Depression or no depression, it was Duveen's principle to pay the highest conceivable prices, and he usually succeeded in doing so. Adherence to this principle required finesse, sometimes even lack of finesse. A titled Englishwoman had a family portrait to sell. Duveen asked her what she wanted for it. Meekly, she mentioned eighteen thousand pounds. Duveen was indignant. 'What?' he cried. 'Eighteen thousand pounds for a picture of this quality? Ridiculous, my dear lady! Ridiculous!' He began to extol the virtues of the picture, as if he were selling it – as, indeed, he already was in his mind – instead of buying it. A kind of haggle in reverse ensued. Finally, the owner asked him what he thought the picture was worth. Duveen, who had already decided what he would charge some American customer – a price he could not conscientiously ask for a picture that had cost him a mere eighteen thousand pounds – shouted reproachfully at her, 'My dear lady, the very least you should let that picture go for is twenty-five thousand pounds!' Swept off her feet by his enthusiasm, the lady capitulated.

Duveen had enormous respect for the prices he set on the objects he bought and sold. Often his clients tried, in various ways, to manoeuvre him into a position where he might relax his high standards, but he nearly always managed to keep them inviolate. There was an instance of this kind of manoeuvring in 1934, which concerned three busts from the Dreyfus Collection – a Verrocchio, a Donatello, and a Desiderio da Settignano. Duveen offered this trio to John D. Rockefeller, Jr, for a million and a half dollars. Rockefeller felt that the price was rather high. Duveen, on the other hand, felt that, considering the quality of the busts, he was practically giving them away. He allowed Rockefeller, in writing, a year's option on the busts; they were to remain for a year in the Rockefeller mansion as non-paying guests. During that time, Duveen hoped, the attraction the chary host felt for his visitors would ripen into an emotion that was more intense. After several months, the attraction did ripen into affection, but not a million and a half dollars' worth, and Rockefeller wrote Duveen a letter with a counter-proposal. He had some tapestries for which he had paid a quarter of a million dollars. He proposed to send Duveen these tapestries, so that *he* could have a chance to become fond of *them*, and to buy the busts for a million dollars, throwing the tapestries in as lagniappe. As the depression was still on and most people were feeling the effects of it, Rockefeller thought, he said, that Duveen might welcome the million in cash. This letter threw Duveen into a flurry. It bothered him more than most letters he got from clients. His legal adviser told him that the counter-offer, unless immediately repudiated, might result in a cancellation of the option. Duveen sat down and wrote a letter himself. As for the tapestries, he told Rockefeller, he had some tapestries and didn't want any more. Moreover, he stated, he was not in the stock market, and therefore not in the least affected by the depression. He let fall a few phrases of sympathy for those who were; by his air of surprised incredulity at the existence of people who felt the depression, Duveen managed to convey the suggestion that if Rockefeller was in temporary financial difficulty, he, Duveen, was ready to come to his assistance. He appreciated Rockefeller's offer of a million dollars in cash, but he implied that, just as he already had some tapestries, he also already had a million dollars. Having dispatched the letter, Duveen, with his customary optimism, prophesied to his associates that Rockefeller would eventually buy the busts at his price. At Christmas time, with a week or so of the option still to go, Rockefeller told Duveen that his final decision was not to buy the busts, and asked Duveen to take them back. Again, Duveen was prepared to be generous, this

'The Ministry of the Marine', Lord Duveen's gallery in New York

time about the security of Rockefeller's dwelling. 'Never mind,' he said. 'Keep them in your house. They're as safe as they would be in mine.' In all love affairs, there comes a moment when desire demands possession. For Rockefeller, this occurred on the day before the option expired. On the thirty-first of December, at the eleventh hour, he informed Duveen that he was buying the busts at a million and a half.

On his visits to Paris, Duveen often gazed admiringly at the building occupied by the Ministry of Marine, a beautiful production of the illustrious Jacques-Ange Gabriel, court architect to Louis XV. The noble façade executed by Gabriel stretches its lovely length to front an entire block along the Place de la Concorde. The Ministry consists of a tremendous central edifice, flanked by great wings. One day, in his lively imagination, Duveen snipped off and reduced in size one of Gabriel's wings and saw it transferred to New York. With his immense energy and drive, he set about materializing this snip at once. In 1911, he engaged a Philadelphia architect, Horace Trumbauer, and a Paris architect, Réné Sergent, to put up a five-storey, thirty-room reproduction of Gabriel's wing at the corner of Fifth Avenue and Fifty-sixth Street, to serve as his gallery. Even the stone was French – imported from quarries near St Quentin and Chassignelles. The total cost was a million dollars, but this was not too much for an establishment that was to house the Duveen treasures. The eight or ten big clients who would enter the building – the handful of men with whom Duveen did the major part of his business – to look at the garnered possessions of kings and emperors and high ecclesiastics were rulers, too, and must be provided with an environment that would tend to make them conscious of their right to inherit these possessions.

In Paris, Duveen always stayed at the Ritz. A permanent guest at this hotel, with whom Duveen had many encounters over the years, was Calouste S. Gulbenkian, the Armenian oil Croesus. Gulbenkian, who controlled a good deal of the oil in Iraq, was often said to be the richest man in Europe, and possibly in the world, and possessed one of the world's most valuable art collections. Of all his achievements, perhaps the most chic is that he several times outmanoeuvred Duveen. One day, happening upon Duveen in one of the Ritz lifts, Gulbenkian told him that he knew of three fine English pictures for sale – a Reynolds, a Lawrence, and a Gainsborough. The owner wanted to sell them in a lot. Gulbenkian proposed that Duveen buy them and give him, as a reward for his tip, an option on any one of the three, with this proviso: Duveen was to put his own price on them before Gulbenkian made his choice known, but the total price was not to exceed what Duveen had paid. Duveen bought the pictures and went about setting the individual prices. As he wanted from Gulbenkian a sum that would become the richest man in Europe, he pondered deeply before deciding which picture he thought Gulbenkian would choose. The finest, although the least dazzling, of the three was Gainsborough's 'Portrait of Mrs Lowndes-Stone'. The showiest was the Lawrence. Duveen concluded that the Lawrence would have the greatest appeal to his client's Oriental taste. He put a Duveen price on the Lawrence, and therefore had to set reasonable figures for the two others. He overlooked the fact that Gulbenkian was a canny student of art as well as an Oriental. Gulbenkian took the Gainsborough. It was one of the few times anyone acquired a Duveen without paying a Duveen price for it.

Altogether, Duveen wasn't fortunate in his dealings with Gulbenkian. He tried hard, but he didn't meet with the success that favoured him in his dealings with his American clients. Not only that, an effort Duveen made in 1921 to get a couple of Rembrandts for Gulbenkian led to an acrid lawsuit in which he found himself in the embarrassing position of having to testify against one of his best American clients, Joseph E. Widener, the celebrated horse and traction man. The paintings, 'Portrait of a Gentleman with a Tall Hat and Gloves' and 'Portrait of a Lady with an Ostrich-Feather Fan', were considered very good Rembrandts. The Russian Prince Felix Youssoupoff, the slayer of Rasputin, had inherited them. He left Russia for Paris rather hurriedly after the Revolution, but he managed to take the pictures with him. Soon, finding himself in need of cash, he proposed to Widener, whom he went to see in London, that he lend Widener the pictures in return for a loan of a hundred thousand pounds. Widener replied that he was not in the banking business; he would buy the pictures for a hundred thousand pounds, but he wouldn't lend a penny on them. Widener returned to New York, and after some weeks of negotiating by cables and letters, Youssoupoff signed a contract in which he agreed to sell Widener the pictures for a hundred thousand pounds, with the understanding that Widener would sell them back for the same sum, plus eight per cent annual interest, if on or before 1 January 1924 (and here Youssoupoff was expressing a nostalgia for the future), a restoration of the old régime in Russia made it possible for Youssoupoff again 'to keep and personally enjoy these wonderful works of art'. Just about this time, Gulbenkian indicated to Duveen a hankering for Rembrandts. Duveen took hold of Gulbenkian's wistfulness and turned it into an avid melancholy. 'If you're interested in Rembrandts,' he said, 'you've just lost the two best in the world to Widener. He bought them both for a hundred thousand pounds, and each of them is worth that.' Gulbenkian was indignant that a man of Rembrandt's talent should sell for less than he was worth; he was willing to give the artist his due. News of Gulbenkian's suddenly developed sense of equity was transmitted to Youssoupoff, who was delighted to hear that Rembrandt was coming into his own. On the strength of the two hundred thousand pounds that seemed about to accrue to the artist, Youssoupoff felt he was in a position to ask Widener to give his pictures back. This he did. Widener wanted to know what revolution had taken place that would enable the Prince to enjoy the pictures again. Youssoupoff said that it was none of his business. Widener said that an economic revolution had been stipulated in the contract, and that if

Opposite Ghirlandaio: 'Francesco Sassetti and his Son Teodoro'. One of the paintings from the Benson Collection which Duveen sold to his 'pupil' Jules Bache. It was one of the prizes of his collection, which he donated to the Metropolitan Museum in New York, and was the frontispiece in the catalogue Duveen prepared for him.

Youssoupoff was going to be so reticent, he jolly well wasn't going to get the pictures. Youssoupoff's reply to this was to bring suit against Widener for the return of the pictures.

This lawsuit, which was heard in the New York Supreme Court in 1925, was something less than urbane. Emory R. Buckner, one of Youssoupoff's lawyers, contended that the Prince had merely mortgaged the paintings to Widener for a hundred thousand pounds at eight per cent, and another of the Prince's lawyers called Widener a 'pawnbroker'. Clarence J. Shearn, a third lawyer, declared that Widener was a sharp trader who had taken in a gentleman. With extraordinary reserve, he abstained from making even harsher allegations against Widener. 'I could shout "perjury" from the housetops,' he said. 'I could say that Widener is a thief, a perjurer, and a swindler. This is not necessary. He has drawn his own picture on the witness-stand.' Duveen, called in by the defence as a witness, gave the court a somewhat different picture of Widener. He testified that Widener had, in the past few years, bought six hundred thousand dollars' worth of art from him, and he, Duveen, had told him that the Widener name on his books was good enough for him. 'You can pay when you want,' he had said. Youssoupoff's lawyers, during their attempt to establish that Widener had taken advantage of Youssoupoff, countered by putting Duveen on the stand as a witness for the plaintiff. Duveen testified that he had once offered the Prince five hundred and fifty thousand dollars for the two Rembrandts and that the Prince had wanted a million. At the Prince's price, Duveen said, he himself could have made only ten per cent on whatever deal he might have effected. Sometimes, though, he said, he did sell at a very small profit, sometimes even at a loss. 'I sold some art once to Mr Widener for three hundred and fifty thousand dollars, and I sold to him losing the interest,' he said. 'That seems to be the usual way with people who deal with Mr Widener,' Shearn observed. There was an objection, and he withdrew the remark, but at least he had had the pleasure of making it. Later in his testimony, Duveen let it be known that his enthusiasm for the disputed Rembrandts had diminished; there were better ones, he said, than the Prince's pair. He mentioned one he himself had sold to Widener. After all, Youssoupoff's Rembrandts had never been Duveen's.

Other unconventional vignettes were drawn at the trial. The art dealer Arthur J. Sulley, Widener's London agent, who had delivered the hundred thousand pounds to Youssoupoff in the form of two cheques – one for forty-five thousand pounds and one for fifty-five thousand – testified that when the Prince came to his office to sign the contract and pick up the cheques, he brought along several friends, who kept snatching at the cheques

Opposite Rembrandt: 'A Young Man Seated at a Table'. The Wachtmeister Rembrandt acquired by Duveen for $410,000, which he later sold to Andrew Mellon

before the contract was signed. Sulley had had to hold them over his head to keep the friends from grabbing them, he said. They told him they merely wanted to look at the cheques. When Widener, who had written Youssoupoff asking him to keep the entire transaction secret, was asked why he had done that, he testified, 'I didn't think it would be a good thing to have it known publicly that large sums of money were being spent for works of art at that time. I thought it might tend to foster a spirit of Bolshevism.' This was one of the many occasions on which the millionaires of the era demonstrated that they thought it expedient for their conspicuous consumption to be kept inconspicuous.

Gulbenkian's name was brought into the suit early. Shearn stated that Gulbenkian, as a *beau geste*, had advanced money to Youssoupoff to buy the pictures back and that Youssoupoff, out of courtesy, had insisted on Gulbenkian's taking a lien on them. The defence, on the other hand, set out to prove that Gulbenkian wanted to get hold of the pictures for himself, not for Youssoupoff, that Youssoupoff was not trying to put himself in a position 'to keep and personally enjoy' the pictures but simply trying to sell them for a higher price. The Prince tried to raise the dispute to a less tawdry plane. On the stand, he made it clear that he considered Gulbenkian's offer the fiscal equivalent of a new régime in Russia, and that he felt that Widener, in his insistence on a return of the Romanovs, was being technical. He went on to say that he came of a Russian family that had been worth half a billion dollars, and that, despite the Revolution, he owned a summer home in Geneva worth a hundred and seventy-five thousand dollars and a house in Paris worth forty-five thousand dollars. There was also an estate in Brittany worth seven hundred and fifty thousand dollars; his family had given it to the French government, but he was expecting to get it back any minute. Several days later, the Prince took the stand again and testified that he had forgotten to mention seventy thousand dollars' worth of jewelry in

Left *Calouste Gulbenkian;* right *Prince Felix Youssoupoff*

The Widener Rembrandts: left *'Portrait of a Gentleman with a Tall Hat and Gloves';* right *'Portrait of a Lady with an Ostrich-Feather Fan'*

England and a New York bank account amounting to $62,250. One of Widener's lawyers said tartly, 'By all this haziness and loss of memory, do you want to appear to the Court as being very simple?' 'I do not want to appear to the Court,' replied the Prince with manly modesty. 'I want only to be myself as I am.'

Widener, unnecessarily complicating matters for himself, mentioned the fact that Youssoupoff not only had signed the contract but also had sent him a cable confirming the closing of the deal. When Widener was asked to produce the cable, he couldn't find it. 'I concede that the cable couldn't be found,' Shearn said generously, 'because it appears quite plain that such a cablegram was never sent.' The Interstate Commerce Commission at that time required that the cable companies keep duplicates of cables for a year, but after the year was up, the companies destroyed them. 'All anyone would have to do if they were impelled by a sinister motive,' Shearn continued, 'would be to wait a year and then testify as to the contents of a fictitious cable, the actual sending of which could never be traced, especially if the plaintiff in such a case were to bring along a host of retainers and secretaries to swear as to the contents of such an unproduced cablegram as against the emphatic denial that such a message was sent from the person who is alleged to have sent it.' Goaded by these remarks, Widener sent several Pinkertons to Lynnewood Hall, his estate in Elkins Park, outside Philadelphia, where they ripped pillowcases open and peered into the secret compartments of antique escritoires, but the missing cable did not turn up. Nevertheless, Widener won the case. The Court decided that his contract with Youssou-poff amounted to a sale, and that if Gulbenkian were permitted to lend the Prince the money to buy the pictures back, Gulbenkian would be the man 'to keep and personally enjoy' them. A year before Widener's death, the Rembrandts went to the National Gallery in Washington, where they now hang. Months after the suit was over, the missing cablegram fell out of an old studbook in the Widener living-room.

When Duveen was in London, he stayed at Claridge's, and his suite there, like his accommodation at all points on his itinerary, was transformed into a small-scale art gallery. He had infallible taste in decoration – even his detractors admit that – and he arranged the paintings, sculptures, and *objets d'art* he travelled with so that his clients and friends could visit him in a proper setting, and possibly take home some of the furnishings. He was never without a favourite picture (invariably the last one he had bought), and he kept it beside him on an easel whenever he dined in his suite and took it along to his bedroom when he retired. At Claridge's, titled ladies from all over Europe, and merely rich ones from America, would drop in to see him. With his long succession of lady clients – the first one he attracted, when he was fairly young, was the remarkable Arabella Huntington, the wife of, consecutively, Collis P. Huntington and his nephew H. E. Huntington – Duveen seems to have had the relationship Disraeli had with Queen Victoria; he gave them the exciting sense of being engaged with him in momentous creative enterprises. The ladies felt that he and they were fellow-epicures at the groaning banquet table of culture.

One of Duveen's closest London friends in the days between the two World Wars was Lord D'Abernon, the British Ambassador to Germany during the early 1920s. Lord D'Abernon used to describe Duveen as an exhilarating companion. It was his interesting theory that Duveen's laugh, which was famous, was a copy of the infectious laugh of a well-known British architect; Duveen's partiality for architects started early. Everyone agrees that his enthusiasm was irresistible, and that he engaged in a kind of buffoonery that was irresistible. Most of his friends were, like D'Abernon, older men, and they enjoyed his company partly because he made them feel young. Duveen was even able to rejuvenate some of his pictures. Once, in the late afternoon, he was standing before a picture he had sold to Mellon, expatiating enthusiastically on its wonders to the new owner. A beam from the setting sun suddenly reached through a window and bathed the picture in a lovely light. It was the kind of collaboration Duveen expected from all parts of the universe, animate and inanimate. When his dithyramb had subsided, Mellon said sadly, 'Ah, yes. The pictures always look better when you are here.'

In London, Duveen occasionally, and uncharacteristically, devoted himself to the artistic tutoring of a non-buyer who was not even a potential buyer. For a period, with the tenderness of a master for a pupil whose aesthetic perceptions were virginal, Duveen piloted Ramsay MacDonald, then an M.P., around the London galleries. This had the look of a disinterested favour, and it was one, for MacDonald came from a social stratum that did not indulge in picture-buying. But even Duveen's altruism proved to be profitable. MacDonald became Prime Minister in 1929, and shortly afterward Duveen was appointed

Duveen with Queen Mary at the Tate Gallery looking at a group portrait by Sargent. On the left is Lord D'Abernon, and on the right King George V.

to the Board of the National Gallery, a distinction that had never before been conferred on an art dealer and that caused a scandal and a rumpus. Was it decorous for a man on the selling end of art to be on the buying end of a publicly supported institution? Neville Chamberlain, who became Prime Minister in 1937, didn't believe it was, and he revoked the appointment. This deposition shadowed the last years of Duveen's life. Earlier, however, MacDonald and Duveen had a good time sitting next to each other at board meetings of the National Gallery, and in 1933 the grateful pupil brought Duveen the apple of the peerage. At a birthday dinner for MacDonald, given by Duveen at his beautiful house in New York, at Ninety-first Street and Madison Avenue, a few years before, the visiting Prime Minister had announced, 'I think I know what Sir Joseph's ambition is. If it's the last act of my life, I shall get it for him.' Very helpful to MacDonald was Lord D'Abernon. An English observer of the scene at the time says that Lord D'Abernon wrought mightily for Duveen to get him the peerage. Lord D'Abernon, this friendly contemporary recalls, was for many years the head of an Anglo-Turkish Bank. 'His lifelong experience in dealing with Turks,' he says, 'had equipped Lord D'Abernon fully to understand Duveen.' That understanding, properly allocated, assisted Duveen in his elevation to the peerage. Duveen had been knighted in 1919; he had been made a baronet in 1927; and now, in 1933, he was made a baron. Very often, Englishmen elevated to the peerage have

Lord D'Abernon, one of Duveen's close friends

commemorated their home town in their titles, as Disraeli did Beaconsfield. But Duveen, who had no settled home for a long time except for the house on Madison Avenue, chose to commemorate the section of London known as Millbank, because that is where the Tate Gallery, to which he had made numerous gifts, is situated. So he became Lord Duveen of Millbank.

Each time Duveen arrived in New York from London, there were fanfares of publicity for him and his most recent fabulous purchases. Past numbers of the *Herald Tribune* are studded with Duveen titbits, such as:

FEBRUARY 19, 1926

Sir Joseph Duveen, the art dealer, has bought the Wachtmeister Rembrandt for $410,000, one of the highest prices ever paid for a Rembrandt, and is bringing it to New York. The painting, which is called 'Portrait of a Young Man', was sold by Count Carl Wachtmeister and it has been in the possession of his family for 200 years.

JULY 18, 1927

Sir Joseph Duveen, international art dealer, bought in London yesterday the entire collection of 120 Italian old masters belonging to Robert H. Benson. It will be brought intact to New York. The purchase price was $3,000,000.

JANUARY 7, 1929

LONDON: Andrew W. Mellon, Secretary of the Treasury of the United States, has purchased

The announcement of Duveen's barony

SIR JOSEPH DUVEEN, BT.
New Baron. Great benefactor to art. Trustee, the National Gallery, the Wallace Collection, and the Imperial College of Art. Director of Duveen Brothers, London, and President of Duveen Brothers, of New York and Paris.

[from Duveen] for $970,000 Raphael's 'Madonna', known as the 'Cowper Madonna'. The painting bears Raphael's signature and the date '1508'.

Once, Duveen brought back Gainsborough's 'The Blue Boy', which he had already sold, in Paris, to Mr and Mrs H. E. Huntington; another time, he brought back Law-rence's 'Pinkie', the portrait of a girl who sat for Lawrence when she was twelve, in the last year of her life, and whose brother became the father of Elizabeth Barrett. There were tearful farewells for both these eminent children when they left their native heath, and jubilant welcomes when they arrived in their adopted land. The circumstances attending Duveen's purchase of 'Pinkie', in 1926, illustrate his tenacity in the fight he made to establish his pre-eminence among the art dealers of the world. His chief rival in America was the venerable firm of Knoedler. When Duveen was starting out, Knoedler had arrangements with Mellon and several other big collectors to make all their art purchases for them, on a fixed commission. From the beginning, Duveen felt that his educational mission was twofold – to teach millionaire American collectors what the great works of art were, and to teach them that they could get those works of art only through him. To establish this *sine qua non* required considerable daring and a lot of money. When it was announced that 'Pinkie' was to be sold at auction at Christie's, in London, a partner in Knoedler's came to Duveen, who was then in London himself, with the suggestion that they buy it jointly. Knoedler's, he said, had a client he was sure would take it. Duveen suspected that the motive for this friendly overture was to keep him from forcing the price up for the prospective buyer, and he politely declined. The Knoedler man said that no one could outbid his client. Duveen said that no one could keep him from buying 'Pinkie'. On the eve of the sale, Duveen went to Paris, leaving behind him an unlimited bid with the manager of Christie's. In Paris, he awaited the result, with increasing nervousness. On the day of the sale, he informed his friends that he was buying a great picture, that he had once sold it himself for a hundred thousand dollars, and that, as a rich bidder was interested, the price might go to two hundred thousand. That evening, he learned that he had paid three hundred and seventy-seven thousand dollars for 'Pinkie'. When he recovered from the shock, he brought the young lady to New York and gave her a lavish reception at his Ministry of Marine. While she was being ogled by an invited throng, Duveen

Opposite *Memmi: 'St John the Baptist'. The painting was attributed by Bernard Berenson to Memmi's brother-in-law Simone Martini, and was sold by Duveen as a Martini to Samuel H. Kress.*

Overleaf left *Franco-Flemish School: 'Profile Portrait of a Lady'; right Botticelli: 'Portrait of a Youth'. Both paintings were in the Clarence H. Mackay Collection, and were later sold to Mellon. Berenson, who attributed the first portrait to Pisanello, said of the second that it was 'more Botticellian than any other Botticelli in existence'.*

telephoned Mellon, in Washington (he had known all along who his rival's rich client was), and offered her to him for adoption. Mellon said that he had indeed been trying to get her but that Duveen had paid an outrageous price for her and he wasn't interested. Duveen admitted that the price he had paid was steep, but he repeated his cardinal dictum: 'When you pay high for the priceless, you're getting it cheap.' Another saying of his, endlessly repeated to his American clients, was 'You can get all the pictures you want at fifty thousand dollars apiece – that's easy. But to get pictures at a quarter of a million apiece – that wants doing!' Duveen now repeated this to Mellon, too. Mellon, having heard all this before, was still not interested. Duveen then told Mellon that 'Pinkie' was being offered to him as a courtesy, because a man of his taste was worthy of her, but that if he thought her price too high, it was all right, because he had another prospective purchaser. Mellon was sceptical, and he was still not interested. The next morning, Duveen tele-phoned H. E. Huntington, at San Marino, the Huntington mansion near Pasadena. The mansion is today a public art gallery and library, and there 'Pinkie' now hangs.

This demonstration to Mellon of the *sine qua non* principle was worth all Duveen's trouble. Mellon did not make the same mistake again. When, shortly afterward, the Romney 'Portrait of Mrs Davenport' was put up for auction at Christie's, Knoedler's once more suggested to Duveen that he go shares with them, and once more Duveen refused. To get revenge, Knoedler kept bidding until the picture cost Duveen over three hundred thousand dollars, the highest price ever paid for a Romney. Duveen was less vindictive than they were; despite Mellon's earlier lapse, Duveen offered him the Romney, and Mellon immediately bought it.

In his five decades of selling in the United States, Duveen, by amazing energy and audacity, transformed the American taste in art. The masterpieces he took there have fetched up in a number of museums that, simply because they contain these masterpieces, rank among the greatest in the world. He not only educated the small group of collectors who were his clients but created a public for the finest works of the masters of painting. ' . . . Years from now,' Lincoln Kirstein wrote in the *New Republic*, 'art historians . . . may investigate the ledgers of Duveen, as today they do the Medici.' The phenomenon of Duveen was without precedent. In the eighteenth century, Englishmen making the Grand Tour bought either from the heads of impoverished families or directly from the artists, as, three hundred years before, Francis I bought from Leonardo da Vinci. Generally speaking,

Opposite *Donatello: 'St John the Baptist'. One of Donatello's masterpieces acquired by Duveen as part of the Dreyfus Collection and subsequently sold to Mellon* the nineteenth-century collectors of all nations operated on the same basis. There had never before been anyone like Duveen, the exalted middleman, and he practically monopolized his field. Fifty-five of the hundred and fifteen pictures, exclusive of American portraits, in the Mellon Collection, which is now in the National Gallery in Washington, came to Mellon through Duveen. Of the seven hundred paintings in the Kress Collection, also in the National Gallery, more than a hundred and fifty were supplied by him, and these are the finest. It has been stated by the eminent American art scholar Dr Alfred M. Frankfurter that except for the English collections that were put together in the eighteenth and nineteenth centuries, America has the largest aggregation of Italian pictures outside Italy. Of these, according to Dr Frankfurter, seventy-five per cent of the best went there through Duveen.

When the twentieth century began, the American millionaires were collecting mainly Barbizons, or 'sweet French' pictures, and English 'story' pictures. They owned the originals of the Rosa Bonheur prints that one can remember from the parlours of one's youth – pastoral scenes, with groups of morose cattle. Those pictures are now consigned to the basements of the few big private houses that still exist or the basements of museums that no longer have the effrontery to hang them. Troyons, Ziems, Meissoniers, Bou-guereaus, Fromentins, and Henners crowded the interstices of the mother-of-pearl grandeur of the living-rooms of the American rich, and their owners dickered among themselves for them. When Charles Yerkes, the Chicago traction magnate, died in 1905, Frederick Lewis Allen says in *The Lords of Creation*, 'his canvas by Troyon, "Coming from the Market", had already appreciated forty thousand dollars in value since its purchase.' Duveen changed all that. He made the Barbizons practically worthless by beguiling their luckless owners into a longing to possess earlier masterpieces, which he had begun buying before most of his American clients had so much as heard the artists' names. Duveen made the names familiar, and compelled a reverence for them because he extracted such over-whelming prices for them. Of the Barbizon school, only Corot and Millet now have any financial rating, and that has greatly declined. A Corot that in its day brought fifty thousand dollars can be bought now even for a few hundred, and Millet is even worse off.

Although the French painter Bouguereau represented the kind of art that Duveen was eager to displace, he was flexible enough to make use of him in order to bring the education of the Duveen clientèle up to his level. A highly visible nude by the French master was used by Duveen as an infinitely renewable bait to bring the customers who successively owned it sensibly to rest in the fields in which Duveen specialized. This Bouguereau travelled to and from Duveen's, serving – a silent emissary – to start many collections. Clients enrolled in Duveen's course of study would buy the Bouguereau, stare at it for some time, get faintly tired of it, and then, as they heard of rarer and subtler and more expensive works, grow rather ashamed of it. They would send it back, and Duveen would replace it with something a little more refined. Back and forth the Bouguereau went. Sometimes, Duveen amused himself by using it for a different purpose – to cure potential customers who had succumbed to the virus of the ultra-modern. Some collectors who had started with painters like Picasso and Braque grew hungry for a flesh-and-blood curve after a while, and presently found themselves with the travelling Bouguereau. Duveen sent it to them for a breather, and afterwards they went the way of the group that had started with the Bouguereau.

Duveen has been called by one of his friends 'a lovable buccaneer'. Whether he was or not, he forced American collectors to accumulate great things, infused them with a fierce pride in collecting, and finally got their collections into museums, making it possible for the American people to see a large share of the world's most beautiful art without having to go abroad. He did it by dazzling the collectors with visions of an Elysium through which they would stroll hand in hand with the illustrious artists of the past, and by making other dealers emulate him. His rivals could no longer sell their old line of goods, and the result was that he elevated their taste as well as that of his customers. An eminent English art dealer whose family has been in the business for five generations and who could never endure Duveen says, nevertheless, that with Duveen's death an enormously vital force went out of the trade. In the 1970s the dealers are still living off the collections he made, from the descendants of the original collectors. Duveen had a cavalier attitude towards prospective clients, and there was a certain majesty about it. He ignored Detroit for years after it became rich. Then its newly made millionaires came to him, and they were delighted to be asked to dine at Lord Duveen's. Once, when he was told that Edsel Ford was buying pictures, and was asked why he didn't pay some attention to him, he said, 'He's not ready for me yet. Let him go on buying. Some day he'll be big enough for me.'

When Duveen entered the American art market, he was barging into a narrow field and one that was dominated by long-established dealers. Duveen not only barged into this field but soon pre-empted it, although, for the most part, his American clients didn't especially care for him. 'Why should they like me?' he once asked one of his attorneys rhetorically. 'I am an outsider. Why do they trade with me? Because they've got to. Because I've got what they can't get anywhere else.' The daughter of one client, who competed with Duveen in a long contest for her widowed father's attention and ultimately lost, would tell in a voice still weary with frustration, how Duveen managed to elude her even when she was sure she had him in a corner. Once, her father had asked several friends to their home to inspect some of his latest acquisitions from Duveen. Among the guests, in addition to Duveen himself, was a distinguished art connoisseur. She showed the connoisseur, a French count, around the gallery in which her father housed his collection of paintings.

The count was full of admiration for them until he came to a Dürer that Duveen had sold her father for four hundred and fifty thousand dollars. Then the expert's face darkened. His hostess urged him to explain what was bothering him. He looked around, spotted his host and Duveen at a distance, and whispered, 'I'm terribly sorry, but I don't think this Dürer is the real thing.' To his horror, his companion triumphantly summoned her father and Duveen. 'Count X—— thinks that this Dürer is not genuine!' she cried as they approached. The host turned a stricken countenance to Duveen. Duveen's famous laugh pealed out. 'Now, isn't that amusing?' he said to his client. 'That's really very amusing indeed. Do you know, my dear fellow, that some of the greatest experts in the world, some of the very greatest experts in the world, actually think that this Dürer is not genuine?' Duveen had reversed the normal order of things. Somehow, the expert who was present, as well as all the experts who were not present, became reduced in rank, discredited, pulverized to fatuousness.

On another occasion, the beleaguered daughter, with Duveen and her father, was inspecting a house that Duveen had chosen for them, and which they eventually bought. She said it was too big – it had eighteen servants' rooms – and running it would be a terrible chore for her. 'But Joe thinks it's beautiful,' her father said. A few days later, the three of them, now accompanied by Duveen's aide Boggis, were looking at the house again. Duveen enlarged on its potentialities, then abruptly looked at his watch. 'No more time today,' he said, firmly but not unkindly. 'What about tomorrow, Joe?' the humble millionaire wanted to know. Again Duveen's famous laugh rang out. He turned to Boggis. 'What am I doing tomorrow, Boggis?' he asked. Boggis knew. 'Tomorrow, Lord Duveen, you have an appointment in Washington with Mr Mellon,' he said. Against this there was no argument. The client automatically accepted his lesser place in the Duveen hierarchy, grateful for the blessings he had received that day.

Sir Osbert Sitwell had an interesting theory about Duveen – that he was a master exploiter of his own gaffes. He expounds it in one volume of his memoirs, *Left Hand, Right Hand!*: *

> Since the following anecdote often appears in the press, I had better recount it myself, correctly. In later years, and especially in 1926, when I visited New York, I used to see a certain amount of Lord – then Sir Joseph – Duveen, and several times went to his house there. The following summer I met him at the opening day of some exhibition in the Leicester Galleries, and he rushed up to me, and said, 'Oh, my dear *Mr Lytton Strachey*, I am so glad to see you again'.
>
> Lytton and I were not much alike, for I was tall, fair, clean-shaven, and certainly by no means thin, whereas he was bone-thin and angular, as well as tall, and bearded, with something of the reflective

* Macmillan, London 1945

air of a pelican. In fact, no two people could have resembled each other less. Consequently, I tele-graphed to him: 'Delighted to inform you that I have this morning been mistaken for you by Sir Joseph Duveen. Osbert'. Lytton telegraphed back: 'One can only say again how utterly duveen. Lytton'. [The 'again' was a reference to a celebrated remark made by the late Belle da Costa Greene, director of the Pierpont Morgan Library, when she was first shown through the art collection in Jules Bache's Fifth Avenue house: 'How utterly duveen!'] Sir Joseph, with his expert amiability, which resembled that of a clownish tumbler on the music-hall stage, heard of these telegrams and sub-sequently always referred to them at some moment of any luncheon or dinner party at which he and I happened both to be present, appealing to me to 'tell the story about Strachey'. Being a remarkably astute man in most directions, I think that, in this different from most people, he enjoyed having the stupid side of his character emphasized; it constituted a disguise for his cleverness, a kind of fancy dress. . . . After the story had been related, he used to add, '*Of course* I knew Osbert Sitwell. I love his books. He's written about *my country*.' At first this statement rather surprised me, until I compre-hended that by it he meant Scarborough and the district round, which are said to figure in my novel *Before the Bombardment*.

Left *Belle da Costa Greene;* right *her employer, J. Pierpont Morgan, 'the Lorenzo the Magnificent of American Collectors'*

Sir Osbert's surprise at Duveen's reference to his 'country' was due to the fact that Duveen was so seldom in England. Indeed, he was sometimes assumed to be an American, he was there so much. (It was only in America that he was always taken for an Englishman.) To counteract this notion, Duveen, who was actually a native of Yorkshire, bought a country home in Kent. He rarely visited it, however. In his New York gallery, Duveen was a stickler for keeping up the correct English tone. The members of his staff, in the words of a former associate, were invariably 'dressed like Englishmen – cutaways and striped trousers'. The censorship of the staff was linguistic as well as sartorial. You could drop an 'h' there with impunity, but under no circumstances pick up an Americanism. One day, a Duveen employee, throwing caution to the winds, said 'O.K.' Duveen was severe. This was unbecoming in an English establishment, a colonial branch of the House of Lords, engaged in the business of purveying Duveens. After that, Duveen was yessed in English.

The S.S. Berengaria, *the liner which Duveen chartered for an exhibition of paintings for his clients*

Duveen looked like a conservative English businessman. He was of middle height, stocky build, and ruddy, almost apoplectic colouring. He had clear, penetrating grey eyes and a cropped moustache. He exuded opulence. He sometimes played golf or went to the theatre, but only half-heartedly; he was interested in practically nothing except his business. He never carried more than a little cash; money in small amounts was something he didn't understand. His valet decided what he would need for incidentals and provided him with it. When he dressed Duveen, he would put in his pocket a few bills to enable him to get about. Once, when the valet was ill, Duveen said that he, too, would have to take to his bed, because there was no one to give him cash for taxi fares. Duveen was meek towards his valet, but in general he was imperious. He had the Oriental habit of clapping his hands when he wanted people; an acquaintance who visited the British Museum with him recalls that Duveen clapped his hands even in that august institution, and that the attendants came running. After becoming a peer, he was proud of being a member of the House of Lords and would occasionally drop in there, to prove that he could. Politics meant little to him, but when he wanted to terminate an interview, he would suddenly remember that he had a political side. 'Sorry, old man, but I've got to go to the Lords,' he would say. 'Important measure coming up.'

His peerage was a psychological implement for Duveen. His American clients appreciated it, perhaps the more because of an obscure, subconscious awareness that they had paid for it. Americans grown great in industry or finance have their little vanities and the routes by which they satisfy them are sometimes indirect. A few years ago, the head of a prosperous enterprise in New England boasted that the specialist at the head of one of his departments was in *Who's Who*; he didn't, he said ingenuously, mind a bit not being in it himself, since those on his pay-roll made it! He had the quiet air of a King-maker. Lord Duveen impressed his American clients more than Sir Joseph had impressed them; the succession of titles had an ameliorative influence on the effect that had been created early, in certain quarters, by plain Joe Duveen. When he was exalted to the peerage Duveen was not above flinging his weight about a bit; this had a business justification in a milieu that flaunted less traditional slogans, celebrating the accumulation of stocks, bonds, copra, rugs, automobiles, advertising accounts and circus elephants. Mr John W. Ringling, the great circus man, was not a regular Duveen customer because Duveen seldom had pictures vast enough to interest him. Mr Ringling was ignited only by enormous pictures; his visual standard was set by the test of what you could plainly see from the ring-side seats at one of his own shows. He bought pictures by acreage and as a result got to own the biggest and also some of the finest Rubens in existence, which are now housed in a museum named after him in Sarasota, Florida.

That Duveen was detached about his Lordship, that he was able to put it on and off in harmony with the occasion, like a white tie, is demonstrated by an instance when he threw it right out of the window of a distinguished drawing-room. This was when he was invited to spend the night at Chatsworth, the historic home of the Duke of Devonshire. A chiselled instinct, sharpened in infinite forays, whispered to Duveen that the Duke of Devonshire would not be impressed by him just because he was a member of the House of Lords. He had the feeling that the Duke must have met a couple and that they were no novelty. After dinner on the day he arrived, his host led him into the drawing-room. Duveen wanted a Riccio bronze that someone had whispered to him the Duke might sell. Duveen didn't settle down to bore his host with aimless chatter about fox-hunting or Parliamentary procedure. He went straight to the bronze, stood behind it, put his hand on it, and invoked a long since vanished avatar. The ducal drawing-room was charged instantly, by the firm tones vibrating through it, with the tingle of a public auction. 'Joe Duveen speakin', Your Grace! Sixty thousand pounds for this bronze! Joe Duveen's price, Your Grace. Going, Going, Gone!' The Duke didn't sell the bronze but he was enchanted. He told his librarian that if he ever sold anything at any time it must go to Duveen.

Like some of his clients, Duveen seldom read anything. (It has been suggested that a number of his American clients gobbled up his wares with such avidity because they could thus indulge in expensive contemplation without making the painful effort of reading.) But if a book said something about a picture Duveen was interested in, he was eager to see it. His impetuosity was sometimes extreme. Once, when the custodian of an immensely valuable collection of books on art he kept in the Ministry of Marine brought him a rare volume he wanted, he seized it and tore out of it the pages he was after, to free himself from the encumbrance of irrelevant text.

The favoured art critics who were permitted to use Duveen's library say that in his time it was in some respects superior to the Metropolitan's and Frick's. One critic, looking up an item in another rare volume, found an irate criss-cross of pencil marks over the passage he was after, and, scribbled in the margin, the words 'Nonsense! It's by Donatello!' Shocked by this vandalism, he took the book to the librarian, who said calmly, 'Oh, Joe's been at it again.' Duveen's habit of editing by mutilation impaired the pleasure of students using the library. To books that weren't in his library Duveen was flamboyantly indifferent. Once, on the witness-stand, opposing counsel asked him if he was familiar with Ruskin's *The Stones of Venice*. 'Of course I've heard of the picture, but I've never actually seen it,' he answered. When his error was later pointed out to him, he laughed and said he'd *always* thought Ruskin was a painter, and not a very good one, at that.

Opposite Lawrence: 'Pinkie'. One of the many fine English portraits which Duveen sold to H. E. Huntington

Duveen was more interested in the theatre than books. His favourite play, which he thought illustrated a great moral lesson, was an English comedy, *A Pair of Spectacles*, adapted from the French by Sydney Grundy, and first produced in London in 1890. It was about a kindly and gentle man who gets into all sorts of trouble because, as he starts out from his house one morning, he picks up the wrong pair of spectacles, and thereafter finds himself becoming mean and distrustful. Duveen said that this play showed how necessary it was to look at life through the right glasses, and that it was his function to furnish his clients with the right glasses for looking at works of art. He joked about it, but he believed it. At the theatre, his appreciation of a funny line was sometimes given audible expression five minutes after the rest of the audience had got the point. He didn't mind at all impersonating the guileless and traditional British Blimp; speaking of himself, he often repeated the formula for giving an Englishman a happy old age: tell him a joke in his youth. He had a fondness for basic humour. A friend, chiding him about his persistent litigiousness, made the mistake of telling a 'darky' story – the one about the coloured man arrested for stealing chickens who, when confronted by irrefutable evidence, said to the magistrate, 'If it's all the same to you, Jedge, let's forget the whole business!' Duveen made the friend repeat it whenever they met. Perhaps, in the steam bath of litigation in which Duveen was immersed all his life, the number of occasions on which his own attitude towards the judge approximated the coloured man's made him such an enthusiastic audience for this story.

Certain men are endowed with the faculty of concentrating on their own affairs to the exclusion of what is going on elsewhere in the cosmos. Duveen was that kind of man, and the kind of man who, if he met you out walking, would take you along with him, no matter where you were bound or how urgent it was for you to get there. One day, walking along Central Park West, he ran into the art dealer Felix Wildenstein, who was going the other way, bent on what was, to him, an important errand. Duveen, with his infectious friendliness, linked his arm through Wildenstein's and suggested that they go for a walk in the Park. Wildenstein explained that he was hurrying to keep an appointment, but they were presently walking in the Park. Duveen turned the conversation to queries and interesting speculations about his own personality, in which he took a detached but lively interest. 'What do people think about me?' he asked. 'What are they saying about me?' Wildenstein quoted a slightly derogatory opinion a friend had expressed; he had to have some revenge for being so abruptly swept off his course. Duveen was not upset by the

Opposite Romney: 'Portrait of Mrs Davenport'. Acquired by Mellon from Duveen soon after he had refused to buy 'Pinkie' as being too expensive

derogatory opinion. 'That's all right,' he said, as if a favourable opinion *would* have upset him, 'but does he think I am a great man?'

Duveen's New York home was filled with rare and lovely things. To an illustrious Englishman invited to a dinner-party there, Duveen said, as they sat down, 'For you, I'm bringing out the Sèvres!' During dinner, the Englishman overheard Duveen say to another guest, 'How do you like this Sèvres? Haven't used it since Ramsay MacDonald dined here.' Duveen seemed to make a point of showing his multi-millionaire clients that he lived better than they did. One evening, he remarked to Frick that his silverware was not quite in keeping with the many Duveen items in the house. Frick asked Duveen what he should have. The work of the greatest of English silversmiths, Duveen replied, and explained that this master was Paul De Lamérie, who had practised his craft in the eighteenth century; each of De Lamérie's creations was a museum piece, and Frick ought to have only De Lamérie silver in his home. Frick asked his uncompromising guest if he could supply a De Lamérie service. It wouldn't be easy, said Duveen, and it would take time, but he would be willing to accept the commission. Duveen made it a marginal chore for years to pick up vagrant De Lamérie for Frick but he never succeeded in accumulating a complete set.

Duveen's clients, as their friendship with him ripened, saw their homes become almost as exquisite as his. A new house that Frick built in 1913 at Seventieth Street and Fifth Avenue was, in the end, thanks to Duveen's choice of its architect and decorator, a jewel of such loveliness that Duveen could have lived in it himself. Duveen chose the firm of Carrere & Hastings as the architects and his friend the late Sir Charles Allom, who had been knighted by King George V for doing *his* place, as the decorator. The collaboration between Duveen and Allom was comprehensive; Duveen indicated to Allom what precious objects he had in mind for the house and Allom devised places in which to put them. It was Duveen who supplied the paintings for the magnificent Fragonard and Boucher Rooms, to mention only the most famous of the pleasances that have attracted many visitors to what is now the Frick Collection. By the time it was done, the place was beautiful, and Duveen had the comfortable feeling that Frick was living as well as he did.

On one occasion, Duveen found it necessary to subject Frick to the same kind of benevolent but firm discipline to which he later subjected Mellon; that is, to teach him that no great picture was to be obtained except through Duveen. On a night in 1916 Duveen noticed in his host an air at once abstracted and expectant. Duveen was adept at following the nuances of his clients' moods, reaching out antennae to probe their hidden thoughts. He knew there was something in the wind, because Frick, always laconic, on this occasion faded out completely. He finally drew from his client and host the fact that he was on the trail of a really great picture, the name of which he refused to disclose.

Duveen went home and pondered. To allow Frick to buy a great picture through anyone else was unthinkable. He cabled his office in London and inquired whether anybody there knew of an outstanding picture that was for sale. Through the underground of the trade, Duveen found out in a few days that Sir Audley Dallas Neeld, whose home, Grittleton House, was in Wiltshire, was about to sell Gainsborough's 'Mall in St James's Park' to Knoedler's. Obviously, this was the picture Frick had in mind. Knoedler's had an even bigger in with Frick than it had with Mellon; Charles Carstairs, one of the heads of Knoedler's and a man of great charm, was an intimate friend of Frick's. Duveen immediately cabled his English agent exact instructions. He believed that Knoedler's man, sure the Gainsborough was in the bag, would be in no hurry to consummate the deal. Duveen told his agent to take the first train next morning to Wiltshire, tell Sir Audley that he was prepared to outbid everyone else for the picture, and offer him a binder of a thousand pounds to prove it. Duveen got the Gainsborough for three hundred thousand dollars. The next time he dined with Frick, he found his host depressed. 'I've lost that picture,' Frick told Duveen. 'I was on the trail of a very great painting – Gainsborough's "Mall in St James's Park".' 'Why, Mr Frick,' Duveen said, 'I bought that picture. When you want a great picture, you must come to me, because, you know, I get the first chance at all of them. You shall have the Gainsborough. Moreover, you shall have it for exactly what I paid for it.' In the first joy of acquisition, Frick was ecstatically grateful, not stopping to think that Sir Audley would probably have sold the picture to Knoedler's for so much less that Knoedler's price with a profit would have been lower than Duveen's without one. Duveen charged the lost profit off to pedagogy. When he brought the Gainsborough to Frick, he pointed to it triumphantly and laughed his infectious laugh. 'Now, Mr Frick,' he said magnanimously, 'you can send it to Knoedler's to be framed.'

The Duveen Brothers' gallery on Fifth Avenue before it was altered

Chapter 2
A BEGINNING IN DELFT

THE original Duveen establishment, the forerunner of the firm of Duveen Brothers, was a blacksmith shop in the little town of Meppel, in Holland. Joseph Duveen, the proprietor, and his wife, Eva, were Jewish. They had four children – Joseph Joel, born in 1843; Henry born in 1854; and two daughters. The blacksmith's wife must have been a remarkable woman. Although her husband, hammering out horseshoes for the farmers in Meppel, often called Joseph Joel to pump the bellows and Henry to hold the metal on the anvil, she managed, in addition to doing her household chores, to give the boys an elementary education – which was all the education they ever had – and to become a collector in a small way, the only disinterested collector the family has produced. She acquired a hobby that must have been a relaxation to her after the grind of her daily existence. She took to buying bits of Holland's celebrated delft pottery with her small savings. Whatever she could spare from the family budget she put into delft, and in time she became a connoisseur of it. She would send her two boys around the neighbourhood to buy or exchange pieces, and for this particular pottery the children developed a taste that was as perceptive as her own. The blacksmith was humorously condescending about his wife's hobby. Delft was cheap, and he doubtless concluded that she bought it only because she didn't have the money to buy land or houses, as her more fortunate neighbours did. Actually, she bought it not just for that reason but because she loved it passionately. After she had been collecting for some years, the news percolated through to Meppel that across the Channel, in rich and mighty England, there were people who wanted to buy delft even if they could afford to buy other things, and this gave her a startling inspiration. She had loftier hopes for her boys than blacksmithing. In 1866, when Joseph Joel was twentythree, she improvised a career for him; she loaded him with all the delft he could carry, and packed him off to England to sell it.

Joseph Joel was quite happy to go to England, but when he got there he had a change of heart. Selling delft struck him as an unmanly sort of work, and since, like so many of the Dutch, he could speak some English, he decided to become a travelling salesman of more substantial commodities. After experimenting briefly with one unmarketable product after another, he finally hit his stride in lard. His slitherings about in lard took him, in

1867, to the city of Hull, and there, one evening, he met a Miss Rosetta Barnett, the daughter of a local pawnbroker. Either Joseph Joel was taken with her charm or he had reached the point when he wanted to settle down, or both. In any case, he proceeded to rush her, and perhaps because he was tired of carrying it around, he showered her with his mother's delft. Miss Barnett, who had never been wooed with delft before, showed her presents to her father, and he was more impressed by them than she was. Possibly he had made advances on delft to Hull collectors who were hard up. He questioned his daughter's suitor and discovered that there was a great deal more good delft where that came from. He also found out that the young man was knowledgeable about delft but somewhat deprecatory about it. Mr Barnett took a firm line. He didn't like the idea of having a son-in-law in lard, but he was titillated by the idea of having one in delft. He said he would give his consent to the marriage if Joseph Joel would get enough delft from his mother to set up a shop in Hull. Moreover, Mr Barnett said, he would finance the enterprise. Joseph Joel gave up his swashbuckling career in lard, married Miss Barnett, and rented a tiny shop with living quarters above it. From delft, he branched out into furniture and objects of art, learning about his merchandise as he acquired it. He attended to the buying and selling; his wife was treasurer, a task that at first consisted largely of getting her father to put up more money from time to time. The Duveens' business and reputation grew, and so did their family. They produced eight boys and four girls. Their eldest was

A family group at the marriage of Anette Duveen to Montague Abrahams. From the left *Uncle Henry, Sir Joseph Joel* and *Lord Duveen* are *fifth, ninth* and *tenth; their wives* are *eighth, seventh* and *ninth respectively.*

Joseph, the future Lord Duveen of Millbank and the greatest art dealer in history, who was born over the delft-and-furniture shop on 14 October 1869.

The blacksmith's wife, having launched her first argosy successfully, felt justified in launching another. She decided that Henry should undergo a course of instruction under Joseph Joel and then move on to America. If rich Englishmen bought delft, so, she reasoned, would rich Americans. In 1876, after a few years of apprenticeship in Hull, Henry landed in Boston. A rotund, flat-footed little man with a walrus moustache, who had never been to school and who spoke English with a guttural Dutch accent, Henry was to become within a few years the confidant, and the adviser on art purchases, of two of the most inaccessible men in America, the elder J. P. Morgan and Benjamin Altman, as well as of a group of more sociable men that included Collis P. Huntington, P. A. B. Widener, and George J. Gould. It is not recorded that Henry ever gave anything away, but he managed nevertheless to generate an atmosphere of Santa Claus benevolence. His clients, and all his fellow-dealers, were soon affectionately calling him Uncle Henry. When he arrived in Boston, though, he was just a Dutch immigrant with hardly any English and a lot of delft. There was no Miss Barnett in Boston to give his delft to, so he began to peddle it from shop to shop. The architects and decorators of Boston liked his pottery, with its graceful blue designs and charming Dutch genre scenes. After Henry had

One of Uncle Henry's early clients, George J. Gould with his daughter Marjorie

covered Boston thoroughly, he decided to try New York. He rented a room on the third floor of a loft building on Maiden Lane, and set up shop there, expanding his line to include various kinds of china, and also furniture. When he had been in New York less than a year, he felt encouraged enough to write home. 'This is a fine place and I think we will do good business here.' Many years later, his nephew Joseph had this letter framed, and hung it in the office of his Fifth Avenue gallery.

The 'good business' probably began when one day there toiled up the three flights of stairs to Uncle Henry's Maiden Lane establishment a short, stout gentleman with thick glasses, who said, after he had recovered his breath, that he was interested in Chinese porcelains. So was Henry Duveen, and they had a porcelain lovers' chat that ended in the visitor's buying two antique Chinese vases of enamelled copper. The visitor was the department store magnate Benjamin Altman, and this visit led to the accumulation by Altman, through Uncle Henry, of a distinguished collection of Chinese porcelains. The two copper vases are now in the Altman Collection at the Metropolitan Museum. 'Mr Altman's career as a collector began in 1882,' the official handbook on the collection says, 'with the purchase of a pair of Chinese enamel vases (Nos. 44 and 45 in Case C, Room 1) which, for sentimental reasons, he always retained as the beginning of a great under-taking. . . . They are of interest as being the first objects of art which attracted Mr Altman's attention, and he always regarded them with affection as the nucleus from which his entire collection grew.' Altman evidently regarded Uncle Henry with an affection almost as deep. Altman was a bachelor and a recluse. He had no social life to speak of, and he lived frugally. Shortly after his death, Lord Duveen said to an interviewer, 'Though he spent millions on art, he travelled like a Cook's tourist.' Altman's business partner and heir, Michael Friedsam, never forgave Duveen. It is the kind of remark that Uncle Henry would not conceivably have made; it is the kind of remark that his nephew Joseph often made, which is one reason he was never given an affectionate nickname. Lord Duveen was called many things in his lifetime, but never Uncle Joseph – not even by his nephews and nieces. Altman's reluctance to spend money on himself was so great that it may have hastened his death. At the age of seventy-three, he became ill at a resort in the Thousand Islands. His regular doctor was in Europe, and he asked a local doctor to call a certain physician in New York and, without mentioning the name Altman, inquire what he

Opposite *Francia: 'Federigo Gonzaga'*

Overleaf left *Benedetto da Maiano: 'The Virgin Annunciate'; right Dürer: 'The Virgin and Child with St Anne.' Three of the works of art sold by the Duveens to Benjamin Altman*

would charge to come up and take care of a patient. The New York physician, who happened to be a friend of Altman's regular doctor, said that his fee would be a thousand dollars a day. Altman thought it was too steep, and stuck with the local man, whose ministrations were more reasonably priced. By the time Altman could be got to New York, his disease had advanced too far to be effectively treated. Perhaps he comforted himself with the thought that he was achieving a considerable economy by dying. Altman's regular doctor, returning from Europe, was horrified to learn of his patient's death. 'Why didn't he give his name?' he asked a member of the family. 'If he had, Dr A—— would, of course, have gone at once, without bothering about the fee.'

Altman seems to have found Uncle Henry a crony after his own heart. Uncle Henry was a constant visitor at his Fifth Avenue house, and they had orgiastic sessions on ceramics – in Yiddish. In dealing with J. P. Morgan, however, Uncle Henry presumably restricted himself to bad English. Though he could not be as fluent with Morgan as he was with Altman, he nevertheless managed to give him a strong push in the direction of ceramics. In fact, before Uncle Henry was through, Morgan's collection was many times the size of Altman's. Uncle Henry did not drop in casually at Morgan's house as he did at Altman's – Morgan had more insistent social obligations – but he was often invited to breakfast. Morgan was the Lorenzo the Magnificent of American collectors, and Uncle Henry explored with him many realms besides ceramics. By then a big-scale dealer in furniture as well as ceramics, he even, in 1882, furnished Morgan's house on Madison Avenue. Miss Belle da Costa Greene, Morgan's librarian, used to recall an incident that demonstrated not only Uncle Henry's continuously developing critical faculty but his detachment. After the elder Morgan's death, his son wished to redecorate the Madison Avenue house. Knowing that Uncle Henry had done the original job, and realizing how fond his father had been of him, he called him in. Miss Greene accompanied them on a tour of the house. 'Well, Uncle Henry, what do you think of it?' she asked when it was all over. 'It iss orful!' Uncle Henry said, and, undaunted by the horrors around him, set about correcting the errors he and his late patron had accomplished together.

Uncle Henry's migration from Boston to New York was paralleled by Joseph Joel's from Hull to London. Mr Barnett, who seems to have been a pawnbroker with imagination, thought that his son-in-law, after twelve years in Hull, should try the big city. Joseph Joel Duveen was a dictatorial, irascible man, but he did what his father-in-law suggested; he transported his stock to a shop in Oxford Street and, as before, installed his family in

Opposite *Luca della Robbia: 'Madonna and Child'. One of the fine works of the Italian Renaissance which the Duveens sold to P. A. B. Widener*

Anthony 1st Earl of Shaftesbury :
by John Hoskins

Mrs. Pemberton: by Hans Holbein the Younger

Sir Robert Walpole, K.G. :
by Lawrence Crosse

Mrs. Parsons :
by Richard Cosway, R.A.

THE FAMOUS PIERPONT MORGAN COLLECTION OF MINIATURES

Messrs. CHRISTIE, MANSON & WOODS

respectfully give notice that they have been instructed by Mr. J. Pierpont Morgan to sell at auction the renowned collection of Miniatures formed by his father,

at their

GREAT ROOMS, KING STREET, ST. JAMES'S, LONDON, S.W.1, on Monday, June 24, 1935

and three following days, at ONE O'CLOCK precisely each day

This famous Collection, both in its quality and in its comprehensiveness, makes the finest gallery of miniatures formed in modern times, and comprises over eight hundred examples representative of the best work of the British and Continental Schools from the sixteenth to the nineteenth century. In addition to the famous Armada Jewel there are examples by Hans Holbein the Younger, Nicholas Hilliard, Samuel Cooper, John Hoskins, Isaac and Peter Oliver, Richard Cosway, John Smart, F. H. Drouais, George Engleheart, Andrew Plimer, Samuel Shelley, J. H. Fragonard, Peter Adolf Hall, J. B. Isabey, J. B. J. Augustin, and other eminent artists.

The Collection will be on view throughout the week preceding the sale

Catalogues may be had on application to the Auctioneers. Illustrated catalogues, containing 53 plates, price £1

CHRISTIE'S, 8, KING STREET, St. James's, London

*Telephone: Whitehall 5056
Telegraphic Address: "Christiart, Piccy, London"*

King George IV. when Prince of Wales :
by Richard Cosway, R.A.

Henry, Prince of Wales :
by Isaac Oliver

Queen Elizabeth :
by Lavina Teerlinc

Portrait of a Nobleman :
by Isaac Oliver

rooms above it. It must have been quite a clutter, for the stock had grown enormously: English, French, and Italian furniture, French and Gothic tapestries, Chinese porcelains, the mingled aromas of Italian velvets and Spanish leathers, the retrieved handiwork of vanished master craftsmen, and, before long, fourteen Duveens. The former Miss Barnett still presided at the till, handling the books and the cash. Joseph Joel was absorbed in buying, without worrying too much about overstocking – a tendency his eldest son inherited. He had unlimited confidence that he would be able to sell the merchandise once he had got it. Like his eldest son after him, he could never buy enough; as for the financial intricacies, he was perfectly willing to leave them to his wife, just as his eldest son was one day to leave them to his comptrollers. Joseph Joel and his wife carried on a running altercation about insuring their property. He did not believe a fire could ever happen to him and held out stubbornly against insurance. But a fire did happen to him – a bad one – and he was in despair. His wife came forward to save the firm. Joseph Joel's absorption in acquiring merchandise had enabled her to put aside sums of money from time to time, so that in this crisis she had enough to rebuild and restock and get going again. After that, the Duveen property was liberally insured.

The four Duveen girls were sent to school, but the boys – Joseph, Charles, John, Louis, Edward Joseph, Benjamin, Henry, and Ernest – went into the business early. Joseph went briefly to Brighton College, quitting at seventeen. From infancy, the boys were spoon-fed on the lore of their father's inventory. They were put to work in the shop, arranging the

Above J. Pierpont Morgan and his wife driving in their carriage in London; Opposite An advertisement of the sale of the Pierpont Morgan miniatures, some of which were bought by Lord Duveen

stock, running errands, wrapping, dusting, learning prices, and studying their father's
sales technique. By the time they reached their early teens, the sons had already become
aware that survival demanded forthrightness in competition. A family conference, an
observer recalls, was usually a pitched battle. The father's decision, however, always
prevailed. In later life, Joseph was fond of telling stories about how autocratic his father
had been. He remembered that when they all sat at the dinner table in their Oxford Street
quarters, his father used to begin the meal with the command: 'Let no one speak unless I
ask a question.' As he didn't feel that his children could tell him much, there were often
long silences at the table. Another recollection of Duveen's was of being taken by his
father to see the elder J. P. Morgan in his London house, at Prince's Gate. His Uncle
Henry, who had by then become a pet of Morgan's, had told Morgan that his brother was,
next to him, the highest authority on Chinese porcelains. Therefore, Morgan wanted
Joseph Joel to see five Chinese porcelain beakers he had just bought. He showed the
Duveens, father and son, into his library. 'Uncle Henry tells me you know a lot about
porcelains,' he said to Joseph Joel. 'Well, here are five beakers. Three of them are authentic
and two of them are reproductions. Now, if you're such an authority, which are which?'
Joseph Joel peered at the beakers, then lifted his walking-stick and smashed two of them.
He offered, if he'd broken good ones, to pay for them. Morgan was relieved to find that
he could not collect.

The Oxford Street business prospered. The advent of William Morris and his wallpapers enabled Joseph Joel eventually to make a killing in tapestries. The craze for Morris's
wallpapers caused the owners of English country houses to get rid of their tapestries as fast
as they could. Joseph Joel bought them up at bargain prices, and waited for the craze to
pass. Then he began selling them at handsome profits to famished customers. His fame
spread, and the nobility and royalty started to show an interest in his shop. He acquired
three distinguished patrons: the Prince of Wales, later Edward VII, and two of the
Prince's close friends, Lord Esher and the financier Sir Ernest Cassel, a grandfather of the
late Lady Mountbatten. There is a trade legend about Joseph Joel's first meeting with the
Prince of Wales. One day, a gentleman of about Joseph Joel's age came into the shop,
showed the proprietor a piece of jewelry, and asked if he would pay a hundred pounds
for it. Joseph Joel examined it, and then his visitor. He asked him where he had got the
piece. 'Never mind about that,' the caller said. 'It's mine and I want to sell it. Will you
give me a hundred pounds?' 'No,' said Joseph Joel. 'It's worth much more than that. I'll
give you five hundred.' According to the legend, Joseph Joel didn't recognize his visitor.
Those who knew Joseph Joel intimately doubted this. They suspected that he was pretty
sure his petitioner was the Prince of Wales. In any case, when the Prince became King,
in 1901, he had Joseph Joel arrange much of the decoration of Westminster Abbey for

the Coronation. This automatically made Joseph Joel the foremost decorator in England. For this and other services, the King knighted him. The reformed lard salesman, the son of the Dutch blacksmith, became Sir Joseph Joel Duveen. Later, his son Joseph was knighted, and, ultimately, raised to the peerage, by King George V. Uncle Henry had a cosy relationship with King George, cemented by the passion both men had for collecting stamps. The King's cousin, Nicholas II, the Tsar of Russia, was also a serious stamp collector, and also became Uncle Henry's friend. Uncle Henry used to reminisce about tranquil evenings spent in Buckingham Palace, with the King and himself working at their albums, and Queen Mary embroidering. He remembered huddles between the King, Nicky, and himself over stamps; during these sessions, though he was not strictly one of the family, he must have felt almost like a cousin. After Uncle Henry's death, his stamp collection, which he had bequeathed to his wife, was privately sold, for a million and a half dollars. King George's collection is still at Buckingham Palace, and what happened to Nicky's collection is not known. The Duveens dearly loved a queen. Queen Mary was a friend and patron of Joseph Duveen. For many years he often accompanied her to art galleries.

Duveen's Father, Sir Joseph Joel Duveen, painted by Emil Fuchs

The firm of Duveen Brothers, dealers in furniture and objects of virtu, was established in 1879; Joseph Joel Duveen, presiding over the Oxford Street shop, and Uncle Henry, presiding over his Maiden Lane walk-up, were partners. In 1886, Joseph Joel sent his son Joseph, then seventeen, on his first trip to America, to get several months' experience in Uncle Henry's place and to size up the country – a country whose art intake he was to boost so astonishingly and whose taste he was to revolutionize single-handed. He crossed

in the Cunarder *Etruria*; he had heard a great deal about her, and he was disappointed by
her smallness. He was also disappointed by the smallness of Uncle Henry's establishment.
It served well enough for Altman, Morgan, and Uncle Henry, but Joseph didn't care for
it. Before Uncle Henry knew what was up, he had been hustled out of Maiden Lane to
what Joseph considered a more becoming location, on Fifth Avenue just below the old
Waldorf. The Cambridge Hotel, then perhaps the most chic in New York, was also close
by. When the landlord asked for security, Joseph, with the lordly manner King George V
was later to make official, paid him six months' rent in advance. The day he got his
bewildered uncle into the new quarters, somebody came in and asked to look at a certain
tapestry. It was William C. Whitney. Joseph parted with the tapestry for ten thousand
dollars. When he got back to London he reported to his father that not only had he moved
Duveen Brothers to the smartest location in New York but he had acquired for them an
American customer who appeared to have taste. Uncle Henry's attitude towards his
prodigious nephew had about it something of the resignation with which one submits
to a tornado. 'This boy is a genius, but he will drive me crazy,' he said.

One day not long after Joseph's return to London, a stocky gentleman with a marked
Irish brogue, accompanied by his wife, a modest, unassuming little woman in a plumed
hat, walked into the shop in Oxford Street. They looked like a country couple dressed
up for a visit to the city. They asked to see some screens. Joseph Joel had recently had
several made up of fine old Spanish leather, and he told Joseph to bring them out. The
lady, in ecstasy, bought one screen after another. As the sales mounted, the elder Duveen
whispered to his son to find out quickly who these people were. Joseph went into con-
sultation with their coachman – an early instance of his lifelong practice of picking up
useful intelligence from servants. He wrote the customer's name on a slip of paper, and
handed it to his father. 'You may think it strange, Mr Duveen, that I am buying so many
screens,' the woman was saying just then. 'Not at all, Lady Guinness,' replied the
proprietor. 'You have many fine homes, and you are quite right to supply them with
screens.' With the delight of anonymity welcoming recognition, Lady Guinness beamed
at her husband. 'You see, Edward,' she said, 'Mr Duveen knows who we are!' When,
years afterwards, Joseph Duveen told the story to one of the sons of the purchaser of the
screens, Guinness said, 'At last I know why we had such a bloody lot of screens in the
house.'

Since the purchaser, Sir Edward Guinness, later Lord Iveagh, was one of the richest
men in England, the elder Duveen was enchanted by the episode, but it had an entirely
different effect on his son. The pleasure the father took in selling thousands of pounds'
worth of screens to the Guinnesses indicated to the son a circumscribed and unimaginative
outlook. For he knew that while Guinness was picking up these knick-knacks in Oxford

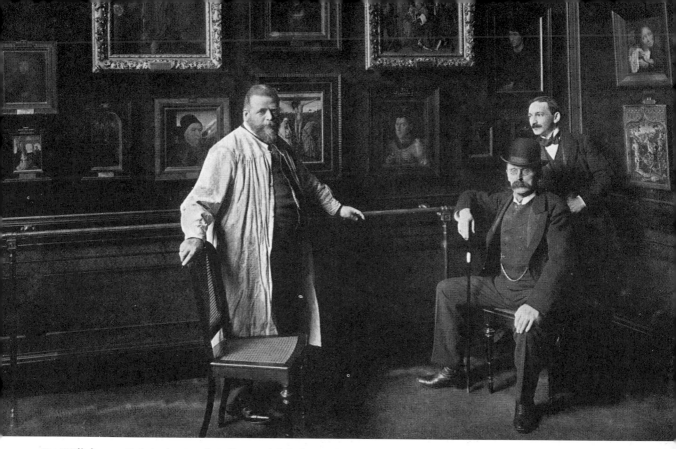

Dr Wilhelm von Bode in the Royal Gallery with left *the picture restorer Professor Hauser, and* right *his assistant Dr Friedländer*

Street for trifling sums, he was spending millions of pounds on paintings and sculptures in Bond Street, chiefly with Agnew's. Guinness, simply by his purchases for his famous art collection at Kenwood House, Hampstead, made Agnew's rich. The inner illumination that sometimes converts playboys into dedicated men, wastrels into saints, must have flared up in Joseph. He determined to deal in paintings and sculptures. His father and Uncle Henry felt that since they knew practically nothing about paintings and sculptures, they had better stick to their own province, which was porcelains, furnitures, tapestries, and silver. Moreover, they were aware that dealing in paintings and sculptures was risky, because of the difficulties in authentication. 'It made me sick at my stomach to see people like Lord Iveagh buying mere art objects from us and paintings elsewhere,' said Joseph Duveen some years later. 'My father was satisfied, my Uncle Henry was satisfied, my brothers were satisfied, but I was not.' His mind, like theirs, was a *tabula rasa* as far as pictures were concerned, but he promptly set about making entries. He began an intensive courtship of experts that was to continue for the rest of his life. The biggest man in the field then was Dr Wilhelm von Bode, director of the Kaiser Friedrich Museum in Berlin, and the world's leading authority on Rembrandt. Duveen went to Berlin and got Dr von

Bode to advise him. He then began to advise his father. With headlong impetuosity, he started to make enormous financial commitments for the firm, and cajoled his father as best he could into stringing along with him. He bought like a man possessed.

Joseph Duveen made his real début as an art dealer in 1901, when he paid the biggest price which up to that time had been paid for a painting sold at a British auction – £14,050. The picture was 'Lady Louisa Manners', by John Hoppner. (He started paying high, and kept stepping it up higher the rest of his life.) The fact that he had to sell his first picture at a loss did not deter him from buying more and more. Finally, in 1906, in Berlin, he soared into the ether and bought for two and a half million dollars the famous Oskar Hainauer Collection, the official catalogue of which had been prepared by Dr von Bode. The price made the newcomer a major figure in the art world. Duveen called his father's attention to the lucky circumstance that the collection contained a vast number of objects of virtu. His father couldn't resist them; indeed, they made the elder Duveen's mouth water so much that he swallowed the paintings too. The objects of virtu in the Hainauer Collection began at once to sell furiously, and this made it easier for Duveen to persuade his father to let him buy another collection – the Rodolphe Kann. Joseph made the point to his father – in talking up the advantage of buying collections, as against buying pictures and sculptures individually – that when one bought a famous collection for a lump sum, the potential repurchaser of a particular item could have no idea of its price, as he would if that item had been sold separately at public auction. You could fix your price at will, and the purchaser had no standard to go by. But the stark fact that stared the elder Duveen in the face was that the art was in his storehouse, the purchasers were non-existent, and the firm's debts were monumental. Joseph bought the Rodolphe Kann Collection at a private sale in Paris, with a loan of five million dollars he got from the firm's bank. As his father suffered from high blood pressure and Duveen didn't wish to send it up still farther, he didn't inform him that this collection consisted almost entirely of pictures and sculptures. His father found it out, however, and the elder Duveen, who had been so happy selling screens and hadn't divined the art hunger of American millionaires, felt that his world was collapsing. Shortly after Joseph's acquisition of the Rodolphe Kann Collection, his father mercifully died of apoplexy.

A few months after his father's death, Joseph Duveen unhesitantly bought still another Paris collection, the Maurice Kann, for which he paid three million dollars. The firm now had nearly ten and a half million dollars invested in three collections – mostly pictures and

Opposite Mantegna: *'Judith and Holofernes'. A Duveen with impeccable ancestry, having come from the collections of Lorenzo de' Medici, Charles I of England and the Earl of Pembroke before the Duveens sold it to Widener*

RAPHAEL SANZIO

[*Umbrian School,* 1483-1520]

The Small "Cowper" Madonna

RAPHAEL (RAFFAELLO SANZIO) *was born at Urbino, April 6, 1483. He died at Rome, April 6, 1520. He was the son of the painter and poet, Giovanni Santi, who died in 1494 and left the orphan to the care of a priest. The boy became a pupil of Perugino and was influenced by Tomoteo Viti and Pinturricchio, and later by Leonardo and Michelangelo. In 1504 he went to Florence, and in 1508 he was called to Rome by Pope Julius II, and painted the Stanze in the Vatican. In 1514 he accepted the office of architect of St. Peter's; in 1515 he was installed as director of the excavations among the ruins of ancient Rome. Among the most important works which he executed, besides the frescoes in the Vatican, may be noted: the Sposalizio, the Madonnas di Foligno, del Pesce, della Sedia, di Sisto, di Loreto, dell' Impannata and Perla; the St. Cecilia, the Transfiguration, the frescoes in the Church of Santa Maria della Pace and in the Villa Farnesina, and several portraits.*

SEATED on a stone bench in the open air, in a quiet landscape, the Madonna holds the naked Child with her left hand, while He thrusts His left foot against her right hand and passes His arms around her neck, at the same time following her gaze in the direction of the worshippers assumed to be present just outside the picture. The hair of both is blond; the eyes brown; the Virgin's dress red and her mantle blue, lined with green. The flesh is radiantly golden, against a sky of pearly blue. On the right there is a country church on a hill, and on the left a stream. The church is probably San Bernardino, a Franciscan convent, a short distance from Urbino.

Wood. *Height,* 23 inches; *Width,* 17 inches.

In the collection of Mr. Joseph E. Widener, Elkins Park, Philadelphia, Pa.

Formerly in the collection of Lord Cowper at Panshanger; purchased by George Nassau, third Earl Cowper, when British Minister in Florence, about 1780, until which time it seems to have remained in a private collection at Urbino.

Exhibited at Manchester, 1857, No. 136; Burlington House, Old Masters, 1881, No. 148; Grafton Galleries, National Loan, 1909-1910, No. 70.

Bibliography:

DR. G. F. WAAGEN: Treasures of Art in Great Britain. London, 1854, Vol. III, p. 9.

J. D. PASSAVANT: Raphael d'Urbin. Paris, 1860, Vol. II, p. 26.

CROWE AND CAVALCASELLE: Life and Works of Raphael. London, 1882, Vol. I, p. 50.

G. MORELLI: Italian Painters. London, 1900, Vol. I, pp. 37 and 79; Vol. II, p. 109.

ADOLPH PAUL OPPÉ: Raphael. London, 1909, plate XXVII.

ADOLF ROSENBERG: Raphael (*Klassiker der Kunst*). Stuttgart, 1909, p. 224, plate 23.

C. HOLROYD: The National Loan Exhibition, Grafton Galleries, 1909-10. No. 70. *Ill.*

BERNHARD BERENSON: Central Italian Painters. New York, 1909, p. 234.

BERNHARD BERENSON: Collection of P.A.B. Widener; Elkins Park, Phila., 1916, No. 17. *Ill.*

ADOLFE VENTURI: Raffaelo. Rome, 1920, pp. 130-131. *Illustrated.*

Above *The page opposite 'The Small "Cowper" Madonna' in Duveen's* Catalogue of Early Italian Paintings Exhibited at the Duveen Galleries, New York, 1924
Opposite *Raphael: 'The Small Cowper Madonna'. The painting which Uncle Henry sold to Widener after Altman's death*

sculptures about which Uncle Henry and Joseph's seven brothers knew very little. Since Joseph did at least know Dr von Bode, he had a great tactical advantage in dealing with his uncle and his brothers. As things worked out, the vast heterogeneity of these three collections formed the backbone of Joseph Duveen's business. Up to the day he died, in 1939, he was still selling pictures and sculptures from these collections: their acquisition so early and the gradual selling of them over a period of nearly four decades has been called, by those close to the art business, the most singular feat of long-range investment in art history. From these three original collections, thirteen pictures eventually went to Altman, three to Frick, and others to H. E. Huntington and Morgan. The last trip Duveen made to see his old friend and client Huntington in California was in 1926. It was not a frivolous trip. He was too modest to think that Huntington wanted to see him for himself alone, so he was accompanied by a freight car containing his wares. Among them were many items from the old Hainauer and Kann Collections. Duveen sold Huntington the entire contents of the freight car. How many times Duveen multiplied his investment of ten and a half million in his first three collections cannot be accurately computed (indeed, as he made clear, that had been one reason for buying them), but the increment was enormous.

Joseph Joel Duveen left his children and Uncle Henry an estate of close to seven million dollars. When the estate was settled, it was found that about two million was in cash. The rest was tied up in the business, of which Uncle Henry owned thirty-five per cent and Joseph fifteen per cent. How the rest was divided up, no one outside the family knows. As long as Uncle Henry lived, he was the *de forma* head of the company and Joseph was the *de facto* head. At Uncle Henry's death, in 1919, Joseph bought his thirty-five per cent and took full command. All the shares his brothers and sisters received at the time of their father's death Joseph ultimately bought, almost entirely on credit. Several of the brothers took an active part in the business – or as active a part as was possible in a firm that contained Joseph Duveen. John, who was the first to be paid off, and in cash, immediately retired. Ernest helped run the Paris gallery, which was opened shortly before his father died, and then left it to become an official in an insurance firm in London, where he handled the Duveen account. Edward worked in the London shop on a salary. Charles had the temerity to go into the decorating business for himself. Duveen paid him £5,000 a year not to use his last name professionally. Duveen grandly ignored the excessive proliferation sometimes indulged in by nature; there was only one Duveen and that was Joseph, and he did not wish the art-buying public to be confused. So Charles became Charles of London. Benjamin, after being bought out by Joseph, became a salaried connoisseur in the New York gallery; he was even permitted to have his own customers. Louis became manager of the London gallery; when he died, in 1920, Duveen bought his share of the business, on credit. Louis's estate was soon threatening lawsuits, but no suits materialized.

The impulse to sue was an endemic family trait. All their lives, the Duveen brothers and sisters pressed for their shares of the estate; all his life, Joseph sought to keep them off balance by unexpectedly paying them large sums of money. At one time, he owed them a total of eleven million dollars, and he doled them out a half million or a million at a time, when he had it handy. When, however, they wanted more than he doled out, or wanted all he owed them, he sat back and blandly invited them to go ahead and sue. This invitation, attractive as it was, they realized they couldn't accept. Most of the firm's money – and a great deal more – was invested in pictures and sculptures, and Joseph was the only one in the family who knew what anything was worth or what it might bring. Their one hope of getting cash lay in Joseph's theoretical ability to sell not only the incalculable jumble of stuff he had to begin with but all the pictures and sculptures he continued to acquire. When Joseph said 'Sue me' he half meant it. Lawsuits gave his life savour; suits against him by competitors, by outraged collectors about whose choice items (bought from rival dealers) Duveen made disparaging remarks, by customers, and, in one instance, by the government of the United States were a ceaseless *obbligato* to his life. He himself got too much pleasure out of litigation to deny the same pleasure to his relatives. But they never really treated themselves to it, no matter how often they threatened to. Their threats sometimes sounded so genuine, however, that Duveen had almost as much fun as if they had actually sued. As a result, he was seldom bored.

Not long after buying his third big collection, Joseph Duveen, confident in the knowledge that he owned the greatest inventory of works of art any art dealer had ever owned, sailed for New York with the intention of making it his headquarters. He had begun to siphon off some of these gems through Uncle Henry, who was permitted to sell them to his American clients. Uncle Henry once more found his nephew's presence not only exhilarating but disturbing. Joseph wanted him to move again. Now the possessor of a princely store of art, Joseph felt that he must have a showcase commensurate with its magnificence. He leased the north-west corner of Fifty-sixth Street and Fifth Avenue, cleared the site, and there put up the Ministry of Marine. Uncle Henry was appalled by his nephew's grandiose ways, but his nephew's optimism and impetuosity overwhelmed him. 'I have it sold,' Joseph told him, referring to his inventory. 'You have everything sold,' said Uncle Henry helplessly. 'Show me the bill of sale.'

Meanwhile, in romance as well as in business, Joseph had proved himself unpredictable. In 1899, he was engaged to marry the daughter of Isaac Lewis, who was one of the South African gold millionaires. The wedding was to be held in London. Duveen's Aunt Dora, Uncle Henry's wife, went over for it and took with her a lovely young friend of hers, Elsie

Salamon, the daughter of a New York tobacco merchant of moderate means. Miss Salamon was just along for the ride. At one of the prenuptial parties, Duveen met her. The effect on him was so powerful that he called off his marriage to Miss Lewis and, with Miss Salamon's consent, married Miss Salamon instead. The marriage lasted till Duveen's death. The Duveens had one child, a daughter they named Dorothy.

Duveen Brothers never advertised specific wares and never employed salesmen in Joseph's lifetime. In the beginning, all sales, except of insignificant items, were engineered by the Duveens themselves: Uncle Henry, Joseph, and Benjamin in New York, Louis in London, Ernest in Paris. The rest of the staff consisted of, in the words of a former member of it, 'gentlemen ushers, who just walked around and knew a lot'. This sophistication extended even to the stockrooms. One day early in 1910, a disgruntled clerk employed there went, after an argument with Benjamin, to Delmonico's for solace. While there, he confided to the head waiter certain facts about some Duveen importations; after discussing them for a while, the two men decided to go to William Loeb, Jr, the Collector of the Customs of the Port of New York, and confide in him. He was willing to listen, because up to 1909 all art treasures had been subject to duty, and the Duveen importations under discussion had come in before 1909. As a result of the clerk's revelations, there fell on the Duveens an unimaginable disaster: the famous Duveen smuggling case, which, in the end, led to the family's paying the government of the United States the biggest settlement fine in the history of American jurisprudence up to that time. At four in the afternoon of Thursday, 13 October 1910, a squad of three customs agents and three special agents from the United States District Attorney's office entered the office of Duveen Brothers with warrants calling for a search of the premises and the seizure of certain art treasures. Wagons drew up at the rear of the establishment and were loaded with books and papers covering the firm's business for the past several years. Warrants also called for the arrest of Joseph, Benjamin, Louis, and Uncle Henry Duveen, on charges that by means of false and fraudulent invoices three Chinese porcelain vases had been brought into the country on 10 February 1908, at less than their true value. The value on which duty was paid had been one thousand one hundred dollars, whereas the actual value – the price paid for the vases in Europe – was not less than twenty-eight thousand dollars.

Benjamin, who must have wished that he had been more conciliatory towards the stock clerk, was the only Duveen in the gallery at the time. He was arrested, taken to the office of the District Attorney, and held in fifty thousand dollars bail, which the firm's laywers, Stern & Corbitt, quickly put up, giving real estate as security. Joseph and Louis Duveen

Opposite Lady Duveen, the former Elsie Salamon

were both in England, and Uncle Henry was due to arrive from England that night on the *Lusitania*. Customs men were waiting to grab him when the ship came into the harbour about ten o'clock. They boarded the ship before it docked and brought Uncle Henry ashore in a revenue cutter. His bail was seventy-five thousand dollars. He signed for it and then went home to try to get some sleep. The next morning, Uncle Henry felt that in making his way through the difficulties that loomed before him he would need more imposing representation than Stern & Corbitt could afford him. He asked some distinguished friends to make suggestions. Five of them wrote out a list of law firms. The name of one firm – Stanchfield & Levy – appeared on all five lists, and Uncle Henry decided on that one. There is a story in legal circles to the effect that Uncle Henry let himself in for more than was necessary when he engaged counsel. He called at the office of the eminent John B. Stanchfield to ask him to handle the case. Stanchfield had just taken on a junior associate, and while Uncle Henry waited in the outer office, Stanchfield discussed with this young man what he should ask for a retainer. 'You go and talk to him,' said Stanchfield finally. 'Try him out on ten thousand dollars.' The novice went out, passed the time of day with Uncle Henry, talked a bit about the case, and then brought up the question of money. Uncle Henry inquired politely what Mr Stanchfield's notion of a retaining fee was. 'Ten thousand,' said the novice. 'Dollars or pounds?' asked Uncle Henry. Instantly, by the utterance of a monosyllable, the novice became a professional. 'Pounds,' he said, and Uncle Henry nodded his assent.

A piquant circumstance connected with the case was the fact that the Customs Collector, having a rather cloudy sense of values about works of art coming into the Port of New York, had been relying for some time on Uncle Henry as his expert. The secret wish-dreams that rival art firms had harboured about the Duveens seemed about to come true when the famous smuggling case started; they were gleeful. Their homicidal gaiety was all the greater because Uncle Henry, in his advice to the Bureau of Customs, had put high valuations on the works imported by his competitors. It now appeared that he had been more modest about his own. It had been an additional exacerbation to some of Duveen's rivals that Uncle Henry, while in a position to appraise their importations, also ladled out to them the pious maxims of a man who is himself immaculate. One of them was 'Avoid lawsuits', a piece of advice that blithely ignored the fact that the Duveens were themselves almost constantly involved in several. It is easy to understand how Uncle Henry got his avuncular nickname. He was plump, geniality radiated from his countenance, and his Bairnsfather moustache belonged to the kind of man addicted to sitting in ample armchairs and dandling children on his knees. When the smuggling case arose, several unemotional men were willing to go to extraordinary lengths to do something for Uncle Henry.

The case hung fire for more than a year. The Duveens, it was charged, were in the habit of putting valuations on the works of art they imported that had no relation to their actual worth. It was also charged that they had a tendency to send over lovely old cabinets whose locked drawers held rolled-up paintings and tapestries that had been absent-mindedly stored away in them and then forgotten. The government held that every shipment including even one undervalued item should be forfeited. The government's demands on the Duveens started at six million dollars, then climbed to eight, and eventually hit ten. After long and patient whittling, the Duveens' lawyers got the government down to a modest one million two hundred thousand. At that moment, a tapestry the Duveens had sold to George J. Gould was found by the government sleuths to have been undervalued. This upped the final claim to one million four hundred thousand dollars. (The government comforted itself for not getting the ten million it had been asking for by slapping a fine of ten or fifteen thousand dollars on each of the Duveens still in the business.) The Duveens didn't have one million four hundred thousand dollars handy. At this point, the aura of Uncle Henry's benevolent personality shone out to save them. It was an awful lot to ask of an aura, but Uncle Henry's made it. J. P. Morgan sent for one of the Duveens' lawyers to come to see him in his private office on the top floor of the Bankers Trust, at Wall and Nassau Streets. When the lawyer entered the office, the great man was sitting behind his desk. On this occasion, Morgan revealed himself as a kind of Grumpy, horrendous in manner but with a heart of gold. He transfixed his visitor with his piercing black eyes and barked, 'Going to get Uncle Henry off?' The lawyer said that he'd like nothing better but that the government had put a trifling obstacle in the way. 'Get him off, get him off,' barked Morgan. The lawyer then became specific about the obstacle. It would require one million four hundred thousand dollars, he was forced to say. 'We've got to get Uncle Henry off,' Morgan said, sticking to the theme. 'Chauncey Jones will take care of it.' Chauncey Jones, it turned out, was Morgan's switchboard operator and handyman, but he must also have been a man of parts. When his boss asked him to get one million four hundred thousand dollars for Stanchfield & Levy, he didn't bat an eyelid. He pulled out his switches and ambled over to the First National Bank. The next day, Stanchfield, whose office was at 120 Broadway, a block or two away from the Bankers Trust, received, in an envelope containing no other communication, a cheque for one million four hundred thousand. Uncle Henry got off. In the process, Joseph Duveen, whom Morgan didn't particularly care for, also got off, but Morgan couldn't help himself.

At the time, all their rivals in the art world were convinced that the Duveens were finished. Joseph Duveen, who ten years before had been a mere furniture dealer, had said things about the works of art owned by his rivals that were not altogether flattering. Because it seemed inevitable that he was now through for all time, they began, somewhat

In the office of J. Pierpont Morgan

prematurely, not to miss him. Certainly the outlook for the Duveens was unpromising, and Uncle Henry's morale had been shattered. But Joseph was imperturbable. The very magnitude of the settlement pleased Duveen, who loved the grandiose wherever he encountered it. 'Who else would have so big a settlement?' he asked one of his friendly enemies a few days after the case ended. There was no answer to this question; his rivals conceded his superiority. The nephew tried to buck up the uncle. The jig was by no means up, he said. He pointed out that neither Morgan nor Altman nor Widener nor Gould had been convicted of any crime, and that there was no reason for the Duveens to snub them. He also pointed out that none of the works of art the Duveens owned had been convicted of any crime, and, further, that since the works of art were now in the possession of what could technically be called smugglers, it was all the more urgent to move them. Besides, he said, the Duveens were the victims of a quirk in legal chronology; inasmuch as a law providing that no duty be collected on works of art over twenty years old had been passed in 1909, the United States government was merely penalizing the Duveens for being prophetic. (In 1930, the law was revised to make all works of art over a hundred years old duty free.) In the days before 1909, Morgan himself had, in order to avoid paying the tremendous duties, kept many of his works of art in his London home. But the Duveens were educators; they were out to elevate American taste, and they couldn't do that if they kept *their* works of art in London. To show Uncle Henry what good company they were in, Duveen pointed out that just a few years earlier Mrs Jack Gardner, of Boston, had also felt that she had a justified grievance against customs. For a long time, her friends in Italy had been trying to buy for her a fresco by Piero della Francesca. The Italian government wanted to keep the fresco in Italy, but in 1906 Mrs Gardner's friends finally won out. When the picture arrived in New York, together with some tapestries from the Charles M. Ffoulke Collection and a marble bust of Cardinal Riario by Verrocchio, the customs agents collected huge duties on her purchases. An indignant editorial in a Boston paper read:

> When the duties of $150,000 on the old masters, valued at $80,000, have been paid, it may perhaps dawn on Mrs J. L. Gardner how grievously she has offended against this great and glorious republic, in trying to import works of art. The law of this republic is very strict with all misguided persons who dare to bring to this land paintings, or statuary, or valuable works of research. What these persons should do, if they wish to be favourably regarded by the law, is import dogs. A snarling, blear-eyed bulldog of uncertain walk and disagreeable temper, valued at $10,000, can be imported free of duty. A yelping, howling, snapping poodle, of no earthly good to himself or humanity, but valued at $8,000, can be imported duty free. An obese, ungainly, and repulsive dachshund of a value of $5,000 can be imported duty free. It is expected that all good and wealthy citizens will spend their money in decorating the land of the free with high art of this variety, and if the animals are 'pedigreed', no duty will be charged. But any millionaire who tries to import works by Titian, Rubens, or Turner, is lucky if he escapes jail. All of which proves us to be a logical, reasonable, and highly intelligent nation.

Troubles, Joseph Duveen found, come not in single spies but in battalions. When the reverberations of the smuggling case were beginning to fade, the firm suffered two blows that were, if anything, more devastating. In 1913, although he was engaged in many negotiations with the Duveens, Morgan died. It was the only time he ever let Uncle Henry down. He owed the firm a quarter of a million dollars, and his estate immediately paid it, but a quarter of a million dollars was small change compared to what the Duveens would have got had he lived. A few months later, Duveen suffered another blow, equally severe, in the death of Altman. This had a special poignance. Shortly after the smuggling

A cartoon predicting Morgan's meeting with his maker: 'That's a nice chair. How much?'

case ended, Duveen had gone after a great picture known as the 'Small Cowper Madonna' by Raphael. For it he happily paid more than a half-million dollars in cash, despite the fact that his firm had just had to pay nearly a million and a half to the government. While Duveen was taking on this new obligation, Altman agreed to buy the picture from him for three-quarters of a million. But when the Raphael arrived, Altman was no longer alive to receive it. Duveen couldn't grieve full time over Altman's death; he had to worry about what to do with the Raphael, since even in his circle three-quarter-million-dollar customers were rare. The agreement between Altman and Duveen had been oral, and, finding no evidence of sale, Altman's executors declined to accept the picture. (Duveen's remark about Altman's travelling like a Cook's tourist did not predispose Altman's executors in his favour.) By this petulance, the executors deprived the departed Altman of what would have been one of the finest things in the Altman Collection.

All his life, Joseph Duveen was in a race with death; his customers were mostly getting on in years. Now, caught in this nexus of disaster, Uncle Henry himself wanted to die, but his nephew forbade it. It was a luxury the firm couldn't afford. Something had to be done about the Raphael. Duveen rallied Uncle Henry, and sent him to Philadelphia to see P. A. B. Widener, the only member of his dwindling band rich enough to buy the Raphael. There was no time to lose; Widener's health was poor. (Two years later, he, too, died.) It may be assumed that when Duveen sent Uncle Henry off on the train to Philadelphia, he made him take an express. Uncle Henry brought home the bacon. He sold the Raphael to Widener for seven hundred thousand dollars. This was fifty thousand dollars less than the picture would have brought if death had not removed Altman from the scene, but then there were a certain few inexorabilities that even Duveen could not subdue.

Chapter 3

A BRISK MARKET IN
IMMORTALITY

THE activities in the United States a half-century ago that made possible the advent of the Duveen Era were on a titanic scale. The tumultuous exertions and accomplishments to be found in the great coal and iron mines, in the flourishing department stores, in the prodigious chains of five-and-tens, in the great public utilities and networks of railroads and banking houses, in the breath-taking corporate pyramiding that reached its climax with the merging of ten giant steel companies into J. P. Morgan's 'billion-dollar trust', in the apogee of finance capitalism, which was bringing its masters a material wealth without precedent – all this was interesting and praiseworthy, as far as it went, but to Duveen it was merely an overture to the fantastic and costly opera he was himself prepared to produce. The emperors of the immense commercial realms of the period were rich in power but poor in panoply. It had all happened so quickly. For the most part, the millionaires of this era could trace the origins of their fortunes to the struggles of their own youth – on farms, in offices, in machine shops or butcher shops, behind the counters of country stores. William Randolph Hearst and Andrew Mellon and John D. Rockefeller, Jr and William C. Whitney were among the exceptions; they were the aristocrats, with a tradition of substantiality that reached back a generation. Most of the rest – H. E. Huntington and Henry Clay Frick, Andrew Carnegie and Benjamin Altman, P. A. B. Widener, E. T. Stotesbury, and Samuel H. Kress – remembered shirt-sleeved rather than imperial pasts. How could they obliterate these memories? How could they drown them in splendour? Duveen showed them how.

The passion of these newly rich Americans for industrial merger yielded to an even more insistent passion for a merger of their newly acquired domains with more ancient ones; they wanted to veneer their *arrivisme* with the traditional. It would be gratifying to feel, as you drove up to your *porte-cochère* in Pittsburgh, that you were one with the jaded Renaissance Venetian who had just returned from a sitting for Titian; to feel, as you

Mrs Anna Thompson Dodge, for whom Duveen assembled one of the richest collections of French furniture and French 18th-century art, painted as Madame de Pompadour by Sir Gerald Kelly

walked by the ranks of gleaming and authentic suits of armour in your mansion on Long Island – and passed the time of day with your private armourer – that it was only an accident of chronology that had put you in a counting house when you might have been jousting with other kings in the Tournament of Love; to push aside the heavy damask tablecloth on a magnificent Louis XIV dining-room table, making room for a green-shaded office lamp, beneath which you scanned the report of last month's profit from the Saginaw branch, and then, looking up, catch a glimpse of Mrs Richard Brinsley Sheridan and flick the fantasy that presently you would be ordering your sedan chair, because the loveliest girl in London was expecting you for tea.

It was Frick's custom to have an organist in on Saturday afternoons to fill the gallery of his mansion at Seventieth Street and Fifth Avenue with the majestic strains of 'The Rosary' and 'Silver Threads Among the Gold' while he himself sat on a Renaissance throne, and every now and then looked up from his *Saturday Evening Post* to contemplate the works of Van Dyck and Rembrandt, or, when he was enthroned in their special atelier, the more frolicsome improvisations of Fragonard and Boucher. Surely Frick must have felt, as he sat there, that only time separated him from Lorenzo and the other Medicis. Morgan commissioned the English art authority Dr George C. Williamson to prepare catalogues of his vast collections. Williamson spent years travelling all over the world to check on the authenticity and the history of certain items and to supervise the work on the catalogues. The last one he completed for his patron was *The Morgan Book of Watches*. For the illustrations, gold and silver leaf was used, laid on so thick that the engraved designs of the watches could be reproduced exactly. Morgan was in Rome when he received this catalogue, on Christmas Day, 1912, and he cabled Williamson, in New York, 'IT IS THE MOST BEAUTIFUL BOOK I HAVE EVER SEEN.' It was lying by Morgan's bedside when he died in Rome, early in 1913.

Duveen boasted that he understood the psychology of his dozen biggest customers much better than his competitors did. In his peculiar semantics, 'to understand psychology' meant to be able to guess how much the traffic would bear, and under that interpretation his boast was not an empty one. He always knew how to shift the interest of his customers – or, more accurately, his protégés – from their original fields of accumulation to his own, and to persuade them, moreover, that his was the more exalted. The truth was that after having spent a lifetime making money, Duveen's protégés were rich enough to go any-where and do anything but didn't know where to go or what to do or even how to do nothing gracefully. After the Americans had splurged on yachts and horses and houses, they were stymied. There were no noble titles to be earned – or bought – and lived up to, as there were in Europe, and if they ever made an attempt to do nothing gracefully, they were hampered by the Puritanic and democratic tradition that held such a life sinful.

Whenever they let themselves go, they had a feeling of guilt. Stotesbury, in a grey business suit and a high stiff collar, with a panama hat clamped down on his head, stood in the blazing sunshine of the tremendous patio of El Mirasol, his Palm Beach home, and said to one of his architects, who had recently added a wing to it, 'It cost too much for ninety days!' And when his wife spent two hundred and seventy-five thousand dollars on Wingwood House, their place at Bar Harbor, he said the same thing again. He felt the same way about Whitemarsh Hall and Winoga, his two places at Chestnut Hill. A European of comparable means who spent ninety days in one of his residences would very likely have felt that whatever it had cost him was justified, on the principle that ninety days was a segment of time that was worth enjoying even if at the end of it he went some-where else. When the American millionaires of the era said, 'I don't care what it costs,' as they often did, they were silently adding, 'So long as I have something to show for it.' And what they had to show for it had to be at once enviable and uplifting. Duveen was like an answer to a prayer.

Duveen's dealings with the American monarchs were conducted according to a care-fully thought-out economic formula. He more than once asked a prospective client, 'Do you realize that the only thing you can spend a hundred thousand dollars on without incurring an obligation to spend a great deal more for its upkeep is a picture? Once you've bought it, it costs you only a few hundred dollars every fifteen years for cleaning.' It was a revolutionary sales argument, and one admirably adapted to American royalty. By advanc-ing it, Duveen satisfied two conflicting desires in his little covey of important customers: the desire for conspicuous consumption and the desire for economy. An effective supple-mentary sales argument, which he used repeatedly, was: 'You can always make more money, but if you miss this picture, you'll never get another like it, for it is unique.' It was the sort of home truth Duveen's clients understood.

After Duveen's death, one of the sunniest of the commentators on him and his era was Mrs William Randolph Hearst. Most people remembered Duveen with a mixture of acrimony, envy, and admiration. In some instances, the acrimony was undiluted, but the mixture was more typical. After Duveen died, in 1939, a famous rival dealer delivered himself of an ambivalent eulogy. 'We miss him, but we are glad that he has gone,' he said. Certainly Duveen did plenty in his lifetime to mitigate for his rivals any melancholy they might have been expected to feel when he died. Mrs Hearst, a woman who viewed most of the phenomena of life with sympathetic detachment, liked Duveen. She saw his side. She regarded the collecting mania of her husband and his friends (a circle that included Rockefeller, Mellon, and many others) as a harmless, if expensive, exercise of vanity, as something they indulged in to relieve the tension of their workaday lives. It was a tax-free time, she once recalled in a reminiscent discussion, and the men in her crowd thought nothing of buying a pair of hawthorn vases at sixty thousand dollars apiece. Mrs Hearst said that the richest man in America – she described him affectionately as a 'stingy feller' – ended up by paying a million dollars for one tapestry. She described Duveen as 'a gentleman salesman in a cut-away,' and added, 'He met you with everything he had.' Duveen's connoisseurship was so respected by her husband and his friends that only with fear and trembling did they show him the possessions they had garnered before they came under his guidance. Mrs Hearst remembered a touching scene. Her own apartment was 'full of stuff' – antique furniture, paintings, sculptures, tapestries. The *clou* of the collection, her husband's pride, was two Rossellino (or allegedly Rossellino) bas-reliefs of angels. Mrs Hearst described Duveen's manner as her husband showed him around the apartment for the first time. Duveen moved through the clutter of antiques, tapestries, and statuary with the air of a man who has plenty of thoughts but is too well bred to voice them. Finally, the increasingly despondent host stood him before the two angels. Duveen made a barely audible remark that cast doubt on their legitimacy, then left, presumably to comfort himself with the contemplation, at his own place, of some genuine Duveens. There was a sad interval after his departure; Hearst was like a college boy who, after cramming hard for an exam, has the terrible feeling that he's flunked it. He was suddenly seized by a devastating doubt about everything he had. He shouted despairingly to Mrs Hearst, 'If those angels aren't right, then nothing is right!'

Duveen's losing fight against the campaigns of attrition undertaken by Mrs Hearst's husband and his friends to loosen his hold on his cherished possessions was something that she was in a position to observe minutely. A pertinent episode began one day when she and her husband had a difference of opinion about something of no real importance. For the moment, Hearst was extremely upset by this difference, and he left the house feeling the need of solace. Unlike many husbands in similar circumstances, he sought it at Duveen's gallery on Fifth Avenue. Duveen was himself just about to leave there, with Van Dyck's portrait of Queen Henrietta Maria with Jeffrey Hudson and a monkey, when Hearst walked in. He gave Hearst a peek at the Queen and her companions. Some-how, for Hearst, this peek was just what the doctor ordered; he felt that if he could only have Henrietta Maria, he would feel better. Unfortunately, Duveen, fond as he was of Hearst, was unable to give him this assuagement. He had promised Henrietta Maria to Lady Duveen, and it was a promise which he could not possibly go back on. Things

Opposite Van Dyck: 'Queen Henrietta Maria and her Dwarf'. The celebrated portrait with Jeffrey Hudson and a monkey which Duveen was persuaded to part with by William Randolph Hearst

were a little delicate in his own home, because of the high degree of mobility of the furnishings and decorations there; her husband's soft-hearted inability to say no to men like Hearst meant that in the morning Lady Duveen often found herself missing familiar and lovely objects that had been there the night before. After this refusal, Henrietta Maria looked all the more desirable to Mr Hearst, and he insisted that he must have her. An imperialist in his own domain, he was not used to being denied anything that he wanted very badly. As Hearst begged, Duveen became plaintive; he implored Hearst to see things from his point of view. Hearst wouldn't. In those few minutes, it had become somehow vital to him to take Henrietta home. To take Henrietta home was, unhappily, vital to Duveen, too. There was a tug of war. After some time, Duveen suggested that if he did let Hearst take Henrietta home, he would have to charge so much for the privilege that he wouldn't advise him to insist. Hearst, poker-faced, now felt he *had* Duveen. The tug of war continued for a while, but Hearst's victory was no longer in doubt. Finally, Duveen, in a sentimental conviction that Hearst's need was greater than his own, weakened. 'All right, take her!' he said. The price was three hundred and seventy-five thousand dollars. By the time Hearst got home, he had begun to cool off about Henrietta. He thought that perhaps he had spent too much to coddle a temporary malaise, and he felt rather sheepish when he had to confess to Mrs Hearst what he had done. 'I've done a terrible thing,' he said. 'I've gone over to Joe Duveen's and bought a picture.' And, he went on to say, he had paid three hundred and seventy-five thousand dollars for it. Mildly, Mrs Hearst remarked that when *she* was upset, she just went out and bought a hat. However, when she saw the Van Dyck, she liked it and told her husband that he should forget the whole thing.

'The fact is,' Mrs Hearst said, in relating the episode, 'you couldn't buy anything from Duveen! Everything was either in reserve for somebody else or he had promised it to his wife or for some reason he wasn't ready to sell it yet. Rockefeller, for example. He used to collect coloured tiles and things in a modest way, and then he heard Duveen had something better and he went into his place one day to buy. But he couldn't buy. Duveen wouldn't sell him anything. That was true of my husband and all his friends.' Among the many people who have wondered at the miracle of Duveen's selling method, perhaps no one has ever put it more trenchantly than Mrs Hearst. With a twinge of genuine sympathy for her old friend, she said, 'Duveen didn't want to sell his stuff, but they always badgered the poor feller till he gave in.'

Opposite: *Ter Borch: 'Curiosity'. A painting of aristocratic provenance, owners before Bache including the Marquis de Removille, the Duchesse de Berry, Prince Anatole Demidoff and Baroness Mathilde de Rothschild*

Left *Mrs William Randolph Hearst* (centre); right *her husband, the newspaper millionaire*

Mrs Hearst recalled another odd fact about her husband and his friends. This was their fondness for catalogues. Speaking of her husband's coterie, Mrs Hearst said, 'They were going after anything that had a book to it.' She watched the men in her circle collecting hard year after year. 'At the end,' she commented, 'they'd get a book all done up.' In this glancing remark, she pithily summed up one of the great basic manoeuvres of Duveen's selling technique. While the American millionaires of the Duveen Era could not become lords and ladies, they could buy the family portraits and other works of art that had belonged for centuries to lords and ladies, and this strengthened their feeling of identification and equality with British nobility and with the great rulers and merchant princes of the Renaissance. In the provenance, or history of previous ownership, of many of the Duveen works appeared the names of kings and the mistresses of kings: Charles I of England, Francis I of France, one or another Louis, Mme Du Barry, Mme de Pompadour. 'It is much easier to sell a second-rate picture that has belonged to any English nobleman than a first-rate one that has belonged to a great name in the Italian nobility,' Bernard Berenson, the eminent art authority, once said in a reference to the American market. The reason for this was that the American millionaires were up on Debrett but had only a sketchy acquaintance with the *Almanach de Gotha*. In an article, Emily Genauer, the art critic of the *Herald Tribune*, once spoke of the 'cachet of the hook'. An example is the cachet that, among American collectors after the elder Morgan's death, attached to the owning of a 'Morgan piece'. Though Morgan was a collector as indiscriminate as he was voracious ('a cheque-book collector', one of his biographers, John Kennedy Winkler, called him), he was able to create, by the sheer weight of his name, a valuable provenance of his own. To solidify for his clients this sense of neighbourliness with the great names of the past, to establish them firmly on the historic field of honour in their own living-rooms, Duveen brought to its apotheosis the catalogue, and, on a lower level, the brochure. A more ingenious apparatus for flattering the ego than these Duveen publications has rarely been seen. For each picture that Duveen sold, his overworked librarian, the late George H. McCall, prepared a free brochure giving the history of its ownership, listing the places where it had been exhibited, noting its relation to its artist's career, and so on. McCall, a gentleman of distinction and a scholar, turned out handsome brochures. H. E. Huntington, who wasn't an avid reader, merely looked at his; Jules Bache memorized his. Once a client had acquired enough brochures, he was in line for an even higher accolade – the Duveen catalogue, which would cover a client's entire collection and which the client would ordinarily pay for himself. Some of the catalogues were prepared by McCall, but for others Duveen called in the greatest art experts in the world. They sometimes devoted months to preparing one. The paper for the catalogues was usually made to order in France, and had as its watermark the name of the collector. On one page was printed the provenance of a picture, the names of the famous owners serving as a decorous overlay to the watermark, and on the opposite page was a reproduction of the painting. The catalogues themselves were costly works of art – they could run as high as fifty or sixty thousand dollars – and they were unwieldy.

One Christmas, Duveen got up for Kress a sumptuous book called *The Collection of Paintings, Sculptures, etc., of Samuel H. Kress*. It was an enormous weight, not easy to lift. Nevertheless, its title was something of an exaggeration, for the book contained histories and reproductions of only what Duveen had sold to Kress; it ignored entirely the vast reaches of Kress's other purchases. But then these came from other dealers, so for Duveen they were non-existent. Another item that Duveen got out for Kress – this one as an *hors d'œuvre* instead of a dessert – was three tremendous and encyclopedic volumes on the medals and bronzes of the Gustave Dreyfus Collection. Duveen had them expertly edited, and they were handsomely printed by the Oxford University Press, all at his own expense. These were noble, if sedentary, volumes. When Duveen showed them to Kress, Kress felt that any objects that could produce such massive and beautiful books were worth owning. He bought the entire collection of medals and bronzes. He bought them, but for several years he didn't send for them; they remained in Duveen's vaults. An acquaintance of Kress's was asked why he didn't take the medals up-town. 'Well, they're awfully heavy,' he said.

Before his book-hungry clients Duveen dangled the canonization of the catalogue as the proverbial carrot was dangled before the donkey, except that they usually had to pay for the carrot. He did not undertake a catalogue for everybody, and when some of his clients asked why *they* could not have one, Duveen would point out that their collections were not yet ready for sanctification. He was prepared to get them ready, he was at their service, but great paintings, unlike money, were difficult to acquire. To acquire a Duveen was no simple matter, even for Duveen. Eventually, he found that there was a slight catch to the issuing of a catalogue; once the donkey had the carrot, he was no longer hungry. The clients refused to buy great pictures not because they weren't fine but because it was too late to get them into the catalogue. Once the client had it, he felt he was registered, accepted in the club, with nothing more to do except lift the heavy tome and turn the pages, peering at his watermarked name in its gallant company. Consequently, Duveen became chary of producing catalogues; he dangled but he did not deliver. The creation of the Bache Catalogue had a somewhat troubled history. Bache asked for one, and Duveen said he would try to get the distinguished art scholar Dr W. R. Valentiner to do it. As it turned out, he had McCall do it. When it was finished, Duveen asked Valentiner to write an introduction. Valentiner said that certain works of art would have to be deleted before he could consent to do so. As the things he said must be deleted were already hanging in the Bache house, Duveen abandoned the idea of the introduction and took the book to Bache. 'Where is Valentiner?' Bache asked. Duveen said that Valentiner had wanted his name too large on it; Duveen did not wish Bache minimized and had refused to let Valentiner appear at all. In the end, Bache took great pride in his catalogue. Its epigraph read, 'We needs must love the highest when we see it: Tennyson.' Duveen agreed with Tennyson.

Duveen was not selling merely low upkeep, social distinction, and watermarks; he was selling immortality. Since most of his protégés were ageing men, the task of making them yearn for immortality was not hard. It was shortly after the First World War that Duveen realized where his future lay; it lay not just in selling individual pictures but in selling the idea of assembling collections that would automatically ensure immortality to his clients. Each of the Duveen millionaires wanted to get the particular intimation of immortality Duveen offered, and, if possible, to get a stronger intimation than the other millionaires were getting. Thus, immortality was put on a competitive basis. When the elder Morgan died, a large part of his art collection was put up for sale. His collection of Chinese porcelains, acknowledged to be the greatest in the world, had been procured for Morgan by Uncle Henry. Duveen now bought the collection. Three of his honour pupils – Frick, Widener, and Rockefeller – wanted it. It offered a quick accession to prestige, and Duveen had to decide where to let the Morgan mantle fall. He decided to let it fall on all three men; each was to have a third of the collection. But how could the division be made equitably? The solution of this dilemma was a nice exercise in diplomacy. Duveen did not wish to offend any of his star pupils, and especially did not wish to offend Frick, who was still dickering with other art dealers and who was a beauty lover with little self-restraint and ample means of gratifying his love. Duveen therefore decided to promise all three men first chance. He would give each of the seekers after immortality first chance at one part. This plan caused a certain exacerbation among the objects of his benevolence, but it is known that Frick believed (possibly without discouragement from Duveen) that he had been given first chance at the best lot, and for all anyone knows today the two other aspirants believed that they had been the favoured ones. Duveen disposed of Morgan's collection of bronzes in the same fashion. Again he gave Frick what Frick believed was first chance at the best lot. All his life, Duveen had to walk a tightrope among the men who were anxious to immortalize themselves with the choicest samples of his taste.

The techniques of trading that the American millionaires had mastered were useless when pitted against Duveen's technique. Again and again, Duveen stressed the point that it was easy to get fifty-thousand-dollar pictures but very hard to get pictures that cost a quarter of a million. An art expert friend told Duveen that he knew of an exquisite masterpiece in London that could be bought very reasonably. 'For how much?' Duveen asked. 'I think you can get it for three hundred pounds,' his friend replied. 'I really cannot afford to buy a picture that costs only three hundred pounds,' Duveen said. While dining in a client's house, he was shocked to see hanging on the wall, among the Duveens, a beautiful Monet. He professed an overwhelming love for it, and his client, whose interest was perhaps piqued by the sudden reversal of their positions, asked him what his love would come to in dollars. Duveen – nobody was better accustomed to Duveen prices than he was – told him exactly what his love was worth. The deal was closed and Duveen took the picture home with him. It was never heard of again. When people who knew of the incident asked him where the picture was, he was evasive. The former owner jokingly accused him of having sold it at an unconscionable profit. To a close friend, Duveen admitted that he had bought it to sequester it in his basement. 'I didn't want that fellow to get used to buying modern pictures,' he said. 'There are too many of them.' Duveen was never eager to sell anything painted after 1800, because the fertility of the nineteenth-century painters would have sadly upset the Duveen economy of scarcity.

Towards the end of his life, Duveen said, 'Except for Rembrandt and Hals, I'll never buy anything but Italians. I can sell any Rembrandt or Hals, no matter how homely, but when you get to the High Renaissance, you get physical beauty. My clients want physical beauty.' Sometimes, however, he violated his own rule. He bought a Mother and Child by Reynolds because he thought it fine, even though the mother was plain. Perhaps he counted on the American principle that denies the possibility of any mother being plain. If so, his faith was misplaced. His clients didn't want a plain mother. The picture was eventually sold at auction; it was bought by John G. Johnson, a Philadelphia lawyer, who was one of the most discriminating of American collectors. Duveen's clients not only disliked plain mothers but were apathetic toward fat women. This created a coolness between them and Rubens, and made it difficult for Duveen to gratify his own fondness for that painter. He was considerate enough not to cater to his personal prejudices; he considered it selfish. In one instance, though, he did forget himself and buy a Rubens Madonna. When he had it cleaned, it proved to portray a nursing mother. This was disheartening to Duveen, but he had to let Rubens have his way. Since his customers, in addition to not caring for plain mothers and fat women, didn't care for nursing mothers, Duveen was compelled to sequester that picture in his basement, too. He later discovered that his customers didn't care for plain pirates, either. He had bought a very bold, striking Velásquez that completely realized his concept of how a pirate ought to look. He was crazy about it, but he couldn't get any of his clients to share his enthusiasm. They thought the pirate looked too much like a desperado – which was exactly why Duveen had liked him. So the Velásquez went into the basement, which was by then crammed with distinguished rejections.

One day, Duveen ran into the American artist Maurice Sterne on Fifth Avenue. 'I have two Tintorettos, Maurice,' said Duveen. 'I'd like you to have a look at them before I put them downstairs.' Sterne went over to the Ministry of Marine for a look, and the Tintorettos – two male portraits – took his breath away. 'Why are you putting them downstairs?' he asked. 'Surely you can sell them.' 'Unfortunately, they're men,' Duveen said. 'If they were women – more particularly, if they were pretty women – I could easily sell them here three times over.' He also showed Sterne two very fine pictures of the Giotto school, but not by outstanding names. Duveen was also putting those downstairs. 'Can't sell them,' he said flatly. 'In America, they want only the topnotchers. If I had the Sistine Chapel, I could sell it tomorrow half a dozen times over.'

It was imperative for Duveen not to make a mistake either over a picture or over the client he offered it to, because once a picture had been turned down by one client, the others heard about it and were cold. Still, he couldn't always avoid mistakes in pairing off clients and pictures, and his mistakes added to his basement stock. There were some dangers even he could not foresee, like his clients' rejection of pictures on moral grounds.

He managed to sell a Gainsborough portrait of Mrs Elliott only because the purchaser didn't find out until too late that she had run off with her gardener. On other occasions, though, some such scandalous gossip killed his sales, and the censored paintings went into the basement. In addition, Duveen became an avid collector of paintings he disliked, among them all the Barbizons and other pardonable errors committed by his clients before they had come under his tutelage. Duveen bought them all, for his basement, and sold his customers suitable replacements, not forgetting when he set the sale prices the liberal prices he had paid for their mistakes.

Over the years, Duveen's basement accumulated quantities of nursing mothers and plain mothers and unappetizing pirates and men without women; of non-topnotch master-pieces; of pictures that had been masterpieces but were beyond the ministrations of the restorers; of pictures that had nothing whatever against them except that one client had turned them down; of pictures that had violated the seventh commandment; of Barbizons; of moderns. That basement contained a fascinating and bewildering miscellany: seepages from the picture collections of kings, kings' mistresses, queens, archbishops, cardinals, and Rothschilds, to say nothing of a wilderness of furniture and *objets d'art* – altarpieces, credenzas, suits of armour, tapestries, and thrones. In a sense, the basement, full as it was of beautiful things, summarized Duveen's eccentricities of salesmanship. Its value became incalculable. His friends and financial advisers kept importuning him to sell some of it. 'Sell your basement,' his comptroller would plead. 'Sell your basement and pay your debts.' But Duveen was fond of his basement, and he was not aware of being in debt. It was once suggested that if he didn't want to sell the contents of the basement under his own name, he might turn the stuff over to Knoedler's, who would get an immense profit on it for him. He couldn't bear to let his prominent rival have a whack at his basement; he felt a pang of jealousy, like that of a man who hears that a discarded mistress is contemplating a new alliance. 'Why should I put Knoedler's in business with my stuff?' he asked pleasantly. He quite ignored the fact that Knoedler's already *was* in business. To the end, he clung to his basement. Basement Duveens were none the less Duveens.

Duveen's purchase of unworthy pictures and art objects sometimes proved profitable. One day, in the drawing-room of an important figure in British diplomatic circles, he noticed a very bad painting the diplomat had bought in his youth for a few hundred pounds. Duveen asked if he could buy it. ('Some Europeans of that era were so very rich that they were always hard up,' Berenson said.) The man said yes, and, without asking him what he wanted, Duveen paid him ten thousand pounds for it, spot cash. The diplomat decided that Duveen was not only a connoisseur but a gentleman who was above the degrading minutiae of haggling, and later he tipped Duveen off from time to time of pictures his friends might be willing to sell. Someone has said that he performed the functions of a runner for Duveen – a highly cultivated, exhaustively informed, unpaid one. Duveen instantly wrote his ten-thousand-pound purchase off as a total loss, but the pictures he acquired from the diplomat's friends returned him a profit many times as large as his investment. Duveen sometimes varied this technique of flattery. Visiting Clarence Mackay at his manor, Harbor Hill, in Roslyn, soon after making his acquaintance, Duveen's gaze took in certain tapestries on the walls. 'Those tapestries, my dear Mr Mackay, are very good but they are not good enough for you,' he said. 'I can't bear you to have them in your château. I'll buy them from you, as I have a customer they're good enough for. I'll pay you thirty-five thousand dollars for them.' Mackay agreed. Duveen's cheque arrived next day, and Mackay incredulously shipped off the tapestries. They went right to Duveen's basement, but Mackay became one of Duveen's best customers.

Compared to his clients, Duveen was a child in business, but he almost always had his way with them. When they started talking about prices, he started talking about values – values that, as it happened, he himself had created. When customers complained about the price of his masterpieces, he brought into play, sometimes subtly and sometimes brutally, his standard threat – that he had a rival collector whose sense of values was more perceptive, whose taste, in fact, was anything but vulgar. The rival collector was his trump card. He capitalized on rivalry in perception, even rivalry in philanthropy. A peculiar aversion was aroused in Frick by Carnegie's propensity for endowing libraries. This quirk of Carnegie's disgusted him. 'What's the point of giving libraries to all those towns that go busted trying to keep 'em up?' Frick asked. Duveen gave him something that had a point, and a chance to do in Carnegie, whom Frick detested.

It has been said of Kress, one of the biggest of Duveen's customers, that he got more pleasure out of haggling with Duveen over a picture's price than he did out of owning it. He bought art on such a scale that when someone asked where a certain picture was, all he could say was that he thought it was in 'that third lot that came from Duveen.' Ordinarily, Duveen showed his clients only one picture at a time. He had it put on an easel in his gallery, gave a discourse on the artist and the special glories of the subject at hand, and ended by working himself up into a spiral of irresistible enthusiasm. Some of his clients, having achieved worldly success by buying wholesale and selling retail, didn't

Opposite Velásquez: 'The Infanta Maria Theresa'. Harry Payne Bingham's painting which Duveen sold to Bache

Overleaf left Verrocchio: 'Lorenzo de' Medici'; right After Raphael: 'Giuliano de' Medici, Duke of Nemours'. Portraits of the great Renaissance patron Lorenzo 'the Magnificent' and one of his sons, bought respectively by Kress and Bache. At the time, experts including Berenson believed the Raphael to be an original, not a later copy.

care for this piecemeal method. Looking at one picture at a time bored Kress, and once when he was visiting the gallery, he finally asked to see a bunch. Duveen, pained, ordered someone to bring in a bunch. Kress admired them and asked the price of the lot. Duveen quoted the price of each picture and added up the figures. 'Isn't there a reduction when you buy by lot?' Kress inquired, out of habit. Duveen said there wasn't. Kress got up abruptly. 'I am not interested,' he said, and departed. Six months later, he returned to the gallery and casually asked Duveen, 'Have you still got that lot of pictures I looked at that day?' 'I have indeed,' said Duveen. 'In fact, I am holding them for you.' Kress looked at them again. 'What did I offer for them the last time?' he asked. 'Your offer last time,' Duveen replied amicably, 'was so small that I can't even remember it.' 'What is the price now?' Kress asked. Duveen named the original figure, and the two men repeated the original routine. 'In that case,' said Kress, getting up – in his relations with Duveen, Kress was always getting up – 'don't hold them for me any more. I am not interested.' Duveen held on to the pictures, and eventually Kress bought them, at Duveen's figure. Later, Duveen said that he knew he had sold the pictures when Kress asked whether he still had them. After his first transaction with Duveen, Kress told a friend that he would never go to Duveen's again, because he objected to the Duveen prices. When, inevitably, he did go back, the friend said, 'I thought you were never going back to Duveen's. What made you?' 'Because he's got things I can't get anywhere else,' Kress said. He was stating a simple truth, and one that each of Duveen's clients had to discover for himself.

Once, Duveen had to grant, to a customer already persuaded of this truth, a far greater reduction than the one he did not give Kress. Mrs Gilbert Miller, a daughter of Jules Bache, walked into Duveen's one day to have a look at some pictures her father contemplated buying. Duveen was not there, but his assistant, Bertram Boggis, was. The pictures did not arouse joy in her heart, but, as her father contemplated buying them and Duveen contemplated selling them, she knew that they would presently be hanging in her father's house and that she would have plenty of time to gaze at them in the future. Somewhat hopelessly, she asked Boggis if there was anything around that was younger than four centuries. Boggis took her into another room and showed her Goya's 'Don Manuel Osorio de Zuñiga' – the little Red Boy, which, in reproduction, has become one of the most popular pictures in the world. Mrs Miller fell in love with the Red Boy, as, on an earlier occasion, H. E. Huntington fell in love with the Blue Boy. Mrs Miller went home and told her father that she could not face the future without the companionship of the Red Boy. Bache was an indulgent father and confided his daughter's passion to Duveen.

Opposite Goya: 'Don Manuel Osorio de Zuñiga'. The Red Boy which Bache bought for his daughter

Duveen, who liked to further love affairs, especially if they got their start on his premises, praised Mrs Miller's taste and asked for two hundred and seventy-five thousand dollars to make the affair permanent. Bache consented at once, with a sense of benefit received.

Bache's son-in-law, Gilbert Miller, the producer, proved to be less grateful. In the first place, he stated flatly, no Goya was worth two hundred and seventy-five thousand dollars. (The general public was less Goya conscious then than it is now; indeed, it is the various exhibitions of this very Red Boy that helped intensify the consciousness.) Also, he was haunted by a feeling that he had met this Red Boy somewhere before, and in surroundings that didn't go with two-hundred-and-seventy-five-thousand-dollar pictures. Miller was tantalized. He hunted around in the picture's provenance and found that it had once belonged to the wife of the French playwright Henri Bernstein. Here Miller was on his home ground. He went to see Bernstein. 'Henri,' he said, 'I feel I know that picture. I feel I've seen that picture.' 'Of course you've seen it,' said Bernstein. 'I used it as a prop in *La Galerie des Glaces*.' *La Galerie des Glaces* is a play of Bernstein's that ran in Paris in 1924, with Charles Boyer as its titular star, and the Red Boy as its wallflower. 'How much did you get for that prop when you sold it?' Miller asked. Bernstein said that in a moment of depression he and his wife had sold it to a Paris dealer for fifty thousand dollars. Miller went in triumph to his wife, and they both went in triumph to her father. Their attitude about Duveen had for a long time been wary, whereas Bache's, of course, had been idolatrous. They were sure that with this information they could easily convert the believer into an apostate. They were disappointed. Bache saw nothing wrong in Duveen's asking him two hundred and seventy-five thousand dollars for a fifty-thousand-dollar picture. The Millers felt a certain frustration. Miller then called on Duveen, and Duveen amiably reduced the price by a hundred and fifteen thousand dollars. This was the best he could do, he said, because he had had heavy expenses in the process of acquiring the picture. Miller again went to his father-in-law, bearing in his hand the gift of the mark-down, and presented it as stunning evidence that Duveen's services came high. 'Under the circumstances, I don't think so,' said Bache imperturbably. Miller inquired what these circumstances might be. Bache broke down and confessed. The price was not as excessive as superficial observers might think, he explained, because he had, years before, made a private deal with Duveen that if Duveen had an outstanding picture to offer him, he would pay him a flat hundred per cent profit. Taking into account Duveen's expenses in getting hold of the Red Boy, the original price he had asked was fair. Miller blew up. 'Why on earth did you make a deal like that?' he asked. Bache explained, and his explanation should certainly rank high in the annals of modesty. 'Listen, Gilbert,' he said, with the patience of practised wisdom before the spectacle of explosive immaturity. 'Duveen has the greatest men in the world as his clients. He has Mellon. Why should he give a first-class picture to me when he can give it to Mellon?' While Bache was explaining, Miller could see that his father-in-law was somewhat amazed that he had succeeded, merely by the promise of so reasonable a profit, in winning Duveen's consideration. Reminiscing with Miller about this episode, a later collector, Albert D. Lasker, made a pertinent remark about his own early days as a picture buyer. 'As a novice in collecting,' he said, with a modesty not unlike Bache's, 'I expected to have to pay the highest prices for masterpieces. What I did *not* expect, what I was to discover, was that I would also have to pay a large premium for the privilege of paying the highest prices!' In effect, Duveen was the king of an unconstitutional monarchy: his leading clients – men like Frick, Morgan, Mellon, P. A. B. Widener, Rockefeller, and Kress – were in the Cabinet, and Duveen managed to hold out to each of them the hope of one day being Prime Minister; clients of lesser rank – Bache, Henry Goldman, Edsel Ford, Elbert H. Gary – were enthusiastic backbenchers content to support the chief.

Duveen was not snobbish in his selection of pupils; he often lavished his knowledge on the backbenchers, and even on what he regarded as the small fry. Hearst was in the small-fry category; he probably spent at Duveen's no more than five million dollars in all. Also, he was what Duveen termed an accumulator, rather than a collector. Duveen made a strong distinction between the two. In Duveen's opinion, Hearst's collateral interest in ibexes, llamas, and Welsh castles kept him from attaining the rarefied heights on which he himself liked to operate. Duveen was always struggling with the aimlessness of his clients' diversions; he laboured tirelessly at the task of focusing them. One day, Bache, who was one of his favourite pupils, absent-mindedly bought from a major rival of Duveen's in Italy, Count Alessandro Contini, for thirty-seven thousand five hundred dollars, an illuminated page from an old book, the work of an obscure artist. Bache showed his master the page. Duveen was gentle. He did not reprimand Bache. He spoke to him mildly. 'Don't scatter, Julie,' he said, with the weariness of the much tried. 'An accumulation is never a collection. Concentrate.' After that, Julie concentrated.

One of Duveen's dear friends was Lady Lavery, the second wife of the painter Sir John Lavery. She asked one day if she might bring a certain California industrialist to see him. Duveen, who never denied anything to a friend, gave her permission, even though he considered the industrialist another of the small fry. Lady Lavery came a little ahead of time and was sitting in Duveen's office when the Californian was announced by an usher. 'Keep him waiting a half-hour,' said Duveen. Lady Lavery protested. 'You can't do that to a man of his importance,' she said. 'Leave it to me and watch,' said Duveen. When the visitor was finally admitted, Duveen took him and Lady Lavery for a stroll around the Ministry of Marine. He showed them a Rembrandt. The industrialist wanted to buy it.

Left *Jules Bache;* right *Lady Lavery, photographed by Cecil Beaton*

'The price is a hundred thousand dollars,' Duveen said. 'That's all right,' said Lady Lavery's friend. Duveen made a few inquiries. 'What other pictures do you own?' he asked, finally. The Californian admitted that he had none of any importance. 'I can't possibly sell a Rembrandt to a man who owns no other pictures,' said Duveen. 'The Rembrandt would be lonely.' He persuaded the ardent customer that for him to take the picture home would constitute a kind of cruelty to Rembrandts. The industrialist saw that he would have to make a more modest start, and here Duveen was able to help him. Duveen sold him a relatively inexpensive picture. Within a few years, the Californian had enough minor Duveens to feel justified in asking for a major one. Duveen shipped the Rembrandt to California with a nice feeling that he had provided for its social life.

Still another of the small fry, in Duveen's opinion, was John R. Thompson of Chicago, the owner of a well-known chain of popular restaurants. Thompson had begun to nibble at paintings through a Chicago art dealer. As his chain of restaurants increased, so did his appetite for paintings. The dealer, drawing upon the resources available to him in Chicago, gradually built up a small collection for him, but there came a time when the dealer's intuition told him that if he tried to keep Thompson to himself, he would lose a valuable customer. The dealer came to New York and advised Duveen that he had a client who had plenty of money and was ripe for higher things. Duveen agreed to give the restaurant man an audience, and the dealer a commission on any sales. 'You mustn't be shocked by my tactics, though,' he warned. Thompson, escorted by the Chicago dealer, presently appeared at the Ministry. He was a small man, and was wearing a derby hat and smoking a big cigar. Duveen kept Thompson and the dealer waiting for an hour. Finally, the two men were admitted to the Presence. Duveen was brisk and genial. 'I hear you are in the restaurant business,' he said. 'Anything like Lyons?' He went on to say that he approved of the Lyons teashops, and that if Thompson's chain resembled them, he approved of that. He revealed that he often snubbed Claridge's in favour of a Lyons in Oxford Street. The absence of formality there was pleasurable. He grew eloquent on the important social service rendered by those who provided good food at popular prices. He asked about the turnover in the Thompson restaurants, and the problems of refrigeration. The restaurant business, it became clear, was Duveen's liveliest and most intimate concern. 'Look here,' Thompson broke in desperately when he could stand the strain no longer, 'I didn't make this trip to New York to talk to you about the restaurant business. I came to see you because I am interested in paintings!' Snapped back so rudely to an activity so marginal, Duveen made a quick adjustment. 'Oh, paintings!' he said, as if recalling an almost forgotten acquaintance. 'Of course, paintings! Oh, well, now, if you're interested in pictures come upstairs with me and I'll show you some.'

Duveen led Thompson, as well as the Chicago dealer, into the lift, which bore them to sacrosanct upper regions. Duveen strode swiftly through a thickly carpeted, dimly lit room that contained six Old Masters reclining on easels. Thompson, in his way, was almost out of the room when, like Mrs Lot, he looked back. He lingered; from the blur of the six pictures he got a quick impression of infinite desirability. He called the hurrying Duveen back. 'Here are some pictures,' he said. 'What about these?'

Duveen took his arm. 'My dear Mr Thompson,' he said gently, 'there is nothing in this room that would interest you in the least.'

'Why not?' argued the new pupil. 'Of course they interest me. What would I be doing here if they didn't interest me?'

'These pictures, my dear fellow, I am reserving, as a matter of fact, for a favourite client,' Duveen said. 'They will interest him far more than they could possibly interest you.'

Thompson protested; he would yield to no one in acuteness of interest. 'Why do you think they wouldn't interest me?' he asked. 'I want you to know, Sir Joseph, that I own some pretty good pictures.'

'I am sure you do,' Duveen said soothingly. 'And if you will just follow me, I am sure that I can add to your collection and, if I may say so, improve it. But not these. You are a busy man, and I don't want to waste your time. Not with these.'

'Why not?' repeated Mr Thompson.

Pushed to the wall, Duveen dropped all pretence of tact. He made it plain that he thought the pictures were over Thompson's head, both aesthetically and economically.

'How much for the six?' Thompson demanded.

'A million dollars, I am afraid,' said Duveen, as if pained at having to demonstrate the truth of an unflattering statement.

Thompson was ready with an answer. 'I'll take them,' he said vindictively.

Behind the façade of Duveen's virtuoso salesmanship, behind the intricate process of converting Midas into Maecenas, operated his even more impressive process of financing. This was, and still is, a source of wonder not only to his competitors and his clients but to the whole world of art. To this day people marvel that he was able over the years to keep his financial structure firm, his credit strong. He tied up immense amounts of capital in his inventory. Altogether, in addition to the many millions he paid for single works of art he picked up at auctions and private sales, he bought eight large collections during his career, investing in them, according to the best estimates, twenty-five million dollars. He carried some items on his books for more than three decades. Works of art that he bought in 1906 and 1907 stayed in his warehouses until he began filling in the crevices of the Mellon and Kress Collections, between 1936 and 1939. The carrying charges on those items, which undoubtedly increased the altitude of the prices he got for them, were beyond calculation. Then, Duveen, who always considered buying, not selling, the main problem of his business, had to pay cash for what he bought, whereas he gave his customers practically unlimited credit. He would allow paintings to hang in a client's house for years, on the theory that where art was concerned, the aphorism about familiarity worked in reverse. To be sure, it almost always did, but in the meantime, again, his capital was tied up. Even when his clients got round to buying, he never hurried them for payment. Although among them they often owed him millions at a time, he never charged them interest. On top of that, it cost him half a million dollars a year just to run his three establishments, in New York, Paris, and London. This included not only paying his staff of runners, ushers, and experts but buying flowers and presents for his clients and their wives on their birthdays and for their sailings to and from Europe, and distributing gratuities among *their* staffs.

Duveen has been called the world's greatest borrower. No one, it has been said, knew so little about interest or paid so much of it as Duveen. Not long after his father's death, in 1908, he owed seventeen million dollars, including eleven million to his eleven brothers and sisters, whose share in his father's business he bought out; and after his Uncle Henry's death, in 1919, he bought his share with notes for an additional six million. Yet he was always borrowing more to expand the business. Fortunately, the Duveen credit was excellent. An idiosyncrasy of the Duveens, the father, Uncle Henry, and the son was having their bankers as customers or close friends or both and this gave their operations in the broad art world a certain compactness. A customer and great friend of the father's was Lord Farquhar, the head of Parr's Bank, who was also a great friend of Edward VII. The Duveens could always count on Parr's for assistance. Early in the century, it extended Duveen a credit of £1,200,000, and it kept renewing this £1,200,000 credit for the rest of Duveen's lifetime. In America, too, some of Duveen Brothers' major clients were bankers, or at least had banking influence. Early in the game, Uncle Henry, operating in the United States, acquired Morgan, Altman, P. A. B. Widener, Collis Huntington, and George J. Gould as both clients and financial advisers. At one point, Duveen counselled Uncle Henry, 'Don't ask Morgan for money. Ask him for credit.' Morgan, who was thinking of buying two million dollars' worth of Duveen objects, was asked to give the Duveen firm that amount of credit at the Morgan institutions. This worked out beautifully for everyone. Morgan got the stuff on approval, and he knew that, in the circumstances, the firm wouldn't press him for cash. In the meantime, Duveen had the prestige of Morgan credit behind him. Later, Mackay, who was a director of the Guaranty Trust, bought from Duveen without making any cash down payment. He agreed to pay off his debt a bit at a time at stipulated intervals, and Duveen mentally earmarked these payments to offset his own debt to the Guaranty Trust.

Mellon was even more helpful. He controlled powerful Pittsburgh banks and had influence in certain New York banks. He was always considering vast amounts of Duveen merchandise, which he might take a long time deciding about but rarely returned. Duveen found that while Mellon was meditating, he was completely willing to extend credit to him. Mellon regarded this as good business. When he finally paid, he ordinarily paid cash – he was the only one of Duveen's big clients who regularly did, the others preferring to pay in securities – and meanwhile he regarded the works of art he had on approval as security for Duveen's debt to his banks, on which he got interest from Duveen. Thus Duveen was paying interest on what he had borrowed from Mellon in order to buy art treasures for Mellon to keep on approval. Nevertheless, there were compensations for Duveen in this arrangement. One day, the manager of the Guaranty Trust called the harassed John H. Allen, at that time Duveen's comptroller, to complain politely that a debt to the bank of three million dollars was past due. Allen succeeded in diverting Duveen's attention from Botticelli's long, unbroken line (which he was explaining to a client) to this minuscule situation. 'Telephone Mr McEldowney, the president of the Union Trust Company, in Pittsburgh,' Duveen said tranquilly. 'Ask him for three million dollars for sixty days.' Allen telephoned the bank, which was Mellon controlled, and got it. The Guaranty Trust man felt more cheerful. Sixty days later, Duveen, his credit with the Guaranty now restored, borrowed the three million back and sent it to Mellon's bank in Pittsburgh, thus bringing cheer to Mr McEldowney. His credit was vigorous at both.

Every spring, before Duveen went abroad on his annual buying tour, whoever happened to be his comptroller would caution him not to buy anything. The inventory was over-loaded already, the comptroller would point out, and the firm's credit shouldn't be subjected to any more pressure. Duveen would promise to be good, and then, once in Europe, would buy two or three million dollars' worth of stuff. In 1927, it was the Robert

H. Benson collection of a hundred and fourteen great Italian paintings, for which Duveen paid over three million dollars in England. In 1930, it was the Dreyfus collection of Italian pictures and sculptures, for which Duveen paid four and a half million in Paris. And so it went on. He would keep the cables to America hot with requests for the money. If the comptroller responded too slowly, he raised it in England. Duveen never worried about money or about credit. He worried only about getting the most famous pictures in the world; that is, not letting any other dealers get them. He always had absolute confidence in the solidity of his financial position, because he was in it. He knew that the value of his inventory, together with what his clients owed him, far exceeded his debts, and that, furthermore, every dollar he put into his inventory automatically went up in value simply because it was an investment in Duveens. He also knew that whereas his Uncle Henry and his brothers and sisters and his comptrollers took the narrow view that it was safer to have money than to spend it, his security lay in his ability to spend it prodigally on what he could sell. He did not think that art should, or could, be sold overnight. He believed in waiting for advantageous moments; he arranged them far in advance, so he was not surprised when they came in. In his grand financial strategy, he calculated in terms of his total life span. The final tally would not be in, he figured, until he had made his last sale and died. His strategy proved sound. It was not until 1937, after he put over his last great deal with Mellon, that Duveen liquidated his £1,200,000 debt to his London bank. When he had made his very last sale, he was out of debt, and had £3,000,000 in the bank, an inventory worth £2,000,000, and his self-confidence intact.

In the early morning hours of 16 April 1912, Duveen found himself sitting with the man who was then his comptroller, Max Bruell, anxiously awaiting news of the steamship *Titanic*. The passenger list was sufficiently distinguished to include several Duveen clients, and Duveen's solicitude for their welfare was almost obsessive. Many, including relatives, waited for news that day, but it is doubtful whether any of them waited with more anxiety than Duveen, who had a passionate interest in the longevity of his clients – an interest not always felt by the relatives of the very rich. Incorrigible optimist that he was, he could not believe the mounting reports of disaster as they came in. He kept repeating to Bruell, 'Don't you think George Widener may have saved himself?' Bruell thought it unlikely. 'I think Widener will save himself,' Duveen kept insisting. Widener, a son of P. A. B. Widener, was the most important Duveen client on board, and Duveen must have felt that Widener's

Opposite *Desiderio: 'The Young Christ with St John the Baptist'. One of the treasures from the Dreyfus Collection, sold later to Mellon*

capacity for survival was commensurate with his position as a client. Through the long hours of waiting, Duveen sat clinging to this life raft, until the bitter reality swept it away from him.

Bruell once cryptically remarked of his boss, 'Anything that Joe Duveen did he thought he could do' – an utterance as prismatic with innuendo as any pronouncement ever made by the oracle at Delphi. The ability to add and subtract is a fundamental part of the equipment of a professional comptroller, and this was an ability that Duveen not only lacked but had no ambition to master. To him, money was merely a convenience, as water is to a fish, and he detested the point of view that regarded the momentary lack of it as an obstacle. He simply didn't want to hear about it. When a stringent financial problem came up, he left it to those who were interested in such matters to work it out among themselves. This inherent difference in orientation between Bruell and the head of the firm often gave Bruell frantic moments. One afternoon, Duveen, having bought some things from Morgan, asked Belle de Costa Greene, Morgan's librarian, to drop in at the gallery. When she arrived, Duveen sent for Bruell and introduced him. He followed up the introduction with a casual suggestion. 'Give Miss Greene a cheque for a million dollars,' he murmured. Bruell remembered that it was, luckily, two o'clock – almost closing time at the bank – so that he was able to ask Miss Greene whether it would be all right if he gave her the million in the morning. Miss Greene said it would. The next day, Bruell got up very early, arrived at the bank at nine o'clock, and spent the morning mixing ingredients that made it possible to carry out Duveen's order. Duveen's insouciance in giving orders like this drove Bruell crazy; he never seemed to understand that, as Bruell later complained, 'it was not quite so simple'.

On the other hand, when Bruell presented Frick, one day, with an invoice for seven million dollars, Frick understood completely and responded precisely. *He* was a man Bruell could talk to. He didn't just make an ample remark and then expect you to leave the room. He gave the invoice a sharp look and wrote down and handed to Bruell instructions to take to his, Frick's, bankers, to deliver in payment fifty thousand shares of Pennsylvania, thirty-five thousand shares of Atchison, Topeka & Santa Fé, and two million dollars' worth of French bonds. Some of Duveen's customers, unlike Frick, were petty when the time came to settle for Duveen's illustrated lectures; they paid in driblets. In a reflective spirit, the harried Bruell wrote an acquaintance:

> Mrs Stotesbury, the former Mrs Cromwell, when she wanted to make a showing in Philadelphia, got acquainted with Duveen. Duveen suggested she go away and leave the entire matter up to him.

Opposite Holbein: 'Edward VI'. One of a pair of outstanding Holbein miniatures which Duveen sold to Bache

Whereupon, he hired trucks, and the whole Duveen establishment was practically dismantled – the stuff going to Philadelphia. There, under Duveen's supervision, the entire Stotesbury house was redone for about $1,500,000 to $2,000,000. At the time, Joe said that nothing would be returned – and nothing was. Stotesbury paid up, though he drew all the cheques himself and never over $25,000 at a time till it was all paid up. Stotesbury's main delight was to play the bass drum at Stotesbury parties.

However petty Duveen's clients were about money (he forgave them because, until he came along, they had had nothing else to divert them), he himself was never petty about it. After a big sale of art objects to Rockefeller, Rockefeller left town – presumably to scrape up the money to pay. During his absence, Bruell recalled, Mrs Rockefeller rushed into Duveen's one day saying that something terrible had happened; one of her maids had dropped a vase, not knowing it was a Duveen. Duveen calmed Mrs Rockefeller down and went at once to her house and examined the vase. The damage was considerable, but he told Mrs Rockefeller not to worry. He took the vase back to his place and got an expert Japanese restorer to set to work on it at once. Duveen insisted that the restorer work day and night on it, so that the job would be finished by the time Mr Rockefeller got back to town. The restorer finished the job on the dot and sent Duveen a bill for seventy-five hundred dollars. At Bruell's suggestion that this bill might legitimately be sent to Mrs Rockefeller, Duveen was shocked. He forbade it. The two men really did not understand each other. Duveen didn't understand Bruell's successor Allen, in his turn, any better; between him and his comptrollers there was always a basic misunderstanding. Another great impresario, a contemporary of Duveen's, was the princely and prodigal Austrian theatrical producer Max Reinhardt. Reinhardt had for years a general adviser who was devoted, informed, practical, and profoundly pessimistic. Of this man, for whom he had an abiding affection, Reinhardt once said, 'In his advice to me, K— is right ninety-nine per cent of the time. But one per cent of the time he is wrong and I am right. It is on that one per cent that I live.' Duveen might well have said the same thing about himself and his comptrollers.

Although Duveen was reluctant to talk about money, he didn't mind spending it, and he didn't even mind giving it away. His benefactions, public and private, were immense. Dr Wilhelm von Bode, the German art critic and museum director who had advised Duveen on the purchase of his first collections (the Hainauer and the two Kanns), had by the late 1920s fallen on evil days; he was ill, poor, and was also going blind. When Duveen heard that von Bode was forced to put his art library up for auction he sent two emissaries to Germany with instructions to make fabulous cross-bids for the books, so that von Bode would realize a handsome sum. This was one time when the pernicious activity known as 'rigging the market' had a pure, philanthropic impulse behind it. Later,

Left *The Elgin Marbles Gallery at the British Museum;* right *the opening of the Modern Foreign and Sargent Galleries, among Duveen's gifts to the Tate Gallery, painted by Sir John Lavery*

Duveen's close friend Lord D'Abernon was in financial difficulties, and Duveen paid Duveen prices for some of his paintings – paintings the dealer could never possibly dignify with his own signature in his personal market. Duveen also gave £200,000 to the British Red Cross, presented to the British Museum the gallery for the celebrated Elgin Marbles, and made large gifts to the Tate Gallery and the National Gallery in London. Altogether, he gave away ten million dollars, and his benefactions compared favourably with those of his great clients. Duveen was sensitive, however, about bringing up the subject of money in conversation just because literal-minded men like Bruell, and, later, Allen, felt he ought to. It was all right for his clients to talk about money to each other; they, poor fellows hadn't much else to talk about. But this was not the case between any one of these clients and Duveen. Between them there was a more intimate and absorbing and exalted subject for discussion. Duveen was a millionaire, as they were. He was a philanthropist, as they were. But there was a difference. He dealt in the aesthetic and the immemorial, they in the prosaic and the temporal. The fact that only through him could they share in the excitements and rewards of his realm aroused his sympathy and, privately, his condescension. (Reproached, once, for putting a high polish on his Old Masters when he restored them, he replied that as his rich clients wanted only to see themselves reflected when they looked at works of art, he found it expedient to give his pictures a mirror surface.) He was perfectly willing, in his conversations with his clients, to give them everything he had in the way of enthusiasm for his works of art. All this was fine, but he wasn't going to clutter the high plateau with dollar signs. It was perhaps in conformity with this principle of his that he never consented to the displaying of a Duveen in Duveen's window. He wouldn't make a sandwich man out of Raphael, nor yet out of himself. If money had to be talked about, there were people to do it – people on his payroll, like Bruell and Allen, and people in banks, like Mellon and Morgan. As for him, he had time only for art.

The late Sir Maurice Bowra, of Oxford, said that Duveen was 'the most symbolic figure of the twenties'. Certainly Duveen was a man of his time. It was a time of monopoly, and Duveen out-monopolized the monopolists who were among his biggest clients. In some people, the impulse to own everything appears to be congenital. Beyond the first victories, the horizons widen; they have to control not only the main stream but its tributaries. The impulse becomes a drive that demands the extermination not only of rivals but of potential rivals – a refusal to allow them to live, or even to be born. This temperament is not confined to businessmen. Some artists, scholars, and professional philosophers have it, and even, frozen in the dicta of ideology, some humanitarians; once you've palmed truth, it becomes logical to destroy those who don't share it. That is why the mass murders of the dictators shine with altruism. Duveen's career was dominated by his monopolistic drive. In June of 1920, it was announced that Mrs Harry J. Hahn, a French lady who had married a United States Army officer and was living in Junction City, Kansas, had put on the market a painting by Leonardo da Vinci called 'La Belle Ferronnière'. The bidding for it was instantaneous and brisk. Anything by the painter of 'Mona Lisa' was newsworthy, and a reporter from the New York *World* telephoned Duveen, as the king of the art world, to ask him if he had any comment to make. He had. He issued a statement on the picture sight unseen. Among other things, he said, 'The Hahn picture is a copy, hundreds of which have been made. The real "La Belle Ferronnière" is in the Louvre.' Duveen's word carried such weight that this simple statement put a dead stop to Mrs Hahn's negotiations for selling the picture. She brought suit at once.

Mrs Andrée Ledoux Hahn at the time of the 'La Belle Ferronière' case

The resulting trial, although it didn't take place until nine years later, was a sensation – a heresy case with a picture as defendant. First, there was a preliminary hearing at the Louvre, where the Louvre Leonardo was placed side by side with Mrs Hahn's Leonardo and peered at by experts. Even at this hearing, the experts revealed a certain astigmatism; a French newspaper made the acrid comment, 'The experts came to examine the Hahn painting, but as it turns out, the painting is examining the experts.' The trial itself took place in New York, and lasted twenty-eight days. A journalist of the time said that the Hahn Leonardo trial was 'a lowbrow and a highbrow circus – the smartest show in town'. Duveen marshalled a gallery of experts for his defence – including Berenson – such as had never before been rounded up for an art suit. The 'La Belle Ferronnière' case has been called 'the world's most celebrated case of art litigation'. In his address to the jury, the Honourable Justice William Harman Black, who presided, gave the twelve good men and true some comfort for the ordeal they had undergone as the involuntary target of a bombardment of disagreements in the arcana of *expertise*. He said, 'You have been privileged to sit in on one of the most interesting cases ever tried in any court.' According to the testimony, neither Berenson nor, by this time, Duveen himself believed the Louvre Leonardo, the exemplar beside which they had found Mrs Hahn's Leonardo wanting, to be genuine. They both stated that they believed the Louvre Leonardo not to be by Leonardo. At the same time, Duveen's experts at the trial made every effort to prove that Mrs Hahn's Leonardo was not like the Louvre Leonardo and therefore, of course, could not be by Leonardo. It was very confusing, but possibly Justice Black's comforting words – which appeared to felicitate the jury just for *being* there – made it up to twelve befuddled victims in their dark hour. Still, it is no wonder that, like the experts, they disagreed. A fatal letter written by Duveen to his manager in London on 5 August 1920, was introduced by the plaintiff into the court records. It read, 'The Louvre picture is not passed by the most eminent connoisseurs as having been painted by Leonardo da Vinci, and I may say that I am entirely in accord with their opinion.' Among the experts with whom Duveen accorded was Berenson. In his book *North Italian Painters of the Renaissance*, published in 1907, he had written of the Louvre girl, 'Paris No. 1600 La Belle Ferronnière. One would regret to have to accept this as Leonardo's own work.' Justice Black, in his charge to the jury, admitted that 'it required a good deal of mental agility to follow some of the experts from their positive evidence on the stand to the diametrically opposite views they had expressed in their books long before.'

This was one lawsuit Duveen did not enjoy; the opposition was too formidable. The jury turned in a mixed verdict – nine to three in favour of Mrs Hahn. Justice Black ordered another trial, but Duveen avoided this by settling with Mrs Hahn out of court for sixty thousand dollars. What the whole thing cost him, in time and money, cannot be

THE LEONARDO DA VINCI DISPUTE: A "SLANDER OF TITLE" ACTION.

"LA BELLE FERRONNIÈRE": A PICTURE IN THE LOUVRE, PARIS, GENERALLY REGARDED AS AN AUTHENTIC WORK BY LEONARDO DA VINCI (FOR COMPARISON WITH THE ADJOINING ILLUSTRATION).

THE SUBJECT OF A "SLANDER OF TITLE" ACTION BROUGHT BY ITS OWNER AGAINST SIR JOSEPH DUVEEN, FOR CALLING IT "A COPY": MRS. HAHN'S PICTURE (FOR COMPARISON WITH THE ADJOINING ILLUSTRATION).

SIR JOSEPH DUVEEN, BT.: THE FAMOUS ART DEALER, FROM WHOM MRS. HAHN CLAIMED £100,000 DAMAGES FOR "SLANDER OF TITLE."

In the Supreme Court at New York, on February 5, a suit for 500,000 dollars (£100,000) damages for slander of title was begun by Mrs. Andrée Ledoux Hahn against Sir Joseph Duveen. The action arose out of his alleged statement, nine years ago, that Mrs. Hahn's picture, "La Belle Ferronnière," purporting to be by Leonardo da Vinci, was only a copy of that master's work. Mrs. Hahn contended that Sir Joseph's declaration had "killed" a proposed sale of the painting to the Kansas City Art Institute. This long-standing art dispute was discussed by a committee of experts in Paris in 1923, and we reproduce above two photographs taken on that occasion and published in our issues of Sept. 22

THE 1923 DISCUSSION OF THE CLAIM OF MRS. HAHN'S PICTURE TO BE AN ORIGINAL LEONARDO: ART EXPERTS IN CONCLAVE IN PARIS—SHOWING PROFESSOR VENTURI (CENTRE BACKGROUND)

EXPERTS WHO PRONOUNCED ON THE 1923 DISPUTE: (L. TO R.) SIR MARTIN CONWAY, SIR CHARLES HOLMES, M. NICOLLE, PROFESSOR VENTURI, MR. ROGER FRY, MR. L. S. LEVY, M. LURFROSE, AND CAPTAIN L. DOUGLAS.

and 29 in that year. It was reported at the time that the experts were understood to have pronounced the Louvre picture to be an original Leonardo and Mrs. Hahn's picture a copy, opinions being based partly on artistic quality and partly on the nature of the pigment. Mrs. Hahn's pending action against Sir Joseph Duveen was also mentioned at that time. It was stated in a message from New York on February 16 last that the suit recently begun there had lasted for ten days, and that Sir Joseph Duveen had been in the witness-box for five days. He was reported to have maintained his ground that an art expert is entitled to give his opinion. In the interests of art and his profession, he had refused an opportunity given him to retract. He submitted that if, as he believed, the Louvre portrait was Da Vinci's original, he had no alternative but to deny the claims of Mrs. Hahn's picture.

computed, but the sum was certainly vast. And the trial did not even enhance his prestige. But it did ruin Mrs Hahn's chance of selling her picture. Since Duveen had not seen it at the time he made his original statement, he could have had no precise knowledge of it. There was one thing, though, that he did know. This was that he did not own it. As he did not own it, he could not sell it. For the moment, then, Mrs Hahn became a business rival, and, as such, she had to go to the block. During the suit, Duveen's associates couldn't understand why he should deny the authenticity of a picture with which he had nothing to do, and thus involve himself in expensive litigation, but his recklessness in expressing his opinions about other people's stuff was not without value. Duveen looked upon himself as the Pontifex Maximus of the art world; he was tolerant of an associate who customarily called him Josephus Rex. His lawsuits, even those he lost, helped to establish his pre-eminence as a monopolist not only of merchandise but of opinion. Absolutism in opinion was as important to Duveen as freight rebates were to his clients in oil, aluminium, or steel. And he achieved it. H. E. Huntington, chatting one day with a member of Duveen's staff in the drawing-room of his house, nodded towards the andirons in his fireplace. They were just two nice, ordinary andirons. 'If Duveen offered me two identical andirons,' he said, 'and told me that they were remarkable and asked me seventy-five thousand dollars apiece for them, I would gladly pay it.'

To establish this kind of absolutism took unremitting vigilance and unremitting ingenuity. Duveen's name must be inseparably associated with not just great works of art but the greatest, and he would allow nothing to tarnish this glittering trademark. That is why when he bought pictures by first-rate painters who had had the bad luck to do their work in periods that he did not specialize in and, having decided for one reason or another not to put them in his basement, he shipped them to London dealers to sell for him, he always stipulated that they must be sold austerely under the names of the artists who painted them, not as Duveens. Just as Duveen would not go into partnership with certain artists on their signatures, so he repudiated more conventional partnerships after he had entered into them. On one occasion he and a London dealer bought two fine Lawrences in England in partnership. Shortly afterward, Duveen sold them to Mrs Stotesbury, but he did not inform the London dealer that he had made the sale. When the dealer began to dun him, Duveen said that the pictures would be tough to sell but that nevertheless he believed in them; he offered the dealer a handsome profit for his interest, and the dealer gratefully accepted it. The amount Duveen paid the dealer was larger than the amount he actually owed him on the Stotesbury sale. But Duveen simply did not wish

Opposite *A contemporary press report of the 'La Belle Ferronière' case* to impede his own flight as the lone eagle. Another partnership that Duveen transmuted into a solo flight involved the purchase of a Velásquez, 'Infanta Maria Theresa'. Harry Payne Bingham, its owner, had promised it to Knoedler's, for a very high price. Duveen knew about it, as he knew about most things that were going on in his world, and he went to Charles R. Henschel, the head of Knoedler's, with the proposition that they buy it jointly. He would put up all the money, and in return he was to have the exclusive right to sell it. Henschel agreed. Duveen took the picture and a long silence followed – two years of it. Henschel became restive and called on Duveen to ask him why he hadn't sold the picture. Duveen said blandly, 'How can I sell it? I don't own it!' In order to make his sense of ownership complete, he was willing to pay Henschel a large sum. He didn't care in the least that the sum he had paid Henschel far exceeded his own profit on the trans- action when, soon after, he sold the picture to Bache. He had proved once more that an important picture could be bought only from him.

Sometimes, Duveen permitted his competitors an unusually generous allowance of rope to hang themselves with. The Marquis de Talleyrand had a Mantegna (though Berenson said it was not a Mantegna but a Girolamo da Cremona). He sold it to Duveen's Italian rival Count Contini. The Count sold it to Bache. Mantegna is an artist of the first rank, and for Bache to buy a Mantegna from a rival dealer was to contradict the major premise of Duveen's philosophy. Duveen settled the matter for eternity when he got out the Bache catalogue. There, Contini's Mantegna is reproduced and listed as a Girolamo da Cremona. Compared to Mantegna, Girolamo is a small potato, and Duveen didn't mind at what shop Bache or anybody else bought his small potatoes. Besides sustaining the major premise, this listing in Bache's catalogue paid Duveen another satisfying dividend. It demonstrated, in Bache's own publication, that he had bought a Girolamo da Cremona when he thought he was buying a Mantegna. Bache never bought from Contini again.

One rival dealer, who suffered much from Duveen, always spoke with mixed resent- ment and awe about Duveen's monopolistic grip on the art market. He also recalled an occasion on which Duveen gave him a chance to retaliate. Duveen was as prodigal of talk as of money, and couldn't resist telling everybody – even his rivals – about his plans. This particular rival unashamedly confessed the pleasure he took in exploiting this weak- ness of Duveen's, though he still refers to him as 'a miracle man in a miracle time'. Duveen had gleefully announced to his rival that he was going to buy the Dreyfus Collection, and he was going to buy it cheap – for a million dollars. As it happened, this dealer himself knew all about the Dreyfus Collection: it had recently been offered to him for a million dollars. Duveen found that the price of the collection was going up – to a million and a half, then to two and to three. It kept ascending. He kept confiding his grievance to his rival. 'Somebody is bidding the Dreyfus up on me,' he said bitterly. The rival sympathized and, knowing that Duveen would never let the collection go, quickly went behind the scenes to add to Duveen's grievance. He bid it up beyond any possibility of buying it himself, but he *did* bid it up. He forced Duveen to pay the four and a half million he finally gave for the Dreyfus Collection. 'Somebody might ask,' the dealer once said, 'why I didn't buy the collection myself when I could have had it for a million dollars. Well, the answer to that is that there would have been no use whatever in my buying it, because I couldn't have sold it. There were only a few men in America rich enough to buy it from me. Those men were all Duveen clients. Had I bought it, all Duveen would have had to say – and he could have tossed it off in the most casual way – would have been "Oh, yes, the Dreyfus. I know all about the Dreyfus. It was offered to me first, naturally. Had it been interesting, of course *I* would have bought it."' Duveen had attained such power that the word 'interesting', properly inflected, would have killed for this rival any chance of selling the collection, excerpts from which now form part of the glory of the Mellon and Kress contributions to the National Gallery in Washington.

One way Duveen maintained his position was to make sure that no picture of his ever declined in price. He was constantly buying back himself – or having his clients buy – Duveen pictures from the estates of customers, to keep the market up. When Elbert H. Gary died, in 1927, Duveen was afraid that an auction of his art works, most of which had come from Duveen Brothers, might bring such low prices that his business would be injured. He therefore offered to purchase the lot for a million and a half, cash. The offer was not accepted, so Duveen took the necessary precautions. At the auction, he bought Gainsborough's 'Harvest Waggon', paying three hundred and sixty thousand dollars for the picture, which he had sold to Gary for one hundred and sixty-five thousand, and he persuaded several of his clients to buy at the auction. The sales totalled nearly two and a half million dollars, which was far more than Gary had spent on his collection. From then on, any client of Duveen's could die secure in the knowledge that as long as Duveen was alive his collection would never depreciate in value. Clients who were so imprudent as to survive him were not so lucky.

It was by methods like these that Duveen kept up the prices of celebrated Old Masters and gradually set up his virtual monopoly. He both paid and got higher prices than other dealers, and he succeeded in selling the pictures for the very reason that he was willing to pay those higher prices. 'You are a great man, and your name is magic,' he once said to Mellon. 'But even *your* name won't get you Duveen pictures.' He let that sink in. 'Neither will *my* name get me Duveen pictures,' he continued, with a rare access of modesty. 'I get them because people know I will pay the highest prices in the world for them. I can't afford to get you these pictures unless you are willing to pay me a profit on them.' He paused for effect, then said, '*You* get them, Mr Mellon, because *I* get them!'

Bernard Berenson in the gardens of his villa, I Tatti, photographed by Cecil Beaton

Chapter 4
B. B.

DUVEEN loved walking. Especially did he love walking through art galleries and along the Bond Streets of the world. On his walks, he usually had with him a disciple or an eager customer, whom he would harangue on his favourite topic – indeed, his only topic: art. The wares he saw displayed in the windows of competitors often stirred him to fury. He would pound the pavement with his walking-stick, shouting 'Rot! Fake! Nonsense!' so loudly that passers-by, whose immediate concerns were remote from Duveen's, would halt and marvel that a few daubs in a window could arouse such expletive passion. In his walks through public galleries, Duveen was less choleric; to be sure, he did not own the paintings displayed in them, but then neither did his competitors. This peripatetic method of instruction was wholly non-Socratic; Duveen did all the talking. He had everything to tell his pupils; his pupils had nothing to tell him. Two doughty American aficionados of medieval armour, Mackay and Hearst, received ambulatory instruction from Duveen on the minutiae of ancient jambs, vambraces, and cuirasses. Other pedestrian companions were Bache, Mellon, Ramsay MacDonald, Mrs Arabella Huntington, and Mrs Horace E. Dodge. Actually, Duveen would take a walk with anybody who was willing to listen and who could afford to satisfy, some day, the desire he kindled.

In all the years of Duveen's ascendancy, only one companion on his walks ever reversed Duveen's role. With this companion, the teacher was the pupil, the haranguer the haranguee, the oracle the listener. On these very special walks Duveen's instructor was Bernard Berenson, an American expatriate who lived in Italy. Berenson was no mean walker himself. He was schoolmaster to a little strolling group of his own, but between the memberships of the two schools there was a disparity that could be measured only in light-years. The two schools had only one member in common – Duveen, master in his own, pupil in the other. Edith Wharton took walks with Berenson and was inspired to write a novelette in which the hero, like Berenson, became devoted to Early Italian art. Another stroller with Berenson was Marcel Proust; embedded in his great book are many reflections on art that passed through the fine filter of Berenson's scholarly mind. Still another fellow-pedestrian was Kenneth Clark, later the director of the National Gallery in London, now Lord Clark, and one of the most eminent living writers and lecturers on art. Another was John Walker, associated with the National Gallery in Washington for thirty years, first as Chief Curator, then Director, and now Director Emeritus, who would go to Italy at the drop of a hat to amble with Berenson. So did Dr Alfred M. Frankfurter, the scholarly editor of *Art News*. Duveen's earliest walks with Berenson resulted in a notable feat of transubstantiation. Without moving from I Tatti, his lovely villa outside Florence, Berenson became the keystone of Duveen's remarkable career. Duveen acquired Berenson's eye, marketed his intuitions, grafted on to himself his instructor's opinions, authority, scholarship, and conscience.

Berenson at Harvard, aged twenty-two

Berenson, a Bostonian of Lithuanian-Jewish origin, graduated from Harvard in 1887. A photograph of Berenson at Harvard shows an extraordinarily sensitive and romantic profile and a superabundance of curly dark locks (they *are* locks, not merely hair), reaching to his braid-bordered coat collar. The photograph reveals intensity and a hint of flamboy-ance, suggesting the Orient rather than the Baltic littoral. Logan Pearsall Smith, who became Berenson's brother-in-law, remarked in his volume of reminiscences, *Unforgotten Years*, that there were two intellectuals at Harvard when he was there – George Santayana and Berenson – and also conveyed the idea that he himself did not have enough intellectual equipment to approach them. At Harvard, Berenson quickly impressed his elders, if not all his contemporaries. In a journal that he kept during the Second World War, while a generous Italian friend was hiding him, near Florence, from the Germans, he recorded that he found his elderly professors far more accessible than the undergraduates. Instinctively, he gravitated to the society of his mentors – William James, Charles Eliot Norton,

Marrett Wendell, Crawford Howell Toy, and Charles Rockwell Lanman, the last his professor of Sanskrit. He also became a fixture at the salons of Mrs Gardner, who felt in this fervent undergraduate an incalculable intellectual promise. From the notoriously volatile Norton, Professor of the History of Art, he received an affection that had in it a certain ambivalence, and from Mrs Gardner an affection that had in it no ambivalence whatever. It was Berenson who eventually selected for her the chief masterpieces in the famous collection at Fenway Court, her home in Boston. Later generations of Harvard undergraduates had to pay a dollar to visit Mrs Gardner's palace on a selected day each year and view the paintings she had collected on Berenson's advice; the young Berenson, in his Harvard days, was allowed to come to see her any time he liked, for nothing.

All her life, the Serpent of the Charles, as Berenson called her – or, as he referred to her on one occasion, 'Boston's first pre-cinema star' – indulged herself in a far-flung genealogical fantasy. She was born Isabella Stewart and she often made, according to Morris Carter, her official biographer*, the flat statement 'that she was descended from Robert Bruce and counted Mary Stuart among her ancestors'. But she wanted to historicize her Christian name also, and therefore she came to identify herself with an earlier patron of the arts, Isabella d'Este. The two genealogies were scarcely reconcilable, but it is one of the advantages of fantasy that it aligns the irreconcilable. Even Berenson encouraged her in this indulgence in mistaken identity; in one of his letters, he urged her to buy a picture because it was a portrait of 'the greatest and most fascinating lady of the Renaissance – your worthy precursor and patron saint – Isabella d'Este, Marchioness of Mantua'. Mrs Gardner didn't like her ancestress's hand, and wrote Berenson to that effect. Berenson wrote back that the hand wasn't 'offensive', and added that he wouldn't urge the purchase solely as a work of art but that it had 'potent attraction as the portrait of Isabella', and Mrs Gardner made the purchase.

Upon Berenson's graduation from Harvard, a group of his Boston friends, in an orgy of blind investment, got up a purse of seven hundred and fifty dollars to send him to Europe for a year. In that time, they felt, his immense but vague promise would focus on some specific ambition that would justify the outlay. His hopes amorphous but high, Berenson sailed. Unhappily, in the course of the year so did a number of his benefactors. They kept looking in on him to see how their investment was going, to try to detect a hardening of the molten promise into a solid core of accomplishment. Berenson was a slow solidifier; at the end of the year, his sponsors felt they had made a bad investment. At this critical point, Professor Ferdinand Bocher, the head of the Modern Languages Department at Harvard, looked in on Berenson in Florence. He was not an investor but

* *Isabella Stewart Gardner and Fenway Court, 1926*

Left *Isabella Stewart Gardner, painted by Sargent, in 1888;* right *the hall of I Tatti, with Berenson's books and paintings of the Italian Renaissance*

he was a friend; he thought that a year was too short a time in which to conduct an experiment so gravid with possibilities. Mrs Gardner was in Europe at this time, and Bocher persuaded her to lend Berenson another seven hundred and fifty dollars. Berenson ultimately repaid this loan, and, by way of dividend, helped Mrs Gardner assemble her collection, which cost her three million dollars. Duveen later offered her fifteen million for it, and the offer was refused.

In Berenson's exceptionally impersonal and self-critical *Sketch for a Self-Portrait*, published towards the end of his life, he mentioned his failure to meet the demand for 'output' by the Boston syndicate. Still sensitive to the stern voice of that unsatisfied demand, he wrote:

> I could retort to the voice, 'All about me, ever since I left Harvard, it was said that I was loafing, that I was wasting my best years in mere amusement, that the little I had published was no proof that I could or did work. I dared not resist the chance offered of proving that I could toil and plod and pedantize and bore with the best of them.'

The chance he referred to was the chance to prepare his first major work, *The Drawings of the Florentine Painters*, a formidable project on which he laboured for ten years. He considered that allowing himself to be 'seduced' into doing it was the greatest error of his life, because the publication of this classic turned him into 'that equivocal thing', an 'expert' on art. The frustration of a writer *manqué* is evidenced on almost every page of *Sketch for a Self-Portrait*. He was eighty when he wrote this book, and thought he had 'nearly emancipated myself from the future and entirely from the past', but he was still disturbed by one thing:

> One habit I have not yet succeeded in getting rid of: the inveterate one of feeling that when at home I must sit at my desk for so long each day to write, not letters whether of business or of friendship, but printable stuff, even when there is no idea of publishing connected with it. If I have failed to do it, I feel morally hangdoggy and physically unclean.

It is possible that a more cheerful view of Berenson's seduction could be taken. For more than half a century, he was generally acknowledged the foremost authority on Italian art of the Renaissance. Many of his pupils and disciples became the curators of the major art galleries of the world. One of them, looking lovingly at a copy of Berenson's *Italian Painters of the Renaissance*, once said to a visitor, 'No curator could possibly do without this.' To Berenson's exquisite villa, I Tatti, with its brilliant collection of pictures and its magnificent library of books and photographs, came the great figures of our time and those aspiring to be the great figures of the future. Berenson, who deplored the fact that he couldn't say no, saw most of them. In one of the smaller living rooms at I Tatti, where luncheon guests were served cocktails and *canapés*, there hung an altarpiece, a gold-framed triptych by Sassetta, depicting 'Saint Francis in Ecstasy' and other subjects. 'You know, this house has a peculiar effect on people,' Berenson said ruefully to one visitor. 'It makes them behave as though they were in church.' Nevertheless, the pre-luncheon conversation in this room was usually gay and secular. Like George Bernard Shaw, Berenson early came to be known by his initials. Even his wife called him B.B. Italians affectionately referred to him as Il Bibi.

In the many years Berenson lived in Italy – 'I cannot be considered a casual visitor,' he once said – he produced a succession of books and monographs on Italian art that are classic works in their field. His contributions to art scholarship are many and diverse. Having observed, in his research, that certain groups of paintings that had long been attributed to well-known masters showed consistent deviations, Berenson felt they must be the work of other, unknown artists. He invented for these unknown artists names that indicated their origins – names like Master of the Castello Nativity, Master of San Miniato, Alunno di Benozzo, Alunno di Domenico. 'Master', as Berenson used the word, has a special meaning. Since the painter of certain works cannot be identified, Berenson chose one painting – the 'Castello' Nativity, for example – that seemed to him to illustrate most clearly the style of the painter and then attributed all the paintings in this style to that artist. 'Alunno di' is the Italian way of saying 'pupil of', and Berenson used the phrase to designate a painter who was himself unknown by name but whose style strongly resembled that of a master who was known.

Two of Berenson's specific creations, Alunno di Domenico and Amico di Sandro, have interesting biographies. In the case of the former, Berenson had a satisfaction that must have come to very few people in the history of scholarship: the lost birth certificate turned up. After he had invented Alunno di Domenico, documentary evidence proved that one artist, Bartolommeo di Giovanni, had indeed painted all the pictures Berenson had attributed to him. Pygmalion, working in the dark, suddenly found his Galatea flooded with light. The history of his other creation, Amico di Sandro, is a gruesome tale of disinterested infanticide. There was, Berenson felt, one artist whose style combined the features of Sandro Botticelli and Filippino Lippi, with a dash of Ghirlandaio; he wasn't any of these, but he leaned most heavily towards Botticelli. Berenson christened him Amico di Sandro and attributed a group of pictures to him. In Amico di Sandro he created an artist who was more consistent, more nearly perfect, more distinctive, and more readily recognizable than any actual artist. This human artifact of Berenson's was in itself a work of art; it grew in beauty as, over the years, he increased the man's production. Amico got better and better. He never had a lapse; he seemed immune to the declensions that afflict other artists. His market value in America went up steadily. One of the greatest American collectors paid altitudinous prices for him, and blessed Berenson for having created him. But then Berenson began to disapprove of Amico. His patient and laborious studies finally persuaded him that Amico was too good to be true. Nobody, Berenson felt, could be that good – so consistent, so distinctive. In the strong solution of Berenson's scholarship, Amico disintegrated. Berenson divided him into three parts; he gave part of him back to Botticelli, part to Filippino Lippi, and part to Ghirlandaio. The effect on the American collector who had paid so high for Amico was catastrophic. He turned on the Pygmalion of I Tatti. In the interest of some such vapourish abstraction as the integrity of scholarship, Berenson had demolished the finest anonym the collector owned. The circumstance that if it hadn't been for Berenson, he couldn't have taken up with Amico in the first place did not mitigate his anger. He had paid a price for Amico commensurate with the eminence of Amico's creator. If Berenson was willing to question the legitimacy of his offspring, *he* wasn't; he suffered a paroxysm of loyalty, and in his anguish he made the categorical assertion, 'Berenson is crazy!' The late Amico's pictures were as lovely as ever, but this did not console him; Berenson said they were not by Amico. There have been many instances of somebody's hitting the ceiling because a picture turned out not to be by the artist who was thought to have painted it, but this was the first instance of somebody's

Opposite *Bartolommeo Bulgarini: 'Nativity'. Attributed by Berenson to 'Ugolino Lorenzetti', an amalgam of Ugolino da Siena and Pietro Lorenzetti*

hitting the ceiling because a picture turned out not to be by an artist that it was not by in the first place. The American collector stuck to Amico, Berenson or no Berenson. And it is not inconceivable that he will some day reap the rewards of his loyalty. Documentation came forth to actualize Alunno di Domenico. Perhaps a similar miracle will occur in the case of Amico di Sandro.

Something of Berenson's legendary quality may be gathered from an anecdote in his journal. After his period of hiding during the war, he had barely settled down again in the somewhat damaged I Tatti when four young men came to see him. One was a painter and two were ambitious to be art critics. When Berenson questioned the fourth, the young man admitted he had no interest in art. 'Why, then, have you come to see me?' B.B. asked. The young man replied, 'Oh, I just thought that you were a sight one ought to see.' And, indeed, Berenson was. It has been said that he was the epitome of what the descendants of an immemorial aristocratic line should look like but unfortunately seldom do. His appearance may have stemmed from the fact that his background, while certainly not manorial, was in a sense aristocratic. He referred to himself as 'a child of the aristocratic and cultural ghetto'; his ancestors were rabbis. He was small and dressed with great elegance, and he spoke in a voice that was at once soft and penetrating. He spoke English like a cultured foreigner, pronouncing each syllable punctiliously: 'When I was a jun⁄i⁄or at Har⁄vard', 'pas⁄sion⁄ate de⁄vo⁄tion'. A high⁄born Italian friend said that Berenson spoke Italian the same way; his Italian, this friend maintained, was straight out of Dante. Once when he lost his temper and mellifluously berated a Venetian gondolier who had taken him down the wrong canal, so that he missed a view he had wanted to see, the lucky boatman thought he was being complimented. In his last years there was no longer in his appearance any hint of flamboyance; his skin was dead white, almost transparent; his blue eyes were clear and lively. He was described by another of his friends as 'a wizard in ivory'. One didn't quite get from his imposing appearance an impression of serenity; Berenson was too minutely aware of what was going on in the world, and too combatively interested in it, for that. When his face was in repose, there was, at the most, the suggestion of a fleeting truce between the warring of what he called his 'many selves'.

Not long before his death, Berenson journeyed from I Tatti to Venice to attend the great Bellini Exhibition, in the Doges' Palace. His name was mentioned on nearly every page of the catalogue; the text describing the hundred and forty⁄one pictures was studded with

Opposite Master of the Castello Nativity: *'Profile Portrait of a Lady'. Though now given to one of Berenson's 'creations', he himself attributed it to Domenico Veneziano, and it was presumably bought as such by Bache.*

references to his works, and the bibliographical index listed eleven books by him. One morning, Berenson, strolling from his hotel to the palace, in the company of an American correspondent he had invited to go along, remarked of Venice, 'The richest, and most exquisite artifact in the history of civilization because she has been spared by that great and beneficent goddess, Poverty. For a century, the Venetians have been too poor to build anything new.' As Berenson and the correspondent walked through the busy narrow streets, over the gentle humps of the bridges crossing the little canals, past the black‑and‑ash‑grey façades of ancient churches that looked like the intricately decorated frontispieces of medieval story books, the crowds swirled past the small, slowly moving figure in brown fedora, brown suit, gleaming brown boots. Berenson kept raising his hat to acquaintances. He spoke of the dozens of American books and magazine articles he had been reading. The correspondent suddenly found himself in the middle of a discussion of Phillips Brooks, the Boston divine. The corners of Berenson's eyes crinkled. What he was about to say seemed so funny to him that he stopped dead to emphasize it. 'Do you know,' he said, 'that when I went to call upon the Spanish philosopher Unamuno, in Salamanca, and happened to ask him whom he preferred to read, who his favourite American author was, he replied, "Phillips Brooks. I love the sermons of Phillips Brooks"?' When B.B. had recovered from his enjoyment of this surprising preference, he started walking again, and the two men emerged presently into the great, colonnaded splendour of the Piazza San Marco. They paused for a moment, as anyone must, even a person to whom the scene is as familiar as it is to Berenson. The corners of his eyes crinkled again. 'Do you know,' he said, 'that one evening, as a petit‑bourgeois French couple, trippers, were coming out of that little street beside San Marco' – he pointed his walking‑stick – 'the man was overheard to say to his wife, his voice twanging with irritation, "I *told* you there was a square here"?'

Outside the doors of the exhibition, a small group greeted Berenson – officials of the show, and various dignitaries. There was much hat lifting and embracing and a flood of Italian. A man whom Berenson evidently had not seen for a long time came up and they embraced affectionately. The two conversed in German, and after a few minutes, the man began to cry and hastily moved away. Berenson, followed by everyone else, walked in to the exhibit. The muscles in his face looked taut. 'That was the director of the museum in Dresden before the war,' he told the correspondent. 'He returned to resume his former post, but the Russians came and carted everything off – all the most beautiful things. They had no right to them, but they took them. What made my friend cry was not alone that they took the things off but that *they were so badly packed*! I execrate those people!' A lady came up to him, smiling and breathless. Berenson greeted her ecstatically and introduced her to the correspondent. 'Miss Freya Stark,' Berenson said. 'Do you know her books? No? Then you have missed an enchantment beyond belief. Of course, you wouldn't know it in

*Berenson at work – using a magnifying glass to study the
brushwork of his Bellini 'Madonna'*

her present conventional dress, but she is a Bedouin. She was intended by Providence to
be a Bedouin.' Miss Stark laughed, and the little procession moved on to the pictures.

Now Berenson went to work with his tools – a flashlight, a magnifying glass, and slung
over one shoulder, a pair of opera glasses. Turning on the flashlight, he peered through
the magnifying glass at the dark, aged backgrounds of the pictures – at a fillet of myrtle
around the head of a saint in one, at the soft contours of the hills behind Vicenza in
another. The torch lit the fading hills. 'Exactly what it is today, isn't it, Freya?' he said,
and he and Miss Stark gazed with delight at an example of the unchanging in a changing
world. 'Do you remember the Latin poet who describes this scene?' Berenson asked her.
'You used to know him.' Miss Stark began to recite the pertinent verse, but after the first
two lines he took over and recited the rest. On the great triptychs and some of the other
altarpieces, Berenson trained his opera glasses. Before No. 80 – '*Il Cristo Morto Sorretto
da Angeli*' – he stopped. The catalogue contained a reference to what Berenson had said
about the painting in 1894, but he was as moved as if he were seeing it for the first time.
The picture shows Christ seated, the head fallen against the right shoulder, the eyes closed.

Four lovely cherubs are supporting him. One of the cherubs stands partly behind the Christ, so that only his small legs and tiny torso are visible. 'The audacity of Bellini!' said Berenson. 'What a dazzling innovator he was to allow that child's head to remain invisible! And look – look at these adorable children! Look at their faces! They know that Christ has suffered; they are aware of it without understanding it. They know that they ought to be sympathetic, and they are doing their best. What they are really longing for is to be off by themselves. And you know that in a few minutes, when they are away from the tragic figure, they will be laughing and playing happily. They really can't wait.' B.B. stopped speaking. He stood in silence, drinking in the picture, and so did his group, for whom it had become a symbol of the chasm between the innocence of childhood and the agony of living. 'And to think that this glorious picture is kept hidden away in Rimini, where, of course, no one ever sees it,' he said as he moved off. He found quick comfort in one panel of a nearby altarpiece – a Church father in a heavily brocaded robe, one hand holding a staff, the other resting on his knee. 'See the *weight* of that hand!' Berenson exclaimed. 'And the *weight* of that *brocade*! You must feel a muscular reaction. If you don't feel it physically, it's mere illustration.' The correspondent did indeed feel the two weights. There percolated into his mind a dim notion of what Berenson's famous 'tactile values' are. B.B. moved on, then stopped, his flashlight and glass focused on a small, dark picture. 'This Bellini is *not* a Bellini,' he said at once, without even turning round to see whether he was overheard. 'But it's very well worth looking at.' The correspondent looked at it, but with the feeling that he was wasting his time. An American in the group was writing a biography of Bellini. 'Please, B.B.,' he said now, 'will you come and look at this predella. I am not at all sure. . . .' B.B. darted across the room, examined it, and was sure. The group drifted on through the exhibition rooms. Berenson linked arms with the correspondent and said, 'Now I should like you to see a most wonderful thing, a work of sublime genius, a picture of the greatest spirit ever produced. Its significance is – if you will forgive me – cosmic. If people looked at it with sympathy and understanding – if everyone did – they would find salvation in it. It would be the salvation of all of us.' They halted before No. 44, 'Il Salvatore Benedicente', lent by the Louvre – a Christ, three-quarter length. The right hand is raised, the lips are parted, the left hand clasps a Bible. The habiliment is brown, rent to show the breast. The eyes are pale blue. At this picture Berenson stared a long time, saying nothing at all.

At lunch that day in the dining-room of his hotel, Berenson, surrounded by eight or ten friends, was in high spirits, despite the strenuous morning he had put in at the Doges' Palace. He said that after living for many years in cherished obscurity he had begun to receive fan letters from America. An excerpt from his *Sketch for a Self-Portrait* had appeared, with photographs, in an American magazine, and this had started the flow. He was forced to conclude that this magazine was read almost exclusively in hairdressing parlours, he said, for many of the letters began, 'While having my hair done today, I happened to read your fascinating....' Berenson had evolved a picture of rows of ladies under aluminium helmets absorbing simultaneously his transient, rueful octogenarian reflections and their permanents. One of the lunch guests, the curator John Walker, whom Berenson referred to as his 'pet biped', was gravely quoted by another guest, an earnest young man, as having said that no person should be engaged for even a minor post in a museum unless he is thoroughly familiar with Berenson's *Italian Painters of the Renaissance*. B.B.'s eyes lit with humorous malice. He turned to his pet biped. 'Do you swear them in?' he asked. 'You should swear them in, the way they do Presidents and Supreme Court Justices in the United States.' He jumped to his feet, put one hand on an imaginary *Italian Painters of the Renaissance*, and raised the other. 'I solemnly swear not to offer an opinion on an Italian picture between 1201 and 1699 without having duly mastered....' He kept improvising until the whole thing was dissolved in self-mockery.

Of all the important American collectors, Berenson admired Frick the most, it appeared. For one thing, he had a beautiful head. And although Berenson never found much to admire in the furnishings and pictures in Frick's Pittsburgh mansion, he was warm in his praise for the French art in the Frick Collection in New York. He told a story about Frick. The American collectors of Frick's era, he said, often felt guilty about paying such vast sums for their pictures, and Frick was no exception. Frick had bought Velásquez's 'Philip IV of Spain' for around four hundred thousand dollars. Learning that Philip IV had paid Velásquez the equivalent of six hundred dollars for it, Frick made an elaborate computation to find out what six hundred dollars at six per cent interest compounded semi-annually from 1645 to 1910 would come to, and found to his joy, that he had got the picture for less than nothing.

Then Berenson recalled a similar story about H. E. Huntington. A friend of Huntington's had once said he was shocked that a sensible man would pay six hundred and twenty thousand dollars for one picture. He was referring to Gainsborough's 'The Blue Boy', which Huntington had bought from Duveen. Huntington, who knew there was no use trying to explain the delights of collecting to a non-believer, tried to justify his purchase on economic grounds; he figured out a way of reducing the price he had paid after he had paid it. 'Listen,' he said. 'I've bought 'em for five hundred, for five thousand, for a hundred and fifty thousand. The one I paid six-twenty for is the greatest in the world. When you average 'em all up, the price of each isn't bad.'

These stories led Berenson to enlarge on the vagaries of collectors and patrons of art. On the whole, he thought the twentieth-century ones an improvement over the historic ones.

He said some harsh words about Isabella d'Este, and spoke as resentfully of her shameful treatment of Mantegna as if the indignity the painter suffered had occurred only a few days before. He circled round to that later Isabella, Mrs Jack Gardner, whose vivacity and charm were, he said, unforgettable. 'But you know that after her husband died – he was the dearest fellow in the world – Mrs Jack made a great discovery,' Berenson said. 'She discovered that things cost money. Mrs Leland Stanford made the same discovery after *her* husband died, and then she lived like a starveling. Mrs Jack, when she came to Europe in later years and returned to the hotels where she had lavishly stayed as the Dollar Princess, asked for the cheapest rooms. On one visit to America, thirty years ago, my wife and I were her guests, and at dinner the first night there was scarcely enough to eat. We thought, well, we are going to the theatre, and when we get back, there will be supper. There was no supper. After we'd gone upstairs to our rooms, Mary and I felt hunger pangs. We couldn't get to sleep, and we stole downstairs to the kitchen to forage in the icebox. In that immense repository we found two dog biscuits!' Berenson touched on the racial influxes that had transformed the character of New England entirely since his day, made some inquiries about the recent acquisitions of the Nelson Gallery of Art, in Kansas City, and then went up to his room to take a nap.

Berenson first saw Duveen in London, in 1906. Lady Sassoon, the wife of Sir Edward Albert Sassoon and mother of Sir Philip Sassoon, and a devoted friend of Berenson – he referred to her as the 'noblest of the Rothschild women' – urged him to go to the Duveen London gallery. Duveen, then thirty-seven, had just bought the Hainauer Collection, and Lady Sassoon wanted Berenson to look at some of the pieces. On her promise that she would not introduce him, he consented. One of the pictures Berenson looked at was first rate, and he decided to try to buy it for Mrs Gardner. 'I'll pay you £30,000 for it,' he said, without preliminaries, to Duveen. Duveen turned to Lady Sassoon. 'This fellow knows too much,' he said, smiling. Berenson and Lady Sassoon left the gallery without Berenson's having been introduced and without Duveen's having either accepted or rejected the offer. Mrs Gardner never got the picture. It went to a favourite client of Duveen's for about £60,000. Berenson had unwittingly put a ceiling price on the picture, and Duveen used it as a floor.

Though Berenson had not been introduced, Duveen had guessed who the visitor was, and their encounter was to have an enormous effect on Berenson's future. Duveen, more definite about his aims than Berenson – after all, truth and beauty are imponderables, offering their pursuer a good deal of latitude – and, in the worldly sense, much shrewder, seems to have had a suspicion of what Berenson's visit could mean to him; Berenson obviously had none. When Berenson left Duveen without having met him, he didn't expect he'd ever have to see him again. He was wrong. Not long afterwards, Duveen sought out Berenson. This time they met. Duveen asked Berenson to become his paid adviser on Italian pictures. Berenson would authenticate pictures for him and would tell him what pictures he considered worth buying. Duveen would give him an annual retaining fee and a commission on sales. Berenson accepted, on condition that he should have nothing whatever to do with the selling. Duveen was perfectly satisfied; after all, when it came to selling pictures, he didn't need anybody's help. This arrangement was to continue for thirty years, and was to bring Berenson an affluence unprecedented in the world of scholarship.

Duveen had the practical man's contempt for the scholar. 'Berenson may know what's authentic, but only I know what will sell,' Duveen would say, laughing. Or he would say, 'If I were to follow Berenson, I would have a basementful of wonderful masterpieces that no one would buy.' From Duveen's point of view, Berenson had a limitation: he didn't care in the least what would sell; he was interested solely in what was beautiful. And between Berenson's aesthetic standards and the standards of Duveen's American customers there was a considerable gap. Duveen's principal clients were ageing men, and they liked bright colours, they liked opulence, they liked youth and beauty; they wanted to be cheered up. Viewing Duveen's wares in his Fifth Avenue gallery, they constituted a kind of collector's baldhead row. Frick would buy only pictures of the first rank that were authoritatively certified, but Mellon had to like a picture. Mellon wanted a picture to be not only first rank but attractive, and this made him a special problem for Duveen, because some of Berenson's recommendations were just first rank. That is one reason Duveen put a high value on his selection from Berenson's selection.

For a long time, there hung in Duveen's London office a superb Masaccio that he had bought only because B.B. was enthusiastic about it. Duveen felt that his clients wouldn't like it very much. The picture was sombre. Duveen had some of his major customers in for a look at it and exercised his panegyrics on it. They didn't work. A picture that wouldn't respond to Duveen's enthusiasm became in Duveen's eyes a picture that was too gross for civilized society. As it stayed on and on in his office, he gradually conceived for it an aversion that amounted to hatred. One day, feeling that he couldn't stand the unwanted guest a minute longer, he summoned his assistant, Boggis. 'Get me an axe!' he said. 'I want to chop up this picture.' 'Don't chop it up, Joe,' Boggis said. 'B.B. likes it.' Duveen forced himself to look at something more saleable, to keep from destroying the masterpiece. Eventually, the adviser to an important collector, who had come upon a description of the picture in one of B.B.'s books, got his client to buy it.

That was as near as Berenson ever came to actually selling a picture. He once gave one away, however, under somewhat spectacular circumstances. A big New York copra man who was a collector of consequence was about to make a business trip to the South Seas when he was told that Berenson was coming to the United States to catalogue a collection of Italian paintings and would be in New York for a month or so. 'Why doesn't he stay in my apartment?' he inquired of his informant. 'It's all staffed, and I'll be going away just as he gets here.' Berenson spent the month there, and felt so grateful to his host, whom he had never met, that he wrote to his wife asking her to send the copra man one of his pictures as a present – something 'really nice'. The catalogue finished, Berenson sailed for home. On his first evening back, he had a reunion with his pictures. 'Where is the little Domenico Veneziano?' he asked his wife. 'Oh,' said Mrs Berenson, 'you told me to send a nice picture to your friend in New York, and I sent him that.' When Berenson had recovered from the impact of his wife's obedience, he said, 'I asked you to send him something nice. I didn't ask you to send him my very favourite.' Copra took a slump, and Berenson's New York host sold his pictures. The Domenico Veneziano was bought by Kress for four hundred and fifty thousand dollars. Berenson's claim that he paid the highest month's rent in the annals of New York real estate may well be justified. His rent payment now hangs in the National Gallery in Washington.

According to Berenson, Duveen himself was an artist of a sort; he got an artist's pleasure out of the tremendous sales he negotiated, and out of his role as purveyor to the most powerful men in the world. He got pleasure, too, out of clowning. His attitude towards people like Berenson and his following might, Berenson said, be epitomized as something like this: 'Now, look here, I am not one of you, nor am I even ambitious to be one of you. I am aware that I don't rate your society, but we have to be together for other reasons, and since I have the gift of clowning, the least I can do is amuse you. That is my passport; that is my price of admission.' Mrs Berenson liked Duveen immensely; she found his vitality and exuberance irresistible. So did Berenson when Duveen was on the premises. There was something about Duveen – 'a Chaplinesque quality', Berenson called it – that captivated him. But as soon as Duveen was gone, Berenson couldn't bear the thought of him. Berenson, who always divided people into the 'life-enhancing' and the 'life-diminishing', was reluctantly forced to put Duveen in the first group. Once, after Duveen had made a flying visit to I Tatti, Mrs Berenson said, 'Oh, Joe is wonderful. He's like champagne!' 'More like gin,' grumbled B.B.

Opposite *Sassetta and Assistant: 'The Meeting of St Anthony and St Paul'. One of the paintings acquired by Duveen from Lord Allendale and sold to Kress*

Overleaf *Giorgione: 'The Adoration of the Shepherds'. The celebrated painting which caused the breach between Duveen and Berenson*

There were a number of Duveen anecdotes in the Berenson memory. While travelling through Central Europe in search of pictures after the First World War, Duveen stopped at a frontier town, and, since no one was allowed to carry more than a limited amount of money across the border, stuffed a wad of bills into his hat. As his visa was being stamped, he saw a friend standing nearby, and raised the hat. All the money fell out. It was confiscated, and Duveen had to borrow from the friend to whom he had been so polite. Another time, when Duveen was in conference in his London office with an assistant named A. E. Bowles, someone brought in an English magazine that contained an article telling how Duveen ran his business. The writer revealed a surprising intimacy with the mechanics of the enterprise. Duveen turned on Bowles in fury. 'How did this fellow come to know all this?' he screamed. 'He must have listened to your talk, Lord Duveen,' said Bowles deferentially. When Duveen's daughter was a very little girl, the family went to Dieppe for a holiday. Duveen took the child to the beach. She dipped her foot in the sea and found the water too cold, so she wouldn't go in. Duveen collected some sticks and borrowed a tea kettle, built a fire on the beach, heated some water till it steamed, and poured it into the sea. His daughter then went in without a whimper.

In the ferociously competitive jungle of the art dealers' world, Duveen was an insatiable tiger who saw no reason why he shouldn't devour everything in sight. 'The difference you have created in the price of first-rate pictures and third-rate pictures is so vast,' Berenson once said to him, 'that you'll drive people into buying the third rate rather than pay the fabulous sums your monopoly enables you to exact.' But Duveen's prices went on spiralling. He believed in keeping the market up, and he kept it up; it collapsed only after he died. Yet, said Berenson, Duveen's 'life-enhancing' artist's quality made him 'a lamb and an angel' compared to some of his competitors. 'He would make you pay outrageously,' said B.B., 'he would exact the last possible penny in a deal, and then would spend thousands of dollars on you with the most open-handed generosity.'

The welding of the personalities of Berenson and Duveen, a welding for which the cold facts of existence were wholly responsible, was an odd one. Duveen, bold and headlong and driving, was the figurehead of a ship that carried as its sole passenger, in its solitary cabin, one of the most civilized and sensitive men in the world. Duveen, who couldn't stand owning only a part of anything, regarded Berenson as his property – the last thing on earth Berenson wanted to be. When, from time to time, Berenson authenticated a picture for a rival dealer, Duveen felt betrayed. Duveen had said to Mellon, and to Kress,

Opposite Crivelli: 'Madonna and Child'. Acknowledged as one of the painter's masterpieces, and sold to Bache by Duveen

The Domenico Veneziano which Berenson gave away: 'St John in the Desert'

and to Frick, and to Bache, and to Altman, and to Joseph E. Widener, and to H. E. Huntington, 'Never buy an Italian picture without a Berenson approval! Never!' He implied that such a policy would protect the purchaser of an Italian picture from everyone in the world – including himself. This was simply good business on Duveen's part. He had almost a monopoly on the supply of Old Masters, and he thought he had a monopoly on Berenson. Berenson had come to be Duveen's hallmark. As Duveen became more successful, he also become more totalitarian. He was convinced that a masterpiece must be sold only through him, that any rival was a poacher on his special preserve. Berenson argued with Duveen that if other professionals bought and sold great pictures, they would in the end help Duveen, for they would expand the market. It was no use. Duveen persisted in regarding Berenson's authentication of other dealers' holdings as a breach of contract, though no contract had ever existed between them.

Still another matter troubled Duveen. He found Berenson as circumspect about expressing an opinion as his American clients were about spending their money. Duveen relied on flair, Berenson on science and what he called his 'sense of antecedent probability'. In Europe, Duveen and Berenson went to museums and exhibitions and private showings together. On a visit to a museum in Munich, Berenson saw much to deliberate over, but it was hard for Duveen to take an interest in pictures he knew he could never buy. He kept crying out, when B.B. paused at length before a painting, 'Next! Next!' Berenson, wielding his flashlight, focusing his opera glasses, refused to be hurried; Duveen's exhortations only slowed down his tempo. And B.B.'s attitude towards pictures that Duveen *could* acquire was even more annoying. Duveen would try to bully him into enthusiasm; Berenson wouldn't be bullied. 'This is marvellous, B.B.! Marvellous!' Duveen would exclaim when he saw something that looked especially saleable. Already phrases he could use while displaying it in the private showroom of his Fifth Avenue gallery were taking shape in his mind; he saw his little circle of American customers listening, enthralled. 'It's not marvellous, Joe,' B.B. would say quietly killing at a stroke a lucrative fantasy. When B.B. did admit that he thought a painting was marvellous, the painting was apt to be a very dark one, and Duveen worried about his American clients' love of bright colours. '*Why* is this picture marvellous, B.B.?' he would ask brusquely. 'I don't think it's marvellous at all.' It was Duveen's method of saying that he wasn't going to buy the painting, and it was also his method of getting an education. He was usually eager to draw Berenson out, so that possibly he himself might one day be able to discover the marvellous in a picture – provided it was painted in bright colours. And he had another motive; he wanted to be able to judge pictures that were outside Berenson's province. B.B. always said, 'I will not baptize outside my parish', which was Italian painting from the thirteenth to the seventeenth century. But Duveen's parish was the universe, and by expressing his opinions to Berenson he goaded his counsellor into expressing *his*. Duveen used the tips he got this way when buying pictures of other schools or other centuries, when he had no B.B. to guide him.

On one occasion, the two men collided head-on over a painting within Berenson's parish. Berenson had gone to America to catalogue the Italian paintings in P. A. B. Widener's collection. A supper-party was given in B.B.'s honour by a New York banker and his wife, who were well-known collectors. His hosts were bubbling with enthusiasm for a Botticelli they had just acquired, and they made haste to lead Berenson to it. He inspected it. 'This is no Botticelli,' he said. 'Where did you get it?' 'We got it from Duveen,' said his host. 'And he's coming to supper, too.' Duveen arrived, and was brought before the picture and confronted with Berenson's disturbing denial. 'Who told you this was a Botticelli?' asked Berenson gently. Duveen foamed authorities. 'Nevertheless, it is not a Botticelli,' B.B. said. Duveen at once offered to take the picture back and refund the money. The supper-party was not a notable success.

Later, in the 1930s, Berenson disappointed Duveen in circumstances which were much more serious. He refused to certify that a picture Duveen was about to sell Mellon as a

Giorgione was a Giorgione. Berenson insisted that it was a Titian. There was a violent quarrel between the two men, and this ended their friendship and their business association. Among art dealers, the difference between Giorgione and Titian is immense; that is, the difference between what you can sell a Titian for and what you can sell a Giorgione for is immense. Titian lived to be ninety-nine and was a hard worker, so his output was colossal. Giorgione, who was Titian's master and friend, died young, so there are very few Giorgiones. When a familiar itch in his fingers told Duveen that he was about to put them on a highly regarded painting reputed to be by Giorgione – 'The Adoration of the Shepherds', owned by Viscount Allendale – he was wild with excitement. He went to Mellon, who had plenty of Titians but was hungry for Giorgiones, and whipped up his enthusiasm. Then he sailed for England, pried the almost unexceptionable Giorgione away from the Viscount for £100,000, and came right back with it. Duveen was aware that B.B.'s still but not small voice had once said that the Allendale painting was a Titian. He felt confident, however, that Berenson by now saw this picture as he, Duveen, saw it. Berenson had been known to change his mind; once, testifying in one of the many lawsuits in which Duveen was the defendant, he had reversed an opinion. When the plaintiff's counsel pounced on this reversal, Berenson said imperturbably, 'I never stick to a mistake.' Duveen, in his incorrigible optimism, was certain Berenson would say that the Allendale was at least partly – that was all Duveen needed – by Giorgione. Berenson was in Cyprus when he received a long cable from Duveen asking him to admit that the picture he was about to sell to Mellon was indeed a Giorgione. B.B. cabled an indignant refusal. When he returned to Florence, one of Duveen's European representatives, accompanied by the picture itself, called upon him and repeated Duveen's request. Berenson studied it carefully for several days and came to the same conclusion as before: namely, that it was an early Titian.

There is a story that news of the perpetual dispute over whether certain pictures were painted by Giorgione or Titian reached Heaven itself and disturbed the friendly relations between the two artists. Titian and Giorgione, who on earth had been so cordial, began to argue fiercely over the authorship of one masterpiece. Titian said that the picture couldn't possibly have been painted by the older ghost, that he had been dead for forty years when he, Titian, finished it. Giorgione pointed to brush strokes that, he flattered himself, only he could have executed. There seemed only one reasonable way of resolving the argument. 'We'll ask Berenson,' they said, with one voice. No decision could be reached, pending the arrival of B.B. But Duveen couldn't wait that long for a decision on the Allendale. Already he was gently ushering Mellon through the silken *portières* of his salesmanship. Duveen beautifully ensconced the Giorgione/Titian all by itself perched on an easel and reverently lighted, in a small, velvet-hung room in the Duveen palace on Fifth Avenue.

When Duveen showed a major client one picture at a time, as he liked to do, he displayed the single picture with the same solicitude David Belasco employed in displaying his stars. Sometimes, Duveen would begin by telling the client that he had just got something wonderful for him. He would press a button to signal Boggis that it was time to bring in the something wonderful and put it on an easel. Other times, he would lead his client into the velvet-hung room, where the thoughtfully lighted masterwork awaited him. Mellon had been completely – or almost completely – sold on the picture in advance, and when he finally sat before it, under the spell of a second Duveen paean, he was enraptured. Duveen wanted three-quarters of a million dollars for it, and Mellon knew that when you were buying a Giorgione you couldn't decently quibble about price. At this ticklish point, Duveen's own special pedagogical method recoiled on him. Mellon, to demonstrate how well he retained what Duveen had taught him, alluded to Lesson No. 1. 'What does B.B. say?' he asked. 'Never mind about that,' Duveen replied sharply. ' *I* say it's a Giorgione. *Everybody* says it's a Giorgione. And there isn't a doubt in the world that B.B. will say it's a Giorgione!' Reassured, Mellon took the picture home. But B.B. didn't say it was a Giorgione. In fact, not long afterwards, he wrote a letter to Royal Cortissoz, the art critic of the New York *Herald Tribune*, in which he said:

> You are acquainted, of course, with the Allendale picture, one of the most fascinating Giorgionesque pictures ever painted. The problem of how to attribute it has preoccupied me for many years. I naturally left no name untried. Finally, some ten or twelve years ago, the light dawned upon me, and I began to see that it must be Titian's, perhaps his earliest work, but only half out of the egg, the other half still in the Giorgione formula – the landscape, namely. Recently I have seen the picture again and was in raptures over its enchantment and beauty. Yet the longer I looked the more and more I saw in it the emerging art of Titian. It is my deepest conviction that this attribution will ultimately win through.

When Berenson's certificate failed to materialize, Mellon returned the picture to Duveen. 'I don't want another Titian,' he said sourly. 'Find me a Giorgione.' The deal was off, and so, in no time at all, was the business arrangement of so many years' standing between Duveen and Berenson.

Having the picture accepted as a Giorgione became a matter of prestige for Duveen; he felt he simply had to sell the Allendale, and as a Giorgione. He could have pointed out in self-defence that B.B.'s opinions on Giorgiones were not upheld by all authorities. Mrs Gardner, for example, had bought on his recommendation a 'Christ Bearing the Cross' that he said was a Giorgione, but Sir Philip Hendy, the art scholar (and later director of the National Gallery in London), stated forthrightly in a catalogue he prepared for the Gardner Collection that it was really a Palma Vecchio. The portrait of Ariosto now in the Altman Collection, at the Metropolitan, had been certified by B.B. as a

Giorgione, but the Metropolitan held it to be either a Giorgione or a Titian. Captain R. Langton Douglas, an eminent British authority, got into the argument over 'The Adoration of the Shepherds' by declaring that Berenson had once attributed the Allendale to Catena – so how could he now so firmly state that it was a Titian? All these facts Duveen knew, but, passionately as he wanted Giorgione to have painted that particular picture, he did not wish to pass his information along to Mellon. By doing so, he would cast doubt on the authenticity of the Italian paintings that B.B. had certified and that he had sold on the strength of B.B.'s reputation for infallibility. Moreover, Duveen was not really daunted. The infallible Berenson might fail him, but not his own salesmanship. He was confident that he would sell the picture, and that it would end up in the projected National Gallery in Washington. When the right moment came, he chose Kress as the conduit. The picture now hangs there, and the label below it says that it is by Giorgione. The controversy is no longer important. The picture is a great one, whoever painted it. To those who see it in the National Gallery, the battle over its authorship means as little as the Shakespeare *v.* Bacon argument means to an audience at *Hamlet*.

Neither Duveen nor Berenson was ever quite the same after the break-up. Duveen never recovered from the separation; Berenson never recovered from the association. How deep a mark it made on Berenson is revealed in his *Sketch for a Self-Portrait*, in which Duveen is never mentioned. Berenson, with his exquisite sensibility, his infinite intellectual curiosity and delicately distilled culture, whose life, it has been said, was itself a work of art, confessed to having misspent it. Above all, it is having become an art expert that he berated himself for. 'In any other field, an expert means a man who knows something about his subject,' he once said to a friend. 'In any field except the field of art.' In his writings, he referred to his intense sense of guilt, which was due, he said, 'to a double dose of Hebraism, an original Jewish one and, piled tower-high above it, a New England Puritan one'. He considered the careers he might have had and regretted that 'accident rather than an invincible tropism' made him become an art expert. This accident led to the accident of his association with Duveen, and the atmosphere generated by that association was abrasive to his spirit. For his singular authority, and for its emoluments, Berenson paid what he regarded as a high price:

> I soon discovered that I ranked with fortune-tellers, chiromancists, astrologers, and not even with the self-deluded of these, but rather with the deliberate charlatans. At first I was supposed to have invented a trick by which one could infallibly tell the authorship of an Italian picture. A famous writer on the Renaissance, Vernon Lee, thought it was close and even mean of me not to let her share the secret. Finally it degenerated into a widespread belief that if only I could be approached the right way I could order this or that American millionaire to pay thousands upon thousands and hundreds of thousands for any daub that I was bribed by the seller to attribute to a great master. . . . Needless to

say that every person I would not receive, every owner whose picture I would not ascribe to Raphael or Michelangelo, or Giorgione, Titian or Tintoretto, etc. etc., turned into an enemy.

Again:

I took the wrong turn when I swerved from more purely intellectual pursuits to one like the archaeological study of art, gaining thereby a troublesome reputation as an 'expert'. My only excuse is, if the comparison is not blasphemous, that like Saint Paul with his tent-making and Spinoza with his glass-polishing, I too needed a means of livelihood. . . . Those men of genius were not hampered in their careers by their trades. Mine took up what creative talent there was in me, with the result that this trade made my reputation and the rest of me scarcely counted. The spiritual loss was great and in consequence I have never regarded myself as other than a failure. This sense of failure, a guilty sense, makes me squirm when I hear myself spoken of as a 'successful man' and as having made 'a success of my life'.

'It is rather awful to think, isn't it,' said Berenson once, while strolling among his cypress groves with a friend, 'that when I am pushing up the daisies, all this will be an institooshun?' He was referring of course to the fact that he had willed I Tatti and all his possessions to Harvard. The 'institooshun' now flourishes there under the directorship of Myron P. Gilmore, Professor of History at Harvard, and B.B. would be delighted at the use that is being made of it. Graduate students – they are called Fellows – come there from all over the world. An Austrian, the foremost authority in the world on Raphael, comes there to complete his Renaissance studies. The Fellows remain for short or long periods; they stay either in the house where Berenson lived and died or in rented quarters in Florence or Fiesole. Mr Gilmore has had the furniture all rearranged and reupholstered. The room in which Berenson died, which was kept intact for a long time, with his slippers beside the bed, has been converted into a lovely music room. The marvellous paintings of his collection remain where they always were. The precious library, his pride and joy, is being put to a use which would have overjoyed Berenson: the books are used as he himself used them; they are not arranged alphabetically; they are 'association copies'. Each book, whether a novel or a historical or scientific work, is the centre of other books which, Berenson felt, had a spiritual affinity with the seminal book. These contain reviews, written at the time, in all languages, and criticism of the time, including B.B.'s own notes and criticisms.

Some years ago, an American young man who was paying a call on Berenson sampled some of the volumes and found the reviews inserted in them. It is a living library, because these are the books that educated B.B. Berenson himself spoke of his library with tenderness. 'The gathering of these books is the only thing I have accomplished in my life which gives me real satisfaction,' he said to his visitor. 'If a young man with moderate equipment were to spend four years in this library, he would emerge a cultivated gentleman.' The visitor, suddenly nipped by temptation, asked his host for a quick definition of 'moderate equipment'. 'Oh,' said Berenson lightly, like one who is diffident about dwelling on the obvious, 'a fluent knowledge of French, German, Italian, Spanish, Greek, Latin and Sanskrit, and some Hebrew, because the books are in all these tongues.' The American, who had only English, which Berenson hadn't even mentioned, decided to become a cultivated gentleman by a less exigent process.

The library has windowseats everywhere; the Fellows read, not alphabetically, but associatively. They find it broadening, very stimulating. Mr Gilmore has managed to correlate, as Berenson did in his lifetime, the life of I Tatti with the social and political life of Florence and the surrounding neighbourhood. The Fellows enjoy this assimilation and profit from it. Mr Gilmore invites, in the spring and in the autumn, when the Fellows are in residence, luminaries of contemporary culture: John Pope Hennessy, Isaiah Berlin, Hugh Trevor-Roper, Kenneth Clark, John Sparrow. To be there, to live there, to be educated there, says one of the Fellows, is to be taking an 'intellectual cure'.

Probably those who go there pursue their studies with more tranquillity than their benefactor did, for he was never very far from the arena of art dealing, and that arena seethes with spite, envy and searing hatred. As he sat there through the years, examining his photographs of paintings, reading his books, and savouring the aesthetic pleasures provided by the Masters on his walls, and as he took his walks, winter and summer, at dawn and sunset on the hills overlooking Florence, Berenson, with all his spiritual alertness, must have detested the scents and stridencies of the jungle overseas, and the sound of the padded prowlings of the insatiable tiger who beat about in it, using his eyes, his sensibility and his name. Of his estate, Berenson wrote:

> When the house was at long last furnished and the works of art in their place, it did not occur to me that I was in possession of more than could be gathered by any student taking advantage of his acquired knowledge and exercised taste. It took the scattering of most private collections all over Europe to make me realize that mine was one of the best remaining.

Opposite *Reynolds: 'Mrs Siddons as the Tragic Muse'. The celebrated portrait which Duveen sold to H. E. Huntington*

Chapter 5
THE BLUE BOY AND
TWO LAVINIAS

CERTAINLY one of the most fascinating unsung heroines of the American scene at the end of the nineteenth century and the beginning of the twentieth was Arabella Duval Yarrington. Born in Alabama in 1853, she married a man named A. D. Worsham, also unsung; in 1884, a few years after he died, she married Collis P. Huntington, the biggest of California's Big Four, the promoters of the Central Pacific Railroad; and in 1913, after his death, she married his nephew H. E. Huntington, who was one of his heirs. H. E. Huntington thus married his aunt, something men don't ordinarily do unless there is an inescapable charm. When the impulse to marry his uncle's widow become irresistible, H. E. Huntington, who had been divorced by his first wife some years before, was sixty-three. Arabella Huntington's early life is obscure. When the newspapers, with a gasp, reported her marriage to Collis P. Huntington – they gasped again when she married, H.E. – one of them noted, in lieu of more definite biographical information that she was 'ambitious'. What she was ambitious for, it let its readers guess. Oscar Lewis, in his book on the Central Pacific Railroad, *The Big Four*, makes it clear that one thing the multiple Mrs Huntington was ambitious for was social recognition. He tells how she induced Collis, a former Sacramento storekeeper who had always prided himself on the fact that he spent no more than two hundred dollars a year on himself, to build a two-million-dollar mansion at Fifth Avenue and Fifty-seventh Street (it looked like a warehouse) and, while he was about it, a comparatively modest two-hundred-and-fifty thousand-dollar mausoleum in Woodlawn. Collis never even went to look at his Woodlawn place; as for the Fifty-seventh Street house, he hated it. Arabella, on the other hand, was enthusiastic about the house. Soon after it was completed, she filled it with tapestries, pictures, and fragile French gilt chairs (Collis, a giant of a man weighing eighteen stone, couldn't sit on any of them), and invited a lot of prominent people to a party. Nobody much came. Arabella transferred her activities to San Francisco, where she remodelled a house, filled *it* with gilt chairs, and gave another party. As Collis was cordially hated in San Francisco,

Opposite *Gainsborough: 'The Blue Boy'. The painting which Duveen bought for H. E. Huntington from the Duke of Westminster* nobody much came to that party, either. In the end, Mrs Huntington was saved from the social isolation that threatened her by Duveen.

Whereas the upper stratum of American society turned its collective back on Arabella Huntington, Duveen received her, whenever she consulted him, with deference. He introduced her to the enchanting realm of the aesthetic, and while doing so treated her, as she herself once said, 'like a queen'. It was a sensation that New York and San Francisco denied her, and one that she enjoyed; Duveen, who knew some authentic queens personally, was in a peculiar position to provide it. There was a special essence of authority about Duveen that eventually made her forsake all others. An eminent New York antique dealer once showed her some very expensive Renaissance furniture; she was delighted with it, and bought it. The furniture was delivered to her New York home at a moment when Duveen was there, giving her a lesson in art appreciation. What he said about the furniture is not known, but her reaction to his criticism is. She telephoned the furniture dealer and told him to come at once and take it back. 'You'll find it in the back yard,' she said. The same antique dealer had another exacerbating experience involving Duveen. Mellon, soon after he became Secretary of the Treasury, asked the antique dealer to come to Washington and give him an estimate on furnishing his apartment. Forehandedly thinking of possible future profits, the dealer made the estimate as low as he could – thirty thousand dollars. Mellon mentioned this figure to Duveen, who pronounced it excessive; he said he could do the job admirably for twelve thousand. Mr Mellon then asked the antique man how it was that Duveen could make an estimate so much lower. 'Because I haven't got expensive pictures to sell!' the dealer answered bitterly.

Oscar Lewis quotes an unnamed phrase-maker as saying of Collis Huntington that he was 'scrupulously dishonest'. He was the epitome of the ruthless business titan of the period. The contribution of men like him to the material growth of America in the latter part of the nineteenth century was incalculable, but it has often been remarked that by using their unparalleled economic power without a corresponding sense of public responsibility they undermined the moral prestige of the leading capitalist country in the world to an extent that is also incalculable. The bad odour that still clings to 'big business' can be traced back to them. In their old age, these men gave out a variety of formulas to those who came to them for the magic word. Collis Huntington advised such seekers to look sharp, and boasted that he had never been out-smarted in business. (He probably listed his transactions with Duveen under the heading of pleasure.) One of his three business partners, Charles Crocker, said that the problem was not to make money but to hold on to it once you got it. In a San Francisco restaurant one day, Collis Huntington berated a waiter who had, by accident, made a twenty-five cent overcharge in a bill. 'Young man,' said Collis as he happily pocketed a refund, 'you can't follow me through life by the quarters I drop.' And yet, thanks to Arabella, he dropped many at Duveen's New York gallery, as well as at his London and Paris galleries. H.E. also dropped many with Duveen. In fact, on Duveen's last visit to H.E.'s California mansion, San Marino, just before H.E. died, the host didn't have enough cash on hand to pay for the freight-car load of merchandise in the guest's caravan. Duveen accepted instead some Los Angeles real estate, a commodity of which H.E. was then the largest owner.

Collis Potter Huntington

Although Collis Huntington did not talk much, he once admitted that he had paid twenty-five thousand dollars for a certain painting, which he called 'a religious scene'. He spent so much time looking at it that he didn't have time to look at any others. This picture seems to have presented to him an allegory of his life; he went to the trouble to set down the reasons for his preoccupation, as follows:

There are seven figures in it – three cardinals of the different orders of their religion. There is an old missionary that has just returned; he is showing his scars, where his hands are cut all over; he is telling a story to these cardinals; they are dressed in luxury. One of them is playing with a dog; one is asleep; there is only one looking at him – looking at him with that kind of expression saying what a fool you are that you should go out and suffer for the human race when we have such a good time at home. I lose the picture in the story when I look at it. I sometimes sit half an hour looking at that picture.

For Collis Huntington, Oscar Lewis suggests, the luxury-loving cardinals represented two of his partners – Crocker, constantly running off to Europe, and Leland Stanford, fiddling with ranches and his university. Huntington always referred to the university his partner's money founded as Stanford's Circus. When the Central Pacific got into financial difficulties, Huntington wired Stanford: 'CLOSE THE CIRCUS.'

After Collis's death, in 1900, Arabella Huntington, guided by Duveen, moved into an artistic realm far above twenty-five-thousand-dollar religious scenes. She bought from him paintings by Rembrandt, Velásquez, Hals, van der Weyden, Bellini, and other ranking masters. Arabella was often brutally rude to other art dealers, but her submissiveness to Duveen's authority not only in the province of art but in clothes, jewels, and coiffures was abject. If he frowned in criticism of her hair-do, she redid the hair-do. She had a passion for blue velvet. Many people offered her blue velvet, but she never took any; she really liked only blue velvet that had belonged to Duveen. When shipments of clothes and jewels came from Paris, Duveen had to see them and pass judgment on them before she changed their status from 'on approval' to ownership. One day, she went to see Mitchell Samuels, president of the well-known antique firm of French & Co., about some minor items that Duveen didn't mind her buying from him, and in his office she left her handbag, containing eleven pearl necklaces worth three and a half million dollars. When Samuels returned the bag, he admonished her about her carelessness. She explained the lapse by saying that she had been irritated with Duveen about something and that her agitation over this had caused her to forget everything else, including the handbag. By the time Arabella married H.E. in 1913 – she relied on Duveen to make all the wedding arrangements – her taste in art had been considerably refined. Her new husband developed a whim of his own; he wanted outstanding English paintings of the eighteenth century. Duveen was quite prepared to indulge this whim, and in the course of doing so he bound H.E. to him for ever. Always a Lucullan, and on occasion a companionable, traveller, Duveen, in the summer of 1921, sailed from New York on the *Aquitania* in a suite adjoining the one occupied by his friends H. E. and Arabella. The Huntingtons were in the Gainsborough Suite, whose walls were hung with copies of that master's paintings. In the dining-room hung a reproduction of 'The Blue Boy'. One evening, the Huntingtons invited Duveen to dine with them. Looking up, between courses, at the picture, H.E. became curious about it. In after years, Duveen enjoyed repeating the conversation that followed.

'Joe,' said H.E., with the confidence of one who knows that he can get the answer to anything, 'who's the boy in the blue suit?'

Duveen said, 'That is a reproduction of the famous "Blue Boy". It is Gainsborough's finest and most famous painting.'

'Where's the original?' Huntington went on, with even more confidence.

Duveen did not let his inquirer down. 'It belongs to the Duke of Westminster and hangs in his collection at Grosvenor House, in London.'

'How much is it?' asked H.E.

Duveen was discouraging. 'It can probably not be had at any price,' he said.

Huntington, impressed, looked up at the unattainable boy in the blue suit with fresh awe. 'It must be a very great painting,' he said.

Duveen seconded this venture into criticism, and went a step farther. 'Indeed,' he said, 'it is the greatest work of England's greatest master and would be the crown of any collection of English pictures.'

In Huntington, aesthetic appreciation was glazing into the enamel of covetousness. 'What do you think would be the price if it ever *were* sold?' he asked.

After a calculated hesitation, Duveen said it would probably be about six hundred thousand dollars – far more than Huntington had ever before paid for a picture.

'I might see my way clear to paying that much,' Huntington said.

Duveen knew many secrets about the owners of fine pictures. His operatives had informed him that this happened to be a moment when the Duke of Westminster might rate higher the temporal easement of a lump of American cash than the permanent delight of owning two or three extra masterpieces. The Huntingtons, on their way to Paris, got off the *Aquitania* at Cherbourg; Duveen continued to Southampton, with the comfortable feeling of having sold at a neat profit a picture he didn't yet own. He deferred all his other engagements and called upon the Duke at Grosvenor House. He found him extremely receptive to the idea of selling 'The Blue Boy', and anything else in the place. Duveen asked to see what was in stock. Three pieces fixed his attention – 'The Blue Boy', Reynolds' 'Sarah Siddons as the Tragic Muse', and Gainsborough's 'The Cottage Door'. Duveen bought them all, agreeing to pay cash within a few days. The price for the three pictures was slightly more than the figure he had mentioned on the *Aquitania* for 'The Blue Boy' alone. The moment the deal was set, Duveen made for his London office and telephoned Huntington in Paris to tell him the good news. He had acquired 'The Blue Boy' and would deliver it for six hundred and twenty thousand dollars – the twenty thousand covered the telephone call – but he needed the money as quickly as possible, because the Duke needed it as quickly as possible. Huntington asked for forty-eight hours. Good-naturedly, Duveen let him have that interval. At the end of it the Duke had his money.

Duveen went to Paris to deliver 'The Blue Boy' in person. The Huntingtons were thrilled at seeing the original, but they were upset by the fact that the Duke's blue boy was

Mrs Arabella Huntington, painted by Oswald Birley

more green than blue; the blue boy in their dining-room on the *Aquitania*, they remembered, was a much bluer boy than the Duke's. Duveen explained that the greenish tinge of *their* blue boy was merely the result of a long accumulation of dust and grime. He promised to have that removed, so that the youth would be restored to his pristine azure, and the Huntingtons were appeased. Duveen congratulated them on being able to take to America this prime glory of English painting, and, when their jubilation had begun to subside, mentioned Reynolds' portrait of Mrs Siddons, explaining that as 'The Blue Boy' was

Henry E. Huntington, painted by Oswald Birley

Gainsborough's greatest, 'Sarah Siddons' was Reynolds' greatest, and adding that he had brought the picture with him. He quoted a pronouncement by Sir Thomas Lawrence, Reynolds' admirer and protégé, upon being asked which portrait he considered the Master's finest. '"Sarah Siddons as the Tragic Muse" is not only his finest portrait but it is also the finest portrait ever painted under the canopy of Heaven,' Lawrence had said. Arabella inquired who Sarah Siddons was. She was, Duveen said, a member of the great Kemble family and the most famous actress in England during the latter half of the eighteenth century. The revelation of Sarah Siddons' profession was unfortunate. Duveen encountered that opposition, more severe than any other, of newly acquired social sensitiveness. Arabella, before her first Huntington marriage, had not only known poverty but had seen more than her share of the sordid aspects of life, yet now the idea of hanging in her house the portrait of an actress shocked her profoundly. Her objections were violent. Duveen was determined to get 'Sarah Siddons' into the charmed circle of the Huntington Collection, even at the risk of treading upon a moral code. 'You are not buying an actress,' he said patiently. 'You are buying a great artist and his finest example. You are ambitious to build a collection of English pictures that will be an honour to America and unique in the world. You cannot afford to exclude this masterpiece. The subject does not matter. It is the artist that matters. If you let this go to another collector, as it inevitably will, you will never forgive yourself for having let it go.' That did it; pride won over moral sensibility. 'Sarah Siddons' went to San Marino. Some months later, she was followed by 'The Cottage Door'.

In accordance with his promise, Duveen subjected 'The Blue Boy' to a professional scrubbing. This started a rumpus – the British newspapers accused him of vandalism – but Duveen hugely enjoyed rumpuses. It was, as a matter of fact, his habit to have an Old Master cleaned the moment he bought it. He felt that a painting should look as nearly as possible the way it looked when it left the artist's studio; the years shouldn't be allowed to ravage and disfigure it. He was often accused of making Old Masters look like new masters. His answer was that they were new when they left the Old Master. An American lady once protested that the Renaissance painting of a girl he was trying to sell her had obviously been restored. 'My dear Madam,' he said, 'if you were as old as this young girl, you would have to be restored, too.' Duveen showed the newly resplendent 'Blue Boy' to Sir Charles J. Holmes, then director of the National Gallery in London. Sir Charles publicly hailed him as 'the saviour of this monumental work', and went on, 'For the first time in over a century, the world can really see this masterpiece as the Master intended it to be seen.'

Duveen emerged from that controversy with honours, but another one was brewing, over the propriety of selling one country's art treasures to the highest bidder in another country. In his autobiographical *Left Hand, Right Hand!*, published in 1944, Sir Osbert Sitwell wrote:

> It is an ironical reflection that while Lord Duveen's magnificent gifts to the nation stand as a memorial to his name, much of the money that paid for them was earned by the sale to the United States of the flower of the . . . eighteenth-century and early nineteenth-century English painting. We have the galleries now, but no pictures to hang in them. He was the greatest salesman of his time.

Duveen's admirers, when they exult over the immense additions he made to private and public collections in the United States, usually end up by pointing out that whereas, before Duveen, art-thirsty Americans had to cross the ocean to see the masterpieces of the world's art, they can now see them at home. That is, of course, an achievement that only chauvinists can take an undiluted pleasure in. Late in his career, Duveen seemingly became sensitive on this point. He acquired – by a stroke of Duveen luck – one of Hogarth's finest paintings, 'The Graham Children'. He had a ready customer in Mellon and he was itching to sell him the Hogarth, but for once he overcame his guiding impulse. He presented 'The Graham Children' to the National Gallery in London.

The departure from England of 'The Blue Boy' gave Duveen an opportunity for advertisement that he did not waste. He permitted the British public a last look, at a public exhibition; it was a farewell to a national heirloom. The lamentation in England over 'The Blue Boy' moved the American composer Cole Porter to elegy. For a Cochran revue, *Mayfair and Montmartre*, he wrote a song that showed that even an American could feel a twinge at the departure of the cerulean refugee. In the course of his threnody, Porter characteristically mentioned Duveen by name and began his chorus:

> For I'm the Blue Boy, the beautiful Blue Boy
> And I am forced to admit, I'm feeling a bit depressed
> A silver dollar took me and my collar
> To show the slow cowboys just how boys
> In England used to be dressed. . . .

Duveen also permitted himself a sentimental indulgence; he was in New York at the time of the exhibition, and he cabled an order to London that his aged mother should be the last person to see the picture before it was crated. This was in fulfilment of a vow made many years before. While he was serving his apprenticeship in his father's antique shop, in Oxford Street, young Duveen came in one day in a state of immense excitement. He had bought a canvas that he had been assured was a Gainsborough. This assurance, as his father was later only too happy to recall to him from time to time, turned out to be baseless. His mother, too, had chaffed him about his naïveté, and Duveen had pledged himself to show her a genuine Gainsborough, and one that belonged to him.

When 'The Blue Boy' reached New York, escorted by two Duveen employees and triply encased – in a waterproof box, a steel box, and an iron-bound case – it was welcomed like an inheritance from an unknown uncle. The arrival was a headline story from coast to coast. The Metropolitan Museum begged Duveen for permission to exhibit it there for a while, but Duveen refused. He didn't think the Metropolitan Museum was safe enough; after all, the Gainsborough had become a Duveen, and he couldn't trust a Duveen to a fragile, jerry-built structure like the Metropolitan. For a few weeks, he exhibited the Boy at his Fifth Avenue gallery, which was solid, and then he personally escorted him to California and to the Huntingtons.

Duveen not only arranged weddings and obtained unobtainable paintings for his clients but he got them steamship reservations and invitations to the right places when they were difficult to get. He couldn't quite insinuate the Huntingtons into American society, but he did pretty well for them in England. In 1914, at the outbreak of the First World War, H.E. was marooned in London, unable to book a passage home. In his distress, he appealed to Duveen, also in London, and Duveen got accommodation for him in a ship sailing in two weeks. Meanwhile, an operative had whispered to Duveen that Lord Spencer, of Althorp, Northamptonshire, found himself in possession of an excessive number of ancestral portraits. It occurred to Duveen that an invitation to visit Althorp might reduce the tedium of Huntington's enforced stay in London. Besides the sixth Earl, Althorp housed the Spencer collection of English portraits, which had come down from the second Earl, a contemporary of George III, and which contained some magnificent eighteenth-century portraits. Duveen got Huntington the invitation and shortly thereafter conducted him through the gallery, thus introducing him not only to the contemporary peerage but to a vanished one. Duveen put him on particular familiar terms with a three-quarter-length Reynolds portrait of Lavinia, the wife of the second Earl. Huntington fell in love with Lavinia at first sight, and Duveen promised to do what he could to further the romance. The gallery also contained a Reynolds portrait of Lavinia with her son, but H.E.'s infatuation with her was apparently so intense that, perhaps unconsciously, he couldn't endure the idea of her having a son by anyone else. Duveen, while he was about it, introduced Huntington to two other Reynolds girls – Georgiana, Duchess of Devonshire, and Frances, Marchioness Camden. Huntington carried on only a mild flirtation with them. They did not engender in him anything like the fierce adoration he felt for Lavinia-without-son. It turned out that the sonless Lavinia was the one ancestor Lord Spencer would not part with. Duveen could supply Huntington with Frances and Georgiana and Lavinia-with-son but not Lavinia-without-son. However, H.E. was stubborn, and he had a considerable record of conquest behind him. When he wanted a piece of Los Angeles real estate or a railroad, he was in the habit of getting it, and when he wanted Lavinia-without-son, he saw no reason that he shouldn't get that, too. Duveen, who

Opposite *News of Duveen buying paintings from the Spencer Collection*

TO ADORN HOMES IN AMERICA: SPENCER COLLECTION MASTERPIECES.

A FAMOUS GAINSBOROUGH SOLD FROM THE ALTHORP COLLECTION FOR EXPORT TO AMERICA: "GEORGIANA DUCHESS OF DEVONSHIRE" (C. 1778).

LONG A SHOW PICTURE AT ALTHORP: VAN DYCK'S BEAUTIFUL "DAEDALUS AND ICARUS," DESCRIBED AS "A MODEL OF PERFECTION IN ART."

PAINTED IN 1775-6 (EARLIER THAN GAINS-BOROUGH'S PORTRAIT): "GEORGIANA DUCHESS OF DEVONSHIRE," BY SIR JOSHUA REYNOLDS.

A FAMILY PORTRAIT SOLD BY EARL SPENCER TO GO TO AMERICA: ANOTHER FAMOUS PICTURE BY SIR JOSHUA REYNOLDS—"LAVINIA COUNTESS SPENCER, AND HER SON, JOHN CHARLES, VISCOUNT ALTHORP."

REGARDED AS ONE OF THE FINEST EXAMPLES OF FRANS HALS: HIS "PORTRAIT OF A MAN" (INSCRIBED "AETA 41, 1626," BUT THE SITTER UNIDENTIFIED) — ONE OF THE ALTHORP PICTURES DESTINED FOR AMERICA.

understood this kind of bullheadedness, cast about for something to assuage the lover's disappointment. He told Huntington that Reynolds had done still another Lavinia, who was just as good and was, happily, sonless. This Lavinia was owned by the Earl of Bessborough, later Governor-General of Canada, who had inherited her from the Spencer family. Huntington commissioned Duveen to get her. Duveen approached the Earl of Bessborough. There must have been something about a childless Lavinia that was infinitely appealing and full of solace; Lord Bessborough didn't want to be parted from his Lavinia, either. Duveen persisted as only he knew how to persist. After negotiations that went on for months, Bessborough agreed to sell on the condition that Duveen would have an excellent copy made to insure His Lordship against loneliness. Duveen had the Lavinia copy made and hung, and sent the original to San Marino.

After Huntington's death, in 1927, Lord Bessborough's Lavinia was the cause of a complicated lawsuit. The trustees of H.E.'s estate hired an English expert to catalogue the great Huntington Collection. He pronounced Huntington's Lavinia a copy; the original, he said, was the painting hanging at Althorp. He also said that certain parts of the Huntington picture were manifestly not Reynolds' work, notably parts of the costume and some areas in the background. Moreover, the Althorp Lavinia wore a white lawn, the Huntington a white dotted swiss. The expert did not know what Huntington, if he were alive, could have told him – that he had known perfectly well he was buying not the Althorp Lavinia but the Bessborough Lavinia. Unfortunately, there was no evidence for this beyond Duveen's word. The trustees demanded that Duveen buy back the Lavinia at what H.E. had paid for her plus interest. As Huntington had paid something like a quarter of a million dollars for the Lavinia twelve years before, the sum asked of Duveen came to nearly four hundred thousand dollars. The parties to the dispute agreed to submit it to arbitration, and put the matter up to Sir Charles Holmes, who had just retired as director of the National Gallery in London.

Sir Charles' first move was to requisition all the private papers of Sir Joshua Reynolds that were preserved in the British Museum. Among these were Reynolds' copybooks of his correspondence and bills, along with letters from his patrons, and a Sitters' Book, in which he had kept the names and dates of all his sitters. A letter was found from the second Earl Spencer, written shortly after his succession to the title in 1783, requesting that Reynolds paint a portrait of his wife, Lavinia. There was a copy of Reynolds' answer, accepting the commission and fixing the date for the first sitting. The Sitters' Book showed the dates of that sitting and subsequent ones, as well as Reynolds' charge for the portrait – a hundred guineas. There was also found in the correspondence an ecstatic letter from Earl Spencer acknowledging the receipt of the painting and asking Reynolds to do another portrait of Lavinia, for the Earl's mother, the Dowager Countess. Reynolds accepted the second commission, at the same price, and his Sitters' Book showed the dates Lavinia sat for the second portrait. For this one, Lavinia changed her dress, but otherwise the two portraits were almost identical. Such a duplication of a portrait by an artist is called in trade circles a replica. When the Dowager Countess died, the replica passed to her daughter, and eventually descended to Lord Bessborough. Sir Charles was so convinced by the documentation and by the similarity of style and composition in the two pictures that he pronounced the Huntington painting genuine after studying a photograph; he did not feel it necessary to see the original. As for the charge that parts of the portrait were not by Reynolds, Sir Charles said that it was a common practice of that busy artist to let lesser hands fill in what he considered unimportant details. Sir Charles cited a letter in which the Earl of Bath referred to the famous portrait of himself by Reynolds, now in the National Portrait Gallery in London. The Earl wrote a friend to the effect that he had just had his last sitting with the Master but did not expect the finished painting for a few days, owing to a practice that he had discovered and that he thought the artist would not be pleased to have him know about; namely, that when the sittings were finished, Reynolds turned the portraits over to assistants, who filled in details of landscape and costume he was too busy or too bored to do himself.

H. E. Huntington strayed from the Duveen fold only once, and Duveen, in his customary fashion, made him aware that heavy penalties attached to such a lapse. One day in 1913, while H.E., then living at the Metropolitan Club in New York, was taking an innocent stroll down Fifth Avenue, he was pulled off the street by an English art dealer who had a Fifth Avenue branch. He wanted H.E. to look at a painting of two ladies in filmy garments sauntering against a background of clouds, which was, he asserted, a wonderful Romney of Mrs Siddons and her sister, Miss Kemble. H.E., who, unlike his wife, had no prejudice against actresses, succumbed to the two sisters on the spot. As Arabella was in California and couldn't bring her scruples to bear, he had the heavenly girls sent to the Metropolitan Club and paid the dealer a hundred thousand dollars for effecting the assignation. Proud of the coup he had achieved on his own, he invited Duveen to lunch to show off his new acquisition. Duveen, whose opinion of paintings he hadn't sold himself was always candid, gave the two tall, lovely, cloud-framed girls a penetrating look. 'I don't think this is a Romney, H.E.,' he said. 'It looks like Romney, it is very like Romney, it is Romneyesque, but it is not a Romney.'

  Duveen's reflection on the legitimacy of the girls ruined Huntington's lunch. 'It must be a Romney,' he insisted. 'Of course it's a Romney. It can't possibly *not* be a Romney.' He told Duveen the name of the respectable firm from which he had bought it. Moreover, he said, the picture had been certified by T. Humphrey Ward and William Roberts, two unimpeachable authorities. Ward had been the art editor of the London *Times* and was the husband of Mrs Humphrey Ward, than which unimpeachability could go no higher. Roberts, a distinguished British art critic, was a specialist on Romney and the co-author, with Ward, of a book about him. The elder J. P. Morgan had engaged Roberts to prepare a catalogue of his English pictures.

'Nevertheless, I do not think it is a Romney,' Duveen said. 'However, let us ask Stevenson Scott.' Scott, a member of the art firm of Scott & Fowles, and a friend of Duveen's, had a little corner on unimpeachability himself.

By this time, Huntington was in a terrible state, and he waited breathlessly for the arrival of Scott. Scott was forced to back up Duveen's opinion. He knew Mrs Siddons' face intimately, if not personally, he said, and he was convinced that neither of the ladies sauntering in front of the clouds was she. This observation only irritated H.E. He didn't care whether it was Mrs Siddons or not. The point was: Was the picture a Romney? Duveen said he recalled that a picture very like it had, years before, been knocked down at Christie's auction rooms in London for a few hundred pounds. This also, cried the unhappy Huntington, was beside the point. *Was the picture a Romney?* Scott soothingly replied that whoever had painted the picture had at least turned out a fine work of art. This remark merely maddened H.E. further. He delivered himself of a summary statement, 'If this picture is a Romney, I won't give it up at any price,' he said. 'If it is not a Romney, I won't have it at any price!'

Duveen was on a spot. Huntington was in no mood for evasion; he wanted his money back if he had been defrauded. The seller of the heavenly twins was so firm in his conviction that the picture was as he represented it that he was prepared to go to law about it. Should the courts sustain the dealer, Duveen's influence with his client would suffer an irreparable setback. But Duveen trusted his eye and Scott's corroboration. Huntington retained Sir John Simon to bring suit against the dealer in London, since his headquarters was there. A number of experts were retained by one side or the other in this *cause célèbre*. Duveen advised Huntington which experts he should hire. All the dealers' experts stated before the trial that the picture was by Romney; all Duveen's experts said that it was close – even hot – but that it was not a Romney. The experts who had certified the picture – the Messrs Ward and Roberts – issued a second, and amplified, certification. In it they mentioned an entry in Romney's Sitters' Book noting an appointment with 'two ladies sitting'; these two ladies, the Messrs Ward and Roberts averred, were Miss Kemble and Mrs Siddons.

It is hard to say how this case would have been decided if a Londoner named Vickers, who was then nearly eighty and who had spent his life working for art dealers, had not come forward. He remembered that when he was a young man, he had worked for a very old London picture dealer who had told him that in *his* youth, in the latter part of the eighteenth century, there had been a famous controversy between one Ozias Humphry (1742–1819), a miniature-painter, and Horace Walpole. Humphry had asked Walpole if he might paint Walpole's two grand-nieces, the Ladies Maria and Horatia Waldegrave. Walpole consented but didn't actually commission the picture. When it was finished and delivered, he didn't like it, and sent it back. Ozias threatened to sue for his money. Vickers suggested that it might pay Duveen's bloodhounds to trace this case in contemporary records. A satisfactory item turned up. Ozias Humphry proved to be a close friend of Romney's, so close that Romney once painted him for nothing – and there is no greater token of friendship between artists. The Duveen men, now off on what seemed a promising scent, came up with another helpful antiquarian. This was Algernon Graves, one more well-known authority on art, who recalled that he had once seen, in the archives of the Royal Academy, a drawing very much like the painting of the by-this-time-alleged Mrs Siddons and the by-this-time-alleged Miss Kemble. The Duveen scouts found the drawing, and it turned out to be the sketch from which Ozias Humphry had made his painting of the Ladies Maria and Horatia Waldegrave. This drawing might equally well have served for the Huntington picture.

Duveen now moved in for the kill. His men got hold of Romney's Sitters' Book and found that on the day Romney had prepared for the 'two ladies sitting', the entry trium-phantly referred to by the Messrs Ward and Roberts, Mrs Siddons was playing in Birmingham; the sleuths dug up a playbill for the performance. As for Miss Kemble, she had taken it into her pretty head to go to France; they found a record of her passport visa. When the case came to trial, Sir John Simon opened for the plaintiff by stating these facts. A recess was instantly requested by the defence, which presently announced that it had decided not to make a fight; it consented to accept a judgment ordering the return of Huntington's money, plus interest, plus £10,000 costs. Counsel for the defence asked, and was granted, a moratorium on the payment until the war was over. In the end, the affair was too much for the firm involved; it went out of business. H.E. had learned his lesson. Duveen had no more trouble with him.

There are some who say that Duveen was a genius as a businessman and salesman but no great shakes as a connoisseur, and there are others who say that those who say he was no great shakes as a connoisseur are rivals whom he constantly outplayed; they claim that his ability to judge pictures was as nearly infallible as his ability to put over a deal. Some of those who take the first point of view are among the leading critical minds in the art world. The layman might wonder, then, how Duveen was able to spot the fake Romney so readily. There is no conclusive answer, since even the experts were fooled. It was the theory of Dr George C. Williamson, Morgan's art adviser, that a good part of the disputed picture actually was done by Romney in an effort to help his friend to execute Horace Walpole's commission satisfactorily.

> It is quite likely [Williamson writes, in *Stories of an Expert*] that Romney himself said, 'I would stretch the hand out. Let me show you how I would do it.' Again, with regard to the drapery I suggest that Romney pointed out to Humphry the awkwardness of the folds, how they hung from a kind of angle, and again, he perhaps suggested how he would like the draperies to fall, and that the greater part of the foot should be shown. It seems to me to be possible that Romney himself was responsible for parts of the picture; the outstretched arm has a close resemblance to Romney's work, in fact it was that arm which made me at first think the picture must be by Romney. The drapery also, especially that of the left figure, resembles the work of Romney, and I am inclined to believe that the better known painter was really responsible for these two portions of the picture, and that it was his work that led the experts astray.

Dr Williamson, himself a witness at the trial, was one of those led astray – possibly because of an excess of knowledge. Duveen, however, conceivably because he was not similarly burdened, guessed right. If Duveen's detractors are correct, there is still, of course, another possible explanation. Perhaps, with the passing of time, he had begun to have suspicions about the authenticity of any picture that was not his, and since there were still a lot of pictures in the world that were not his, he sometimes suspected with a gratifying accuracy.

In his estimate of pictures that weren't his, Duveen occasionally made a costly mistake. One of the most painful occurred in the summer of 1911, when he was taking the cure at Carlsbad to recover from an intensive wooing of Frick and to gather strength to continue it. Frick was then the greatest prospect in the world, and Duveen was, in his own eyes, the greatest dealer. Duveen was willing to concede the first distinction to Frick, but Frick was still not willing to concede the second to Duveen. Frick had dealt with and liked Duveen's Uncle Henry, but he had always been somewhat chary of the nephew. And Frick had close social and business connections with Knoedler's. He had bought many paintings of the Barbizon school from them. Duveen had gradually succeeded in displacing most of them with Old Masters, but Frick was so fond of some of the Barbizons that he held on to them to the end, an indulgence that Duveen, even when he got the upper hand, as he inevitably did, permitted him. For a long time, Frick played on the rivalry between Duveen and Knoedler's. He thought that it kept both firms on their toes, and that this was to his benefit.

Opposite Reynolds: *'Lavinia, Countess Spencer and her son, Viscount Althorp'. The 'Lavinia' that Duveen persuaded Lord Spencer to part with and sold to H. E. Huntington*

While Duveen was in Carlsbad, a free-lance runner pursued him with a photograph of a three-quarter-length portrait of King Philip IV of Spain, by Velásquez, which he said was for sale. Duveen knew that Velásquez had painted many portraits of his sovereign. That very year, Duveen had sold one to Altman, and he had earlier sold one to Mary M. Emery, of Cincinnati. 'The original of this particular painting hangs in the Dulwich Museum, in London,' he told the runner, 'and, as that is the acknowledged authentic one, the Velásquez of your photograph must be a fake.' Later, in the lounge of his hotel, Duveen saw the runner in conversation with Charles Williams, of Agnew's. When an hotel clerk told him that Williams and the runner had booked reservations to London, his malaise became acute. Duveen knew that Agnew's was acting as the London agent of Knoedler's, and he figured that the picture, if after all it was the original, would certainly go to Frick. Selling pictures to Frick when Frick liked somebody else better was not an occupation that allowed one to take it easy in Carlsbad. Duveen got on the train Williams and the runner were taking, and was no sooner aboard than he was assailed by an agonizing recollection. He remembered that Aureliano de Beruete y Moret, a Spanish expert on Velásquez, had for years clung to the notion, as persistently and obdurately as Galileo had clung to *his* notion, that the Velásquez in the Dulwich Museum was only a copy. Duveen tried to reopen the discussion with the runner, but the man told him he needn't bother; the picture had been sold. Could it be that the fanatical Beruete, like Galileo, would turn out to be right – that the Dulwich Velásquez, which had been raptly stared at by generations of art-loving English, was merely a copy? When it came to the point – that fine point where a collector was willing to pay four hundred thousand dollars for a painting, provided only that it was an original – Beruete delivered. He proved to the satisfaction of other experts that he *was* right, and Frick bought the Velásquez. Duveen had not simply lost a sale; he had lost a prime opportunity to demonstrate to Frick his theorem that if a great picture was to be had, it could be had only from Duveen.

A bold move was necessary to capture Frick's attention. In Paris, in 1913, one of Duveen's runners reported to him that a Russian noblewoman, the wife of an important general, owned a painting she believed to be the work of Leonardo da Vinci. Getting wind of a new da Vinci was like discovering a new planet; Duveen was aquiver. But, as he had mistaken a genuine Velásquez for a false one, he could not risk mistaking a false Leonardo for a genuine one. He invited the Russian lady to come to Paris with her painting and bring it to his gallery in the Place Vendôme. Duveen took her and the

Opposite Hals: 'Balthasar Coymans'. A masterpiece which Duveen acquired in the Rodolphe Kann Collection, and which was later sold first to Mrs Huntington and then to Mellon

Henry Clay Frick

painting upstairs to a room where there was sunlight and a small man with a magnifying glass. The man was Berenson – a fact Duveen did not mention to the lady. Berenson peered at the picture, then looked at it through a magnifying glass, then took it to the window. He finally put it down and gave Duveen the high sign. It was indeed a da Vinci. On the way down to Duveen's office, Berenson found an opportunity to tell him that it was a long-lost picture known as the 'Benois Madonna'. Duveen, tingling with realization of what he could do to Frick and to Knoedler's with this painting, invited its owner to discuss a deal. She named what was then the highest price ever asked for any picture in the history of art – one and a half million dollars. Duveen felt that Frick could afford it. He didn't see, in fact, how Frick could afford not to afford it. The lady asked that a million dollars be placed in escrow as a binder, then explained that, under Russian law, she could not sell the painting until she had offered it to the Tsar at the price she had quoted Duveen. A contract of sale, subject to an option to the Tsar for a certain period, was signed, and the million was placed in escrow. Duveen, who thought it unlikely the Tsar would have the effrontery to compete with Frick, sailed for America in a joyful humour. He told Frick what he was going to get him. The two men went through the motions of their daily lives waiting for the moment when the option would expire. Duveen was an ebullient man and Frick was a cool one, yet Frick's excitement far exceeded Duveen's.

The man who had taken it in his stride when the radical Alexander Berkman came into his office and shot him in the neck, who, with the country clamouring against him, had refused to negotiate with the Amalgamated Association of Iron and Steel Workers, who had calmly lost Benjamin Harrison the Presidency in the campaign of 1892 by his intractability towards the unions in the Homestead Strike – the man whom no one could stir and nothing could move – fumed while the Tsar was making up his mind. Just before the option was to expire, a cable arrived from the owner of the picture saying that the Tsar had met the quoted price. In the dawn of his bitter disappointment, Duveen realized that he had been used. The Russian lady had manoeuvred him into providing a Berenson opinion for nothing. He and Berenson had got the da Vinci into the wrong gallery. It had by-passed Frick and landed in the Hermitage, in Leningrad. Still, the incident was not a total loss from Duveen's point of view, for he had learned how much Frick was willing to pay for what he wanted, or what Duveen could convince him he wanted.

Duveen had one advantage over other dealers, even those who were close friends of his major clients. His rivals offered only pictures, whereas he had other things to provide, too. He knew *décor* and architecture, and could be of great assistance to a man like Frick. Many a time, when a client was building or furnishing a house, Duveen had a hand in it.

The architect of Frick's house on Fifth Avenue,
Thomas Hastings

Rose Terrace, the Detroit home of Mrs Horace E. Dodge

He had more than a hand in furnishing the Detroit and Palm Beach homes of Mrs Horace E. Dodge, the Philadelphia and Palm Beach homes of Mrs E. T. Stotesbury, and Mrs A. Hamilton Rice's home on Fifth Avenue. Mrs Dodge spent so much that her lawyer called her up to find out whether she had gone crazy. He was told no, that she just liked furniture – especially Duveen's. The Rice home Duveen furnished from top to bottom, including the beautiful eighteenth-century *salon* that Mrs Rice later gave to the Philadelphia Museum of Art. The carpet of this room belonged to Louis XIV before Duveen got it. When, in 1913, Frick decided to build his town house at Fifth Avenue and Seventieth Street, and Duveen chose Carrère & Hastings as the architects, Duveen worked with Hastings on the plans. Hastings was quite familiar with the exquisite collection of furniture and tapestries in Duveen's warehouses, and Duveen helped him out by indicating exactly where certain of these items would look their best in the projected mansion. When Hastings submitted the plans, Frick raised his eyebrows at their unconventional character, but Duveen's extravagant admiration of Hastings' work persuaded him to lower them. Later Duveen managed to persuade Frick to make room for the famous set of eleven Fragonard panels he had just bought for him. The four largest panels were commissioned by Mme du Barry in 1770, to hang in her home. Du Barry refused the present, because she considered one of the panels, 'Storming the Citadel', too forthright a comment on her relations with the King. She didn't mind being a citadel, she didn't even mind being stormed, but she didn't want it suggested to posterity that the citadel had fallen. Fragonard had to take his panels back. He kept them for eighteen years and then sold them to a cousin, Alexandre Maubert, for the equivalent of seven hundred and twenty dollars. From M. Maubert, they descended to a grandson, M. Malvilan, and from M. Malvilan they went, by a more commercial route, to Morgan. While Duveen and Hastings were working on the Frick plans, Morgan died. The Morgan estate offered Duveen first chance to buy the panels, but they asked more than a million dollars; even Duveen hesitated. His position was ticklish; Frick, a close friend of the Morgans, would have no trouble finding out the difference between what Duveen paid the Morgan estate and what he was charging *him*. The estate told Duveen he must make up his mind quickly; if he didn't want them, it had another purchaser. He bought the panels and went to see Frick. 'Mr Frick,' he said, 'I have just made a marvellous purchase. I have bought the Fragonard panels from Mr Morgan's estate. I paid a high price, but I had to have them for you. You shall have them at exactly what I paid for them.' Frick bought the panels, and Duveen wrote off the lost profit as an investment in conditioning.

Panelled in the Louis XVI style, with furniture, porcelain, sculpture and tapestries of the Louis XV and Louis XVI periods, the floor covered with Louis XIV Savonerie carpets, this was the salon of Mrs A. Hamilton Rice.

The eleven Fragonard panels are of various sizes and shapes. It was not easy to compose them into a harmonious pattern in a room. There was only one man to do the job, Duveen advised Frick and Hastings – Sir Charles Allom, of London, who had received his knighthood after harmonizing interiors for King George V. Frick and Hastings thought it was a wonderful idea, and called Allom in. When he arrived, Frick offered him the job of doing not only the Fragonard Room but most of the other rooms in the house. Allom, a prima donna, wanted all or nothing, and sailed back to England in a huff. Duveen had a harmonizing job of his own to do. He did it. Frick recalled Allom and put the whole job in his hands. The Fragonard Room was a transatlantic collaboration between Duveen and Allom, who had returned to England again, this time to work on the problem. Frick agreed that the chamber should be provided with a mantel, andirons, mouldings, candelabra, and whatever else should go into harmonizing a Fragonard Room. Duveen sent full-size copies of the panels to Allom, and Allom built a full-size model room to contain them. For accoutrements, Duveen concentrated on the eighteenth century. He managed to acquire for it a marble fireplace that had once graced the Bagatelle, Marie-Antoinette's little château built in 1777 in the Bois de Boulogne by the Comte d'Artois,

Madame du Barry, by Elizabeth Vigée-Lebrun,
a French masterpiece of the 18th century
which was in Duveen's own collection
for some time

who reigned as Charles X from 1824 to 1830. When Allom had arranged the fireplace and the panels to his satisfaction, Duveen went abroad to inspect the job, and passed it. Allom disassembled the roof, accompanied it to New York, and set it up again in a ware-house. Hastings, Allom, and Duveen took Frick down to have a look. Duveen's enthusiasm for it was overflowing, Frick apparently thought it wasn't bad, but, as always, he didn't say much. There was still plenty to be done; when you decide on an eighteenth-century room, you can't just pick up the furnishings anywhere. But fortunately, if expen-sively for Frick, Duveen had just what the room needed: a Riesener commode, a Marie-Antoinette writing-table, some pieces of Clodion sculpture, chairs covered in Beauvais tapestry, and other titbits. After it was finished, Frick was satisfied. Even Duveen seemed to feel satisfied. True, he had sold the Fragonard panels at cost, but when he moved in the other Duveens he was more equitable.

The Fragonard Room was only a start. The Frick house was a big one, and it needed paintings and sculptures as well as furniture. Duveen was able to supply them. In 1916, he built the Boucher Room around eight panels commissioned by Mme de Pompadour for her salon, which were entitled 'The Arts and Sciences'. In 1917, he sold Frick Gainsborough's 'Mrs Peter Baker' and the Hals 'Portrait of a Man'; in 1918, Van Dyck's 'Sir John Suckling' and two Paters, 'Village Orchestra' and 'Procession of Italian Comedians'; and in 1919, Vermeer's 'Mistress and Maid'. Then, still outfitting the Frick establishment, Duveen got a break that partly made up for his bad luck with the Velásquez and the da Vinci. While he was in Paris, one of his runners brought him photographs of a set of tapestries in a château in the Loire District. He wasn't much impressed by the photographs, and, besides, he was about to sail for America, but the runner persuaded him to drive down to the château to look at the tapestries anyway. The château was unoccupied except for a caretaker. Duveen quickly decided he didn't want the tapestries, but, being there, he asked the caretaker if there was anything else in the place. He was invited to look around and see for himself. In a storeroom on the top floor stood a dilapidated bookcase, and on top of it a begrimed bust with a smashed nose. Duveen took the bust down, gave it a good inspection, and instructed the caretaker to tell the owner that he would buy the tapestries if the owner would throw in the bust. The deal went through. Duveen was sure the bust was by Francesco da Laurana, who had worked in Italy and southern France in the latter part of the fifteenth century and was famous for his elegant and imaginative work, and his quick judgment was confirmed. The smashed nose was no problem; Duveen had an expert restore it with marble taken from the base. Duveen's rating with Frick was boosted by this find; the Laurana became one of the most esteemed treasures of the Frick Collection.

Duveen's rating with Frick shot up even higher when he was able to pull a Houdon bust nonchalantly out of his hat. It was a fixed policy of Duveen's to establish a high market value for anything he had a lot of. One thing he had a lot of, early in the century, was Houdon busts. He had fifteen. There was a happy time when you could get a Houdon bust for twenty-five thousand dollars. After buying several at that price, Duveen began to feel sorry for Houdon. Twenty-five thousand dollars was a stodgy and humiliating figure, and if Houdon was worth collecting at all he was worth more than that. Duveen set about correcting what he now realized was a scandalous state of affairs. At a public auction, he paid seventy-five thousand dollars for a Houdon bust – an unprecedented figure. He then returned to his Fifth Avenue gallery and looked at his other Houdon busts more respectfully, and with a righteous feeling of having vindicated their honour. The world market in Houdons followed Duveen's lead; presently, you couldn't get one for less than a hundred and fifty thousand. 'If you owned one that had cost twenty-five thousand dollars,' an observer of Duveen's Houdon operation has said, 'you had to apologize.' In the steeply rising market, Duveen held on to his Houdons; he found their society restful. Besides, his instinct told him that they might come in handy in emergencies. One emergency arose when he had to furnish the Frick house. The sculptor who was invited to America by Thomas Jefferson to do a statue of George Washington also permitted himself less austere assignments. He did, for example, a marble portrait bust of the Comtesse du Cayla. It ended up in the Duveen collection. Duveen may have done a good deal for Houdon, but Houdon did something for Duveen – and, incidentally, for Frick, too. When it came to deciding what to put on the mantelpiece in the Fragonard Room, Frick's brain stopped functioning. Duveen's brain became active; the Comtesse du Cayla occurred to him. (Similarly, years later, the mansion's Oval Room needed something; it couldn't go on indefinitely just being oval.) No wonder it was hard for Frick to suppress an impulse of gratitude towards Duveen; he found himself being rescued from such acute dilemmas almost hourly, and not by frustrated, undervalued artists but by perfectly adjusted Duveens.

The technique Duveen had applied to adjusting Houdon he also applied to Rembrandt. He owned a lot of Rembrandts, and by paying tremendous prices for additional ones he raised the value of those he had acquired when Rembrandt was lowly. There are penalties even for large-scale beneficence, and the penalty Duveen had to endure was that in the course of this process Rembrandts and Houdons that belonged to other people went up in value, too. Duveen forced himself not to think about that. There came a day when Duveen saw his labours on behalf of levitating Houdon crowned so magnificently that he was dazzled by his handiwork. This happened at the auction of the huge Elbert H. Gary Collection in 1928. It being always Duveen's aim to prove that the value of Duveens went up and never down, that all ownership save his own was ephemeral, and possibly even irrelevant, Duveen was determined that none of the objects he had sold Gary should be undervalued just because Gary had died. Duveen, by bidding the prices up, saw to it that one Duveen after another went for a price that was far above the one for which he had sold it to Gary. Then there appeared on the auction block one of his Houdons – a bust of the sculptor's daughter Sabine at the age of ten months. Duveen had bought it in Paris in 1912. His campaign for Houdon had by then advanced so far that he paid ninety-six thousand dollars for it. He had sold it to Gary for a hundred and ten thousand dollars. The bidding for it was sharp, and Duveen participated in it. It narrowed down to a contest between Duveen and Knoedler's, who were acting for Edward S. Harkness. As the bids rose to new heights, Duveen became more and more impressed by what he himself had wrought. Finally, bemused, he allowed Knoedler's to buy the bust for Harkness, for two hundred and forty-five thousand dollars. Later, Duveen was a little rueful about having let his old friend go to somebody else, especially as that somebody else was Harkness, whom he considered sufficiently well bred to belong in the Duveen stable but who would never buy from him, being married to Knoedler's. Still, when Duveen went home from the sale, he must have looked back over the long history of his efforts on behalf of Houdon and remembered incredulously a time when you could actually buy a Houdon for twenty-five thousand dollars, and he may have reflected pleasantly that if Houdon had been alive he would surely have written him a grateful bread-and-butter letter. Rembrandt, also, might well have dropped him a line.

A few days before Frick died, in December 1919, Duveen was startled to get back from him two million dollars' worth of painting he had had on approval. The explanation offered was that, in his poor physical condition, Frick could not swing the financing. Frick had always engaged in protracted, and enjoyable, haggles with Duveen – not over price but over methods of paying the price – and perhaps he felt that now he was deprived of them, he might as well be deprived of the pictures, too. But Frick was not deprived of a certain kind of immortality – an immortality he can be said to have sought in collecting his pictures. The art patrons of the Renaissance had themselves painted into the pictures they commissioned; because their American counterparts lived too late to have this service performed for them, they had to gain their immortality by buying collections and putting them in public museums. It is human and perhaps touching, this impulse to project one-self beyond one's mortal span. The article on Frick in the *Encyclopaedia Britannica* runs to twenty-three lines. Ten are devoted to his career as an industrialist, and thirteen to his collecting of art. In these thirteen lines, he mingles freely with Titian and Vermeer, with El Greco and Goya, with Gainsborough and Velásquez. Steel strikes and Pinkerton guards vanish, and he basks in another, more felicitous aura. The old boys take him cosily under their wings; they carry him along. For the pleasure of their society on the golden shore, Duveen made Frick pay heavily, but they are earning their keep.

Andrew Mellon

Chapter 6
THE SILENT MEN

ALL his adult life, Duveen ran a race with his clients' mortality. This race was a close one, for his major clients were well along in years, and from 1934 on it was complicated by his race with his own mortality. In that year, Duveen fell ill with cancer, and he knew from the beginning that he could not recover. For much of his remaining five years, he had to have a nurse with him constantly, and, one by one, he gave up all the little indulgences that for most people relieve the pangs of existence. The only indulgence he did not give up was selling pictures; here his tempo, if anything, accelerated. To many individuals the approach of a deadline has a paralysing effect; to rarer ones it is a stimulus. In 1926, when Duveen went to San Marino ahead of a freight-car load of his merchandise, to make sure that H. E. Huntington, one of his best clients, would not die without an additional several million dollars' worth of Duveen's taste to leave behind, Huntington's age and physical condition made speed essential. Previously, in similar situations – notably those involving the elder Morgan and Altman and Frick – Duveen had lost. Death had got there ahead of the pictures. Having learned his lesson, he worked fast with Huntington, and he did the same with himself. He was like an ageing painter who feels he has to complete a masterpiece in the brief time left him. Duveen's masterpiece, and from his point of view his monument, is the National Gallery of Art in Washington.

Duveen's career had beautiful composition. Early in the century, he inherited from his Uncle Henry three gigantic clients – Morgan, Altman, and P. A. B. Widener – and thereafter time, and the swelling American prosperity, supplied new ones. There were great millionaires who spent little and small millionaires who spent vast sums. Duveen saw fortunes come and go. When they went, Duveen, following his lifelong principle of keeping the market up, usually bought his pictures back for more than he got for them and sold them – at an increase over the increase he had paid – to clients whose fortunes were still intact. Even depressions were lucky for him, and so, finally, were the rising income and inheritance taxes. The era of big houses was ending, and as the artistic appetites of Duveen's clients increased, a new problem developed for them – a critical shortage of wall space – and that, too, Duveen turned to his advantage. Some collectors met the exigency by providing a building for their paintings and an apartment for themselves and their

J. P. Morgan Jr

families. The pressure of space made it inadvisable for Duveen's customers to keep buying pictures for their homes; the pressure of inheritance taxes made it unattractive for them to leave valuable collections of pictures in their estates. Duveen had pegged the art market so high that no man was now rich enough to live with Duveens or to die with them. On the whole, Duveen was not interested in politics or political change – he cared not who wrote his country's laws so long as he could sell its pictures – but he was keenly sensitive to social change, and he saw before most people did that, between them, income taxes and inheritance taxes were going to make it impossible for men of wealth to buy art for themselves or leave collections to their heirs. The public bequest, impervious to taxation, was the way out. Specifically, the public bequest of Duveens was the way out. By earmarking his purchases for museums, a collector could afford to buy art; at least, he could let the art pass through his hands on the way to the museums from Duveen. Gifts to museums offered his clients not merely economy but immortality. Using Duveen's method, an aged American millionaire could, in good conscience, circumvent oblivion and the Collector of Internal Revenue at a single stroke. Under Duveen's spell, one after another of his clients – H. E. Huntington, Frick, Mellon, Bache, Kress – took up this form of philanthropy. For Duveen the advantage was double; with museums as the terminal for his pictures, he no longer had to worry about the passing of the big houses – the museums were larger than the houses – and he no longer had to worry that the pictures would be dumped on the market at a time when it might be difficult for him to sell them, especially at the prices he would have to charge after buying them back at Duveen prices. Ultimately, in the National Gallery, Duveen provided a place that was big enough to absorb everything any client had bought or could buy. It was Duveen's final solution to the problem of wall space.

Most of the big names in American industry and finance – except those of the benighted millionaires who didn't collect anything and the benighted (and to Duveen snobbish) millionaires who collected first editions instead of works of art – appeared in Duveen's Callers' Book. Throughout his long and fantastic run, there was always someone to relight his torch. When Collis P. Huntington and Altman and Morgan and P. A. B. Widener died, Frick showed up, and John D. Rockefeller, Jr, and Stotesbury, Mackay, Bache, Gary, Joseph E. Widener, Henry Goldman, H. E. Huntington, Philip Lehman and his son, Robert, and a host of lesser collectors. And then, as late in his life as in theirs, Duveen met two men whom he was to help make almost as great collectors as he was: Mellon, the founder of the National Gallery, and Kress, the Gallery's most lavish contributor. In the case of the former, the word 'met' is ludicrously inadequate. It is like saying

Left John D. Rockefeller and his son, both of whom were important Duveen clients; right Rockefeller Sr shortly before his death

that Napoleon ran into Alexander at Tilsit. Duveen and Mellon moved in different social spheres. They didn't belong to the same clubs: Duveen couldn't encounter him in the bar. For him to meet Mellon, a campaign was necessary. In his management of it, Duveen displayed that scrupulous attention to detail that has distinguished the careers of other celebrated generals.

In a way, Duveen's determination to meet Mellon began with an extraordinary meeting with Henry Ford. For American art dealers, 1920 was a very bad year. The important buyers had been dying off, and their replacements were not yet visible. The year 1920 was one of crisis – of such acute crisis, in fact, that it forced the major dealers, for once, into solidarity. The lone wolves at last decided to pack up. Even Duveen consented to merge his talents with the talents of those he regarded as stumbling pedagogues whose function it was to prepare American art buyers for his finishing school. Looking around for new clients, the purveyors of art were discouraged. Save for one towering monolith, the horizon was blank. That monolith was Ford. The dealers – Duveen, Knoedler's, Wildenstein, Seligman, and Stevenson Scott – decided to make a mass assault on him. Ford was an objective so big that there would be enough for them all, and too big, they felt, for just one of them to tackle and risk fumbling. It was like annexing Texas. The five dealers reconciled themselves to pooling their inventories as well as their aggressiveness. They decided to prepare a list of the Hundred Greatest Paintings in the World and offer them to Ford; thus in one transaction they could convert America's richest man into America's outstanding collector. Like most other collectors, each of the five dealers had persuaded himself that the paintings he owned were better than any owned by his rivals, and the task of selecting the hundred greatest resulted in many acrimonious debates, during which the surf of controversy often rose so high that the scheme was in danger of foundering. But the gravity of the crisis and the grandeur of the objective made for compromise, and finally the hundred paintings were agreed upon.

The pictures, each of which was accompanied by a scholarly text, were reproduced in three magnificent volumes; the dealers were going to present these books to Mr Ford as an invitation to the dance. Representatives of the five firms and the three magic books went, by appointment, to Dearborn. Representing Duveen Brothers, as always, was Duveen himself. The international worldlings from New York were astonished at the simplicity of Ford's style of living; compared to Duveen's house on Madison Avenue, or even to some of his clients' houses, Ford's house was almost primitive. Mr Ford was unaffectedly pleased to meet them, and when they displayed the superbly illustrated volumes of the hundred greatest pictures, his delight was immeasurable. He jumped up and called Mrs Ford in to share his enthusiasm. 'Mother, come in and see the lovely pictures these gentle-

Henry Ford, with his son Edsel beside him, driving the twenty-millionth car from his Detroit works

men have brought,' he said, as Duveen later told the story. Mrs Ford came in and admired the books as much as her husband had. 'Yes, Mr Ford,' said Duveen, the spokesman for the delegation, 'we thought you would like them. These are the pictures we feel you should have.' Ford teetered on the narrow threshold between admiration and possession. 'Gentlemen,' he said, 'beautiful books like these, with beautiful coloured pictures like these, must cost an awful lot!' 'But, Mr Ford, we don't expect you to *buy* these books,' Duveen hastened to explain. 'We got them up specially for you, to show you the pictures. These books are a present to you.' Ford turned to his wife. 'Mother, did you hear that?' he said. 'These gentlemen are going to give me these beautiful books as a present. Yes, gentlemen,' he continued, 'it is extremely nice of you, but I really don't see how I can accept a beautiful, expensive present like this from strangers.' For perhaps the first time in his life, Duveen was inarticulate. Such innocence was confounding. It was a classic example of the worldling defenceless against the Man from Home. When at last he found speech, he explained that the books had been got up to interest Ford in buying the pictures whose simulacra they contained. At this revelation, Ford's amazement vanished and he became again a man of business. 'But, gentlemen,' he said, 'what would I want with the original pictures when the ones right here in these books are so beautiful?'

The fiasco left the four other dealers in a state of dejection from which they did not recover for some time, but for Duveen it was just a tonic. Attributing his failure with

Ford to his having broken his own rule against combining forces with other dealers, he decided to turn his attentions to the biggest potential collector of them all: Mellon. From the defeat of Dearborn, he went on to the conquest of Pittsburgh. Probably no other single episode in Duveen's career illustrates his nonchalance in the face of the impossible as well as his campaigns to acquire Mellon. Mellon had never bought anything from Duveen; he was a confirmed client of Duveen's greatest rival, Knoedler's. Mellon had a standing arrangement with Knoedler's under which they acted as his exclusive agent on a fixed commission. Duveen thought the business of selling pictures on a fixed commission was thin, lacking in substance, texture, resiliency, promise – above all, promise. It made a dealer a mere merchant. It divested the game of adventure, of the mystery of the incalculable. Duveen was advised by a friend to give up any idea of selling to Mellon; the advice contained a strong hint that there was something about Duveen that the aristocratic Mellon would find uncongenial. 'Not only will Mellon buy from me but he will buy *only* from me,' Duveen replied. 'And it won't be on commission.' In a commemorative article on the Frick Collection written in 1943 for the leading American publication dealing with art matters, *Art News*, H. G. Dwight, then assistant director of the Frick Collection, spoke of 'the stormy human equations of collecting, the gnawing obsessions, stealthy pursuits, crushing disappointments, and intoxicating triumphs that lie in the background of the most beautiful things'. The stratagems Duveen used to acquire and hold customers were not unique, but he used them better than anybody else. However little his clients knew about the masterpieces they bought, they did understand competition, but no more clearly than Duveen understood it. Monopoly was his method. Once he had cornered an Old Master, he knew that the 'gnawing obsessions' from which his customers suffered would bring them to him.

What proved to be as helpful as anything else in enabling Duveen to gain the coveted entrée to Mellon was Duveen's unusual spirit of friendliness. He wore friendliness like a nimbus, and let it shine upon an enormous miscellany of people connected – sometimes directly, sometimes very indirectly – with art: critics, museum directors, restorers, architects, decorators and servants of all grades, including deck stewards on ships. Accustomed to doing things *en prince* he scattered largess, often for no specific purpose but with a touching faith in the emotion of gratitude. Unimpressed himself by sums that were less than colossal, he was continually being pleasurably surprised by the welcome that people who had a different scale of values accorded smaller amounts. Because he couldn't resist a lawsuit even

Opposite de Hooch: 'A Dutch Courtyard'. Acquired by Duveen from the collection of the Countess of Carnarvon and sold to Mellon

when he didn't care particularly about winning it, he once found himself mixed up in one over a claim made by a young artist who had been engaged to do some special work for him. The artist kept asking for more and more pay, until, at last, Duveen's comptroller gave him a cheque marked 'In final payment'. The artist accepted this cheque and cashed it, and then came back and asked for more money. The comptroller refused to give it to him, the artist brought suit, and Duveen spent several enjoyable days in court. (He said one time that he was sorry he hadn't become a lawyer, because he so loved a fight.) The case was thrown out, and Duveen and his comptroller left the courtroom together, flushed with victory. In the car on the way back, Duveen inquired what the amount involved was. The comptroller told him it was $14,095. This minuscule sum had a quaint sound to Duveen. 'Why quibble over fourteen thousand and ninety-five dollars?' he asked. 'Send him the money.' To a man to whom fourteen thousand and ninety-five was nothing to quibble about, it seemed strange that a deck steward on a liner would be enchanted with a mere hundred dollars in return for putting Duveen's deck chair next to one reserved for an American millionaire, but that is what the deck steward was. Over the years, Duveen became very popular with deck stewards.

Among the American millionaires Duveen met through a deck steward who liked him was the late Alexander Smith Cochran, the Yonkers carpet man. Duveen and Cochran met on a boat going to Europe and, while they were chatting, Cochran happened to mention that he would like some day to see Buckingham Palace and St James's Palace. Duveen said casually that he would be delighted to take him through both places. When they got to England Cochran found himself strolling through the two palaces; they seemed as accessible to Duveen as the lobby of Claridge's. While he was showing Cochran the royal pictures, Duveen spoke warmly of Queen Mary and told Cochran what a high regard he had for their absent hostess as a connoisseur of art. He never mentioned that he had things he considered as good as hers in his own galleries. In fact, he never mentioned his galleries at all. When they parted, Cochran felt a certain obligation to Duveen, a healthy respect for his connection, and a sharp curiosity about why a stranger should be so kind. They met again in New York, and Duveen took him to see the wonderful Duveens hanging in the private houses of some of his clients. But he did not tell him they were Duveens; he let them pass under the pseudonyms of Raphael, Botticelli, Donatello, and the rest. Again, he neglected to mention his great New York gallery. This display of benevolence went on for three years, in this country and abroad, until finally Cochran

Opposite van der Weyden: *'Portrait of a Lady'. One of the masterpieces of Flemish painting bought by Duveen in Germany, and sold to Mellon*

could not stand it any longer, and he broke down. 'Lord Duveen,' he said, 'I would like to see some of *your* things!' His back to the wall, Duveen took Cochran to his gallery. He could not spare any paintings – they were all on reserve – but he did let Cochran have five million dollars' worth of art objects.

Duveen's generosity towards the household staffs of his clients equalled his generosity towards deck stewards, and it was no less endearing. He was aware that his sales to their masters and mistresses caused the servants a lot of extra work. When he felt that a room needed what he called 'lifting', he would refurnish it entirely. The hanging of his pictures was an elaborate and intricate ceremonial, which he supervised in detail. All this meant work for the staffs, and Duveen was not one to allow services to go unrewarded. So he rewarded. He rewarded liberally. The staffs of the great houses hung with Duveens came to realize that he was a man they could rely on to pay time and a half for overtime, even when the shifting and heaving and wiring they had to do took place in their regular working hours. One rather celebrated butler in a Fifth Avenue house that stocked Duveens put in so much overtime that, before he retired, his emoluments from Duveen totalled over a hundred thousand dollars. The gratitude of servants was a fine silt from which burgeoned the flower of remembrance. They developed a feeling that it was only fair to transmit to the generous nobleman any information that might interest him: what rival dealers (who had no comparable sense of the value of a servant's time) had the effrontery to offer works of art to their masters, what purchases the masters were considering, what was said about Duveen's emissaries on the walls – in short, all the minutiae of relevant gossip that in the art world are as pregnant with significance as the secret memoranda exchanged by chancelleries. A rival of Duveen's who was a friend of Frick's found, for example, that he could never see Frick alone. Whenever he dropped in, Duveen was there. Another dealer had the same experience whenever he called on Bache. Duveen's generosity even extended to the household staffs of people who were not clients of his but merely potential clients. Eventually, his circle of friends included almost every valet and butler of any distinction whatever.

In the higher strata – with museum directors, say – Duveen assumed a helpful, avuncular role, and here, too, the emotion of gratitude asserted itself. It often happens that a museum director gets on the trail of some things that he would love to have for his institution but that his budget won't allow. In situations of that kind, Duveen could usually be counted on to help out with a cash gift. He loved the role of benefactor. One of his beneficiaries was the director of a museum in Dijon, France. As a result, the Dijon director, without realizing it, turned himself into an unpaid runner for Duveen. He came upon two early French masterpieces by artists whose names were not known but who were members of the Avignon school. The authenticity and the quality of the pictures were indisputable, but they were altogether beyond the range of the Dijon museum, and the director immediately put Duveen in touch with them; Duveen bought them, and sold them to Rockefeller for three-quarters of a million dollars.

With architects and decorators, Duveen was, of course, completely at home. Once an architect won his affection, there was almost nothing he wouldn't do for him – from his early favourite, Horace Trumbauer, to whom he gave the job of building his Ministry of Marine; through Thomas Hastings, whom he talked Frick into selecting to build Frick's house; down to his last, John Russell Pope, for whom he performed a similar service in connection with the job of building the National Gallery in Washington. Earlier, Duveen had donated to the British Museum a wing to house the Elgin Marbles, and he had given Pope the job of designing that, too. After the death of Mrs Frick, in 1931, Pope, thanks to Duveen, was chosen to convert the Frick mansion into the Frick Museum. It is said that in the beginning Duveen's regard for Pope was not wholly disinterested. Pope was a stepson-in-law of an important Baltimore collector, Henry Walters, and Duveen hoped to get Walters as a customer. He failed in this but came to like Pope for himself alone. For Hastings, Duveen had a vociferous enthusiasm. Some of Frick's friends were sceptical about Hastings' plans for the partially one-storey Frick house; they thought it was too low for a city that went in for altitude. These sceptics Duveen demolished; to Frick he expressed as much satisfaction with Hastings' plans as if they were a Duveen, which, in a sense, they were to become. It was when Duveen, with his exhaustive solicitude, began worrying about the interior of the house that he had Sir Charles Allom brought in. Just as Duveen would sometimes furnish an entire room to sell a picture, so, conversely, he would some-times sell a picture to furnish a room, as happened in the case of the famous Fragonard Room that he got Allom to set up for Frick. Not only did he inspire the emotion of gratitude in others, but he was capable of feeling it strongly himself. He never forgot Allom's appreciation of his taste in furnishing the Fragonard Room, and got him job after job: the Bache house; Mrs Horace E. Dodge's house, which Duveen furnished entirely; and, for good measure, Hearst's castle in Wales, so that at least once Allom wouldn't have to go too far to go to work.

Besides architects and interior decorators, Duveen had a great affection for restorers – those men who perform the nice task of revivifying pictures that have lost their bloom. Restoration evidently has its limits; it stops short of resurrection but, given sufficient skill on the part of the restorer, it can accomplish wonders. To those who suggested that, for instance, a Dürer that Duveen sold to Bache had very little of Dürer left in it, Duveen answered wistfully that anyway it *had* been by Dürer. Duveen had a pet restorer in Italy for Italian pictures, one in France for French pictures, and one in England for English pic-tures. Oddly, his pet restorer of all was a man born in New York City, Stephen S. Pichetto.

Pichetto, who was of Italian parentage, attended Townsend Harris High School and then went to C.C.N.Y. He had ambitions to be a painter himself, but he gave them up in favour of restoring the works of other men, especially those who flourished in Italy during the Renaissance. Duveen began using him early in his American career; by 1928, Pichetto had an official position as 'consultant restorer' to the Metropolitan Museum. As Duveen sold many more Italian pictures in America than anybody else sold, he had many more of them to restore, and Pichetto was kept busy. Duveen's generosity – that is, his conviction that anyone who worked for him, high or low, should be compensated in a manner commensurate with the dignity of the association – paid off marvellously in Pichetto's case. Pichetto became not only restorer but art adviser to Kress. Kress came to rely on Pichetto's judgment, and it was convenient for Duveen that coincidentally Pichetto was (as a friend of both Kress and Pichetto once put it) 'extremely Duveen conscious'. This adventitious awareness of Pichetto's came in handy for Duveen when he wanted to sell a picture to Kress, even if it didn't have to be restored. Pichetto, brimful of goodwill, must have outdone himself when he had to restore a picture that belonged, successively, to Duveen *and* to Kress. In Duveen's final years, when he was at his height, Pichetto was at *his* height; he was so busy that he leased an entire floor of the Squibb Building and had twelve men on his staff. When Pichetto died, in 1949, at the age of sixty-one, he was himself a wealthy man. Such was the era and such was the trade, as Duveen practised it, that even a restorer who worked for Duveen could leave a fortune.

When at last the moment came for Duveen to meet Mellon, he found himself bountifully rewarded for his unremitting and democratic friendliness. For one thing, although Mellon knew very little about Duveen, apart from the fact that he didn't want to deal with him, Duveen was thoroughly informed about Mellon. Duveen was much better prepared to know Mellon than Mellon was to know Duveen. For another thing, the mechanics of the meeting were so much simpler than they would have been had Duveen been an unfriendly man. The meeting was effected by a delicate feat of co-ordination. Duveen could not depend on coincidence unless he himself created it. In 1921, Mellon, visiting London, occupied a suite on the third floor of Claridge's. Duveen had a permanent suite on the fourth floor of Claridge's. Stirred suddenly by premonitions of intimacy, he had himself moved to the floor below Mellon. Duveen's valet was, inevitably, a friend of Mellon's; the two valets seem to have wished the contagion of their friendship to spread to their masters. One afternoon, Duveen was apprised by his valet that Mellon's valet was helping Mellon on with his overcoat and was about to start down the corridor with him for the lift. Duveen's valet hastily performed the same services for Duveen. The timing of the valets was so exquisite that Duveen stepped into the descending lift that contained Mellon. Duveen was not only surprised, he was charmed. 'How do you do, Mr Mellon?'

he said, and introduced himself, adding, as he later recalled, 'I am on my way to the National Gallery to look at some pictures. My great refreshment is to look at pictures.' Taken unawares, Mellon admitted that he, too, was in need of a little refreshment. They went to the National Gallery together, and after they had been refreshed, Mellon discovered that Duveen had an inventory of Old Masters of his own that, although smaller than the museum's, was, Duveen thought, comparable in quality. He gave Mellon, as he gave all his clients, the sensation of, in H. G. Dwight's words, 'intoxicating triumphs' to come. So heady was this sensation that Mellon appears to have forgotten altogether that Duveen did not work on a commission.

Mellon, 'the Apostle of Silence'

The personalities of Duveen and Mellon were widely disparate. Duveen blurted out everything; Mellon was the Apostle of Silence. When Mellon was appointed Secretary of the Treasury by Harding, he had to be introduced to the public; his footfall was so light that his name had rarely appeared in the papers, and then most inconspicuously. (At the time of the appointment, Duveen was asked how he felt about it. 'I don't care whether Mr Mellon is Secretary of the Treasury or not, as long as he keeps buying pictures,' he replied. Duveen was not interested in what he called his clients' 'outside jobs'; he was interested only in their *main* job, which was buying Duveens.) In 1928, Mellon was the featured speaker on Founder's Day at Carnegie Institute, in Pittsburgh. Carnegie Institute was hard up, and there was a rumour that Mellon would come through with a donation. The honoured guest, reading almost inaudibly from a prepared text, had his audience straining for the news of a bonanza. Presently, the inaudibility became complete. Mellon had lost his place. He made an effort to find it, and then gave up. 'That's all,' he murmured, and sat down. The audience filed out, not knowing whether Carnegie Institute had got anything or not. They didn't find out till the next morning, when the speech was reported in

the Pittsburgh paper, and then they were disappointed. Mellon had been describing a
monumental plan he had for rebuilding Washington.

In his Cabinet days, Mellon was a small, frail man with silver hair, a narrow, finely
moulded head, and a well-trimmed moustache. His admirers considered him patrician;
one of them has said, 'He was princely but not prodigal.' A more detached observer of
him said, however, that he looked like 'a double-entry bookkeeper afraid of losing his job
– worn, and tired, tired, tired'. To call Mellon laconic was to accuse him of garrulity.
Feeling, after he became a public figure, that he should make an effort to be hail-fellow-
well-met, he often tried to force a smile. He didn't have to force one, though, when
Coolidge succeeded Harding. 'Coolidge will become one of our greatest Presidents,' he
said. The two men saw much of each other, conversing almost entirely in pauses.

Perhaps there is some mysterious relation between the possession of great wealth and
parsimony of speech. A characteristic of practically all the Duveen millionaires was the
feeling that speech, like money, was to be held on to – or, at any rate, doled out very slowly.
If silence was indeed golden, then this was an easy way for them to increase their capital.
When Morgan was in Rome, he liked the society of Salvatore Cortesi, an Associated
Press correspondent. According to Morgan's biographer, Frederick Lewis Allen, Morgan
would drive through the streets of Rome with Cortesi for hours, 'without feeling any
necessity to say or hear a word'. When someone asked Leland Stanford, when he was
Governor of California, 'How do you feel this morning, Governor?' the Governor threw
the questioner an uneasy look, on guard against this dangerously leading question, and
countered with another question. 'Wouldn't you like to know?' he said. The Governor,
who had been, like one of his business partners, Collis P. Huntington, a Sacramento
storekeeper, once sold some groceries and hardware to a couple of prospectors who were
broke. In exchange, they gave Stanford seventy-six of the ninety-three shares in their mine.
On these shares, Stanford subsequently cleared half a million dollars. An inquiring
psychologist in search of the connection between money and silence might discover a
sound one – a suspicion that talk breeds friendship and that friendship can be expensive.
The rich man's intuition is probably right. Once you have achieved some sort of human
relationship with a man, it is hard to bring yourself to sell him a few groceries for half a
million dollars. In addition to founding his university, Stanford splashed his will with
munificent bequests. He called in his wife and another of his partners, Mark Hopkins, to
consult with him about it. Despite all his acquisitiveness, his affairs were in bad shape.
'Don't you think, Leland, that you are being too liberal to some of these people?' Mrs
Stanford asked. 'They won't think I'm so liberal when they come to collect,' said Stanford
compactly. On the way up, reticence is important; once one is there, it is obligatory.
Speech is alive with the germ of commitment. The less you say, the less vulnerable you are.

According to a biography written by his close friend George Harvey, Frick's childhood dreams centred about the ambition to have, one day, a million dollars. When he was thirty, he had it and he felt justified in blowing himself to a jaunt in Europe. A cautious and conservative young man, he went to call on another cautious and conservative young man in Pittsburgh, Andrew Mellon, to propose that they join forces on a holiday. Mellon nodded his head, and the trip was on. But that genius for organization which Frick had already begun to apply to his coal-and-coke business and which was to multiply the realization of his modest early dreams by the hundreds he applied instinctively to the organization of his first European trip also. Harvey tells about it as follows:

> Naturally, after three years of close and continuous application at his desk, the young banker [Mellon] eagerly welcomed the suggestion of a trip abroad and, having his affairs in perfect order as usual, he readily arranged for an absence of four months. Presently Clay proposed to increase the party by inviting two acquaintances to join them. One of those suggested was a popular young man who wrote poetry, sang gleefully, and told amusing stories. Andrew readily assented to this thoughtful provision of entertainment enhanced by the desirability of having 'someone along to do the talking'. The other was an older man, no more loquacious than themselves.

As Harvey does not tell us, one can only imagine that this industrial principle of division of labour worked out beautifully on the European jaunt. As Frick and Mellon – except possibly in their relations with Duveen – always got something in excess of value received, it is safe to assume that the fellow they took along to do the talking worked hard and incessantly and made it blissfully unnecessary for his two hosts to open their mouths in speech except in emergencies. On occasion, though, Frick, if sufficiently stimulated by a colleague, permitted himself to be expansive. One day during a stock-market crisis, he was in the office of James Stillman, the president of the National City Bank. The two giants were besieged by a financial reporter, who asked for a statement. The reporter waited a full hour while Frick and Stillman evolved it. Finally, it was sent out by Stillman's secretary. It read:

> The U.S.A. is a great and growing country.
> >   (Signed) JAMES STILLMAN
> >   HENRY C. FRICK

> This is confidential and not for publication unless names are omitted.

Although Duveen got what he wanted that day in the lift in Claridge's, although Mellon became a customer, and his best customer, Duveen had to pay a high price, for Mellon, by not talking, made him suffer acutely. He took for ever to decide about a picture, and during these endless periods of indecision gave Duveen no hint of what he was thinking. In an impulsive, indiscreet moment, a rival art dealer once heard himself saying to Mellon, 'Duveen tells me you drive him crazy. You drive him crazy because he never knows what you feel about things. He says he can never get a word out of you.' At this testimony to his inscrutability, Mellon permitted himself a smile, unaccompanied by speech. Duveen used to cheer Bache up when he was low, and H. E. Huntington used to cheer Duveen up when *he* was low. But Mellon was simply withdrawn. Not only was he withdrawn; he had to be satisfied that a picture was indisputably authentic and that it was the best the Old Master had to offer. Moreover, he felt that he must like it – without saying so, of course – almost as well as Duveen did. Without speaking a word or even altering his expression, he let Duveen's spirals of ecstasy envelop him. Through all the long and, on Mellon's part, silent struggle, Duveen sought, by all the devices at his disposal, to uncover the well-spring of emotion he was sure lay within. He came nearest to it the day he found Mellon in a mood bordering on irritation. This was promising. He plumbed it, only to discover that Mellon was annoyed because his haberdasher had asked him an exorbitant price for a fourteen-carat-gold collar stud. He had left the shop without a word and without the collar stud.

During the 1920s, Duveen moved extremely cautiously with Mellon. He did not regard Mellon as the kind of man who should be rushed. He was satisfied to sell him one or two pictures at a time, and to put up with the fact that Mellon still saw a great deal of Knoedler's. And somewhere along the way Duveen began to plant in Mellon's mind filaments of suggestion – the merest gossamer, at first – that were to lead Mellon to wake up one day with the awesome idea that he would found a national art gallery in Washington. As a close observer of the National Gallery's genesis has said, 'It was a gleam in Duveen's eye long before Andrew Mellon ever thought of it.' Towards the end of the decade, with a view to making a start towards filling up the gallery of his imagination, Duveen, hearing that the Soviet government was eager to sell some of its famous collections of paintings in the Hermitage Gallery, went over to have a look at them. The Soviet government proved to be the first seller in his experience whose price he did not care to meet. The outlay was too great, he thought, especially since Mellon was the only potential purchaser, and

Opposite *Filippo Lippi: 'Madonna and Child'. A painting which Duveen 'abducted' from the Kaiser Friedrich Museum in Berlin, and sold to Kress*

Overleaf left *Giotto: 'Madonna and Child'; right Daddi: 'Madonna and Child with Saints and Angels'. Two outstanding early Italian paintings which Duveen sold first to Goldman, and on his death to Kress*

Mellon had not seen the pictures. Duveen contented himself with telling Mellon about the expensive opportunity. After several years of negotiation, Mellon, in 1930 and 1931, using Knoedler's – still working on a fixed commission – as his agent, took advantage of it. Mellon bought twenty-one of the Hermitage paintings, for seven million dollars. For Raphael's 'Alba Madonna' alone he paid over one million one hundred thousand dollars. Mellon's taciturnity about his Hermitage buy equalled his taciturnity about everything else. David E. Finley, who was Mellon's right-hand man and at his request was appointed the Director of the National Gallery, has been quoted in the *Saturday Evening Post* as saying, 'Mr Mellon wanted to keep the thing a surprise until the right moment. It probably would not have been good politics for the Secretary of the Treasury publicly to spend millions for rare paintings at a time when the government was swamped with unemployment, bank failures, and general distress.' To keep quiet about this was no strain on Mellon.

To anybody else, Mellon's purchase of the Hermitage pictures would have been a lethal blow, but to Duveen it was like finding a gusher. After it had been announced, a rival dealer came to offer him some gloating consolation. He was startled to find Duveen radiant. 'Mellon has arrived,' Duveen said. 'He's ready for *me*.' Duveen felt that any man who would spend that much money on pictures he had never seen was a buyer for whom he was prepared to endure any anguish. He knew that Mellon would make no more such purchases except from him; there was no other source of supply. The Hermitage affair showed that Mellon meant business. Duveen meant business, too. In congratulating Mellon on his acquisition, he said, 'These pictures are wonderful, but let me remind you, Mr Mellon, that you paid Duveen prices.' Finley recalls that when the paintings finally arrived in Washington, they were secreted in a vault in the Corcoran Gallery. Finley has said that Mellon would retire there to commune with 'treasures like Raphael's "Alba Madonna", and his "Saint George and the Dragon", the second of which cost $745,000; Botticelli's "The Adoration of the Magi", which cost $838,350; Jan van Eyck's "The Annunciation", which cost $503,010; and Titian's "Venus with a Mirror" – a very nude painting that Mellon never would have hung in his home – which cost $544,320'. That was a lot of money to spend on a picture you couldn't hang in your home, to say nothing of the upkeep on a place where you *could* hang it. Finley has said that Mellon had strict ideas about what could be hung in one's home; he 'did not care for nudes or contemporary paintings, and he was careful not to hang religious pictures in a room where his friends might be smoking and drinking'. His private museum must have been governed by the

Opposite Bellini: 'St Jerome Reading'. A painting which Duveen bought in the Benson Collection, and which was sold to Clarence H. Mackay and later to Kress

sort of regulations that public museums had late in the nineteenth century, when the hours at which men and women were permitted to look at Greek sculpture were staggered, like the hours at a Turkish bath.

During the early 1930s, Duveen, quietly plugging away at his plans for a national gallery, sold Mellon art on a grander and grander scale. Everything was going along rosily for both Mellon and Duveen when, in the spring of 1934, the United States Attorney General sent Mellon a notice claiming that in 1931 he had not paid enough income tax. Bluntly the government asked Mellon for $3,089,000 for back taxes and penalties. Mellon denounced the government's implied charge of tax evasion as 'impertinent, scandalous, and improper', made a counter-claim that in 1931 he had, in fact, overpaid his taxes by $139,000, and, ostensibly to get a refund but actually to clear himself of the Bureau of Internal Revenue's charge of fraud, asked for a hearing before the Board of Tax Appeals in Washington. The government's case against Mellon was enormously complicated; before the hearings were over, ten thousand pages of testimony had been recorded. Mellon had to withstand a terrific barrage from the government's lawyers, and his defences were sometimes puny. The hearings whipped up a turbulent sea, filled with knobby islands, on which the Mellon lawyers were shown to have erected intricate and diaphanous structures: labyrinths of 'shadow security sales' and 'coalesced corporations'. But, fortunately for Mellon, the stormy sea of this litigation led into a comparatively tranquil and sunny cove, on which the Mellon art collection, bought from Duveen and others, sailed serenely. In this cove – which to Duveen *was* the sea – the talkative peer thrashed about prodigiously. The nub of Mellon's defence – a nub that the government apparently had not anticipated – was that in 1931 Mellon, without talking about it, without even bothering to mention it to the government, had given more than three million dollars' worth of pictures to the Mellon Trust, a foundation he had set up the year before for charitable purposes. The government answered that the foundation itself was a tax dodge, that the pictures were hanging in his apartment and were inaccessible to the public. (Those that were in a vault in the Corcoran were even less publicly accessible.) Mellon's reply to *that* was that though these works of art were still privately displayed, it had for years been his intention to turn them over to the nation as soon as he had acquired enough to provide a decent start for a national gallery he was planning to give the American people. To prove that Mellon had had this intention even earlier than 1931, Mellon's counsel called to their aid the man who had shared this intention with him – Duveen. In his testimony, Duveen swept clear of the ingenuities of lawyers, the importunities of tax collectors, the avidities of the over-rich. He was able to slant a shaft of benevolent, lateral light on Mellon: here was the government insisting that Mellon was trying to cheat it out of over three million dollars; Duveen was present to prove that Mellon had spent vastly more than that on a project he had long been

'Art experts testify at Mellon tax appeal': left to right *Duveen, Mellon, Frank J. Hogan, Mellon's attorney, and*
William R. Valentiner, Director of the Detroit Art Institute

preparing to hand over to the government he was supposed to be defrauding. As Mellon's
attorney, Frank J. Hogan, put it, 'God doesn't place in the hearts and minds of men such
diverse and opposite traits as these; it is impossible to conceive of a man planning such
benefactions as these and at the same time plotting and scheming to defraud his government.' Duveen supported God's and Hogan's view of the eternal homogeneity of human
nature.

Duveen's lawyers, who, over the years, had had to pilot him through countless lawsuits,
had despaired of him as a witness; he never saw any reason, even in a court-room, to curb
his habit of talking too much. They had seen him off to Washington with sinking hearts.
But on this one occasion, even they later admitted, Duveen acquitted himself nobly. That
exuberance in Duveen that subtle men like Sir Osbert Sitwell and Lord Clark – weary,
perhaps, of their own subtleties and grateful for big, colourful splashes of untested generali-
zation and unpremeditated gusto – delighted in, overflowed at this trial and captivated
everyone in the crowded hearing room except opposing counsel. Duveen entered with the
assurance of a popular comedian who knows he is irresistible and knows he is funny. He
addressed opposing counsel – headed by Robert H. Jackson, attorney for the Bureau of
Internal Revenue – with the condescension of an Olympian talking down to worthy, but
fumbling and misinformed, groundlings. Duveen must have quickly sized Jackson up

as a man who didn't own any Duveens, and he set about educating him. He made a broad introductory statement, by way of breaking him in, about the Mellon Duveens. 'The ex-Secretary's collection,' he said concisely, 'is the finest in the universe.' This gave Jackson little margin, but he tried to manoeuvre on his narrow shelf. He had evidently peeked into Duveen's income-tax reports as well as into Mellon's, for he replied by asking Duveen whether it was not true that his art firm had lost $2,950,000 in 1930 and 1931. Duveen looked at him pityingly. 'I've never asked for the last fifteen years what I've made or what I've lost,' he said. 'I'm simply not interested.' Even for a non-customer, Jackson showed an ignorance about Duveens that shocked the art dealer with its Philistinism. Nevertheless, Duveen took the time to give him some elementary instruction in picture values. Jackson asked about the value of van Eyck's panel 'The Annunciation'. Duveen looked at him reprovingly, as you could not help looking at a man who would ask a question about a thing like that. 'Perhaps you don't realize that there are only three small van Eycks in America,' he said. 'And they cannot compare with Mr Mellon's van Eyck.' He threw a compliment at Mellon for his shrewdness in getting this panel for a mere $503,010. It was worth a million, he said, and added, 'Why, even I would give $750,000 for it now.' He was asked about the 'Cowper Madonna' of Raphael, which he had sold Mellon. This turned out to be another example of Mellon's shrewdness; he had wrested it from Duveen for $836,000. 'I thought it a very low price. Mr Mellon thought it a very high price. One day after lunch, I gave way,' said Duveen, with the candour of a man who was not above admitting defeat. He beamed at Mellon to show that he bore no grudge. Mellon nodded in acknowledgment.

Jackson blindly persisted, and Duveen had to go on lecturing him. The government's counsel tried to get Duveen to admit that there was a great fluctuation in the values of works of art. Duveen tried to lead counsel gently to the plateau on which he himself resided. Leonardo da Vinci, Michelangelo, Raphael, Perugino, van Eyck, Titian, and Rembrandt were all great men, said Duveen, 'because only great men can become great artists'. And, he pointed out, their prices must be commensurate with their greatness. Jackson then asked, bloody but unbowed, 'Is it nevertheless true that art works do fluctuate greatly in value?' Duveen, forced from where he dwelt to the lowlands, became paternal. 'Really, my dear fellow,' he said, 'art works don't rise and fall in value like pig iron or sheet copper or tin mines. They have a value and that is all there is to it.' He added that he did not have to depend on certificates to assure the authenticity of his pictures. The audience laughed. 'I have received certificates from emperors and kings,' Duveen continued, 'but usually I find that the picture in question is no good. My clients just accept my word, for they have been dealing with me for years.' Again he beamed at the defendant, who had been dealing with him for years and who rewarded him with another nod.

When the issue was really joined and Jackson tried to prove that Mellon had formed his foundation to escape taxes and had never intended to let the public enjoy his art collection, Duveen testified that as early as 1928 he had discussed with Mellon the project of a national gallery to house the art treasures he was helping get together for him. He had introduced to Mr Mellon 'a noted architect', who had drawn rough plans for the building, which were still in his possession. Jackson tried to interrupt Duveen's description of his talks with Mellon about the plans for the building, but Duveen in full flight was not an easy man to interrupt. He went on describing the talks and the plans. Not only had he discussed the plans and introduced an architect to Mellon but he had even suggested a site in Washington. Hogan asked him a question about the site. Jackson didn't want to hear any more about it, but Duveen saw to it that he heard more. 'Oh, yes, there was a site,' Duveen said. 'By the obelisk near the pond.' At this deft transposition of the Washington Monument to the Sahara, and its reflecting pool to some English county, the spectators howled with laughter, and attendants had to shout for order.

Duveen went on, and the case went on. Commentators on the hearings, which at moments looked very bad for Mellon, have said that Duveen's testimony did much to dispel the sinister atmosphere that surrounded the case. In a dramatic fashion, Duveen's pictures – which he had always told his clients they were getting cheap no matter how much they paid for them – and even Knoedler's pictures, rallied to Mellon in his dark hour. In the end, the Board of Tax Appeals exonerated him of the government's charges of fraud. It came round, at last, to a belief in Mellon's and Duveen's charitable intentions. The Old Masters, it turned out, were useful to have as contemporary pals.

The end of the tax hearings in Washington left Duveen in a handsome position; the idea of the National Gallery was now out in the open, and Mellon could not very gracefully change his mind about it. Duveen's only problem was how to provide Mellon with the works he had testified he needed to give the gallery a decent start. In 1936, for the second time in his dealings with Mellon, Duveen decided to take an apartment directly below his, this time in Washington. As he later recounted, he said to Mellon one day, 'You and I are getting on. We don't want to run around. I have some beautiful things for you, things you ought to have. I have gathered them specially for you. You don't want to keep running to New York to see them; I haven't the energy to keep running to Washington. I shall arrange matters so that you can see these things at your convenience and at your leisure.' Then, in an allusion to the National Gallery, he added, 'Of course, these things don't really belong to us. They belong to the people.' Mellon lived in an apartment house near Dupont Circle. Duveen prevailed upon the family living below Mellon to transfer its lease to him, and then moved in the wonderful things that belonged to the people. The result was very beautiful and very expensive. He installed a caretaker, engaged several guards to keep an eye on the apartment, gave Mellon the key, and went back to New York.

In New York, to divert himself while waiting around for the silent potentate to make up his mind and speak, Duveen decided to have some fun at the expense of a potentate who was not silent at all, Adolf Hitler. Duveen thought that except for Holbein and Dürer, whom he consented to deal in, German art was gross and tasteless. In speaking of German pictures, he was repeatedly able to employ his favourite epithet for a picture he didn't like – 'vulgar'. Hitler's preferences in art had a strong nationalist tinge; he deplored the fact that so many early German artists had been displaced, in museums and private collections, by decadent Italians. Duveen went to considerable trouble to see that Hitler's preferences were indulged. Working under cover of an English firm of unblemished Aryan genealogy – a firm that, in turn, employed a similarly impeccable Dutch concern – Duveen furnished the funds for a large and long-term operation that funnelled back into Germany early German art works which came quite cheap, in exchange for the decadent Italians. He thus managed to abduct from the very walls of the Kaiser Friedrich Museum, in Berlin, and the Alte Pinakothek, in Munich, among other prominent German museums, some of the finest examples of Italian art – a Duccio di Buoninsegna, a Fra Filippo Lippi, a Raphael, and the like – and transfer them to the walls of the more catholic Duveen clients.

Meanwhile, Duveen kept in touch with his caretaker in Washington. The caretaker confided charming vignettes of the tenant on the upper floor, in dressing-gown and carpet slippers, leaving his own apartment to bask in Duveen's more opulent environment. Sometimes, the caretaker reported, Mellon found it more agreeable to entertain guests in Duveen's place than in his own. Gradually, Mellon must have begun to feel that the paintings he showed off to his friends as Duveen's were his own. There came a moment when he felt he couldn't go on living a double life. He sent for Duveen and bought the contents of his apartment, lock, stock, and barrel. This was the largest transaction ever consummated in the world of art. Duveen had easily outdone the Soviets. There were twenty-one items in the Soviet deal, forty-two in Duveen's. Mellon paid the Soviets seven million dollars; he paid Duveen twenty-one million. For once, Mellon found himself short of cash. He paid Duveen in securities. Duveen was able to liquidate credit of £1,200,000 his London bank had been extending him for thirty years and to arrange trust funds for his wife and daughter. The deal was a remarkable feat of salesmanship, but it represented an even more remarkable feat of collecting. After all, the Soviet government had inherited the Hermitage collection from a government that had been collecting pictures far longer than Duveen. The agents of Catherine the Great had brought back many of the Hermitage pictures from their tours through England, Flanders, and Holland in the early eighteenth century; Nicholas I and the Alexanders, in the nineteenth century, were responsible for further acquisitions. Since Duveen was able to assemble a large part of the Mellon Collection – and a large part of so many others besides – in one lifetime, it can be argued that he was the greatest collector in history.

A few months after Duveen sold Mellon the apartment in Washington, Mellon wrote President Roosevelt offering to build a national art gallery and give it to the nation, along with his entire art collection and a five-million-dollar endowment fund. As soon as the President and Congress had, in March of 1937, formally accepted the National Gallery in the name of the American people, Duveen formally called in Pope, the architect anonymously referred to during the trial, to draw up more definite plans. After Duveen had passed them, they were shown to Mellon. Duveen was as fastidious in planning the National Gallery as he had been in planning the apartment he sold to Mellon. He had a prejudice against limestone. His soul revolted against limestone. He thought it was dirty. Mellon, however, had made up his mind to build the Gallery of limestone, for which he had already exhibited a noticeable fondness. President Coolidge had put Mellon in charge of a $190,000,000 District of Columbia architectural programme, and Mellon had chosen limestone for one government building after another. 'Three Presidents served under Mellon,' Senator George Norris once said. Unlike Harding, Coolidge, and Hoover, Duveen refused to serve. He didn't want the National Gallery, to which he had given so much thought and which was to house so many of the best Duveens, to look like the Mellon National Bank in Pittsburgh. He arranged a conference with Mellon and Pope, and praised marble. Pope said marble would cost at least five million dollars more. Mellon said that that was much too expensive; limestone was good enough. After all, he had rebuilt the District of Columbia out of limestone. Duveen said that what was good enough for the District of Columbia was not good enough for his and Mellon's pictures. He suggested an automobile ride round town. As they rode, he pointed out to Mellon many examples of his crowning glory. They were of limestone, and they looked shabby and dirty, or Duveen said they did. All the time, Duveen kept selling marble as if he were selling marble. Mellon yielded. 'Thanks for the ride,' he said. 'It has been the most expensive ride of my life.'

Once Duveen had persuaded Mellon that marble was the only substance suitable for a building that was to house Duveens, Mellon insisted on choosing the *kind* of marble, and Duveen let him have his own way. Mellon decided on Tennessee marble because it was, like himself, unostentatious, and austere. He chose it because it didn't look like marble. Here, too, perhaps, his choice indicated an expression of his desire for silence; he didn't want the marble to admit that it was marble. He struck a snag, however. It was the middle of the depression, and the marble people were highly inactive. The hibernating marble men woke up, warmed to life by Mellon's big order. They set about turning out the largest amount of Tennessee marble ever ordered at one time. When it arrived in Washington, it was seen to be in a variety of shades, from quite intense pink to quite pale pink. When a sample wall was finally put up, it looked as if it had scarlet fever. What made the operation enormously costly was that it was decided, in order to avoid the hectic look, that all the dark marble should be at the bottom and the light at the top, so that the walls would present a non-pathological gradation of colour. This meant that it had to be determined in advance where each block should go. With the passage of a few years, the colour differentiations disappeared; the infinite trouble and expense of the elaborate block-matching might have been spared.

'Why did you make such a fuss about the marble?' someone asked Duveen. 'What difference does it make to you? Besides, Mellon will have five million less to spend with you.'

'I'll have other customers besides Mellon,' Duveen said, as if diagramming the obvious. 'They'll want *their* pictures to go into the National Gallery. They'll be impressed by marble.' Foremost among the customers Duveen had in mind was Kress.

Relating the history of the National Gallery, John Walker, the Director Emeritus, wrote:

> The building for the National Gallery was designed to provide five and a half acres of exhibition space, and Mr Mellon's original collection contained a hundred and thirty-two works of art. It goes without saying that he hoped for a greater density than twenty-four to the acre. He was thoroughly confident that the beauty of the new building would have a magnetic effect on other collections.

Duveen, as well as Mellon, was anxious for an increase in density and an intensification of the magnetism. As a friend of Mellon's once said, 'Mellon had an art museum six blocks long on his hands and enough paintings to decorate a good-sized duplex apartment.' Duveen co-operated loyally. One opportunity arose because Mellon didn't care for sculpture at all; his ambition for the Washington gallery was that it should model itself after the National Gallery of London, which Mellon loved and which contained no sculpture. At the same time, however, Pope, whom Duveen admired as much as Mellon admired the National Gallery of London, had designed the Washington gallery with beautiful and spacious halls intended to receive sculpture. The sculpture halls were almost tenantless; the density, as far as sculpture was concerned, was just about zero. Duveen

Opposite Vermeer: 'The Smiling Girl'. Discovered by von Bode, this painting was acquired by Duveen and sold to Mellon.

came to the rescue. Fortunately, in the Dreyfus Collection, which he had bought in 1930, he had a great many marvellous sculptures. Faced on the one hand by an architectural *fait accompli* – sculpture halls with no sculpture – and on the other by Duveen, who had plenty of sculpture, Mellon found himself overcoming his prejudice against sculpture, and he allowed Duveen partially to fill the yawning cavities. It was another neat example of Duveen's prefabricated coincidences.

In the delicate art of rivalry-whetting, Duveen was unexcelled. He had practised it earlier with Morgan, Frick, the Wideners, and Rockefeller; he had made Bache, Goldman, Hearst, and the lesser fry conscious that they were lucky to be dealing with a man who was gracious enough to take time off to see them when he might be dallying with such giants as Mellon. The National Gallery gave him an ideal vantage point for stimulating competition for his favour among the giants themselves. It enabled him to immortalize rivalry, to keep it at fever heat even after the death of one of the rivals. Kress wouldn't consent to deal with Duveen until after Mellon was dead. He felt that it was no use, because Mellon, as far as Duveen was concerned, was No. 1. Mellon died in August of 1937, and immediately afterwards Duveen managed to convey to Kress the fact that there was no longer any reason in the world he should deprecate himself; he had the stature to make himself No. 1. There was that agoraphobic ratio of twenty-four to the acre; with Duveen's assistance, Kress could drastically increase the density. Duveen found himself, in a way, the sole administrator of a vast cultural Homestead Act. Everything worked here for Duveen, including Mellon's modest decision not to have his name put on the Gallery. Mellon did not believe in the value of this kind of personal fanfare; he told an intimate that although the Smithsonian Institution was named after James Smithson, not one man in a million could tell you who under the sun Smithson was. Perhaps Mellon's refusal to put his name on the Gallery was, again, an extension of his principle of silence. Whatever the cause, the anonymity was a wonderful help to Duveen. Kress had bought so much art that he had no place to put it all and had planned at one time to build a gallery of his own; he had gone so far as to set aside land for it in New York. But the National Gallery, because it was national, was better. The anonymity of the pink marble building on Constitution Avenue gave Duveen a better chance to offer Kress *his* chance.

Duveen had known Kress for eight years, and had waited and waited while Kress dabbled around, buying from other dealers. The patience Duveen perfected while waiting

Opposite Rembrandt: 'Aristotle contemplating the Bust of Homer'. A masterpiece from the Rodolphe Kann collection, which Duveen bought and sold three times

for Mellon stood him in good stead. Duveen had an extraordinary sense of timing. 'Mr Kress isn't ready yet to be a customer of mine; he's got to make a few more mistakes,' he said. Kress made them. Duveen had come to think that in permitting anyone to deal with him he was bestowing a special accolade, like an invitation to tea at Buckingham Palace, and he waited for Kress's perceptions to ripen. When he felt that they had ripened enough, he moved in. 'You're not going to let Mellon have the whole National Gallery to himself, are you, Mr Kress?' he said. Kress, with a quick sense that Mellon was crowding his immortality, saw the point.

It is an oddity of geography that the three greatest American five-and-ten-cent-store magnates, Kress, S. S. Kresge, and F. W. Woolworth, got their start in eastern Pennsylvania. Woolworth was born in New York, but he went to Pennsylvania as a young man. Kresge was born in Bald Mount, Pennsylvania. Kress, one of the few clients of Duveen's who survived him, was born in Cherryville, Pennsylvania, in 1863. His ancestry was Pennsylvania Dutch; he was brought up in modest circumstances, and his fortune was his own handiwork. He never married; he devoted his long life to five-and-ten-cent stores, to the acquisition of art treasures, and to the preservation of his health. His stores were so numerous and far-flung that for one period of eleven years, as he made the rounds, he didn't sleep in the same bed for two successive nights. The accommodation he had to accept in small towns and villages may have accounted for the hypochondria from which he long suffered. His worry about getting hygienic and properly prepared food caused him, during the First World War, to move into three rooms in a New York hospital, where he felt the food would be at least clean, and he stayed on for a year and a half.

Kress led a singularly lonely life. He died in 1955 at the age of ninety-two, and in his last years was bedridden, seeing no one except his brother Rush, fourteen years his junior, his doctors and nurses, and specialists in the art field. New York had been his home for over thirty years, but even when he was well he knew almost no one there, and no one knew him. Outside his art collecting, his passion was travelling, but he did not indulge it directly. When he went abroad, it was to look at pictures, and he saw little else; when he was at home, his chief relaxation was the gratification of his wanderlust offered by Burton Holmes and his travelogues. Kress could never see enough of the Holmes lantern slides, and his appetite for the lectures was insatiable. He had his secretary paste all the programmes and even his seat stubs in a scrapbook, so that he would have a permanent log of the voyages. This passion was sometimes a trial to those in his small circle whom he induced to accompany him. 'He could have chartered the *Olympic* and gone anywhere in the world he liked,' one of them has said sadly, 'but he preferred to do his travelling in Carnegie Hall.'

Kress's caution, like that of so many very rich men, seemed to extend to the spending of even small sums of money, but on at least one occasion his instinct for haggling overcame this caution. Taking his ease on the veranda of an Italian watering place, he stopped a Levantine pedlar staggering by under a load of tablecloths and mufflers, and asked him what he wanted for a dozen mufflers. The pedlar told him. 'What do you want for six mufflers and six tablecloths?' Kress asked. The pedlar scratched his head and named a figure. Kress became fascinated by the possibilities of permutation, and settled down to a nice, complicated haggle. A gross of tablecloths and more than a gross of mufflers offer the most beguiling vistas in that direction if you care to study them, and Kress studied them. He studied until the poor Levantine was perspiring from his effort to supply figures that wouldn't bankrupt him; he endured agonies of indecision, of quick revision, of abrupt estimates, and finally he lost touch with reality altogether. Kress enjoyed the game. At last, the virtuoso casually asked what the pedlar would take for the lot. The pedlar gasped out a figure and, suddenly recovering his business sense, dumped his stock in Kress's lap. Kress, not sure how to argue this point, paid him. The pedlar, suddenly out of business, walked away. Kress found himself with a gross of tablecloths and an infinity of mufflers on his hands. There was something in Kress's nature that could not resist a gross of anything. He sent his new stock to his storehouse in downtown New York.

In his interminable hagglings with Duveen over batches of paintings and miscellaneous art objects, Kress tried to confuse him with swift permutations, as he had the Levantine. ('How much for the Houdon bust without the nine pictures? How much for the nine pictures without the bust?') But Duveen had a firmer grasp than the Levantine, and a firmer grasp than Kress. Kress prepared himself carefully for his sessions with Duveen. Like all the other big clients, he was a slow talker and a slow decider. He had photographs taken of the pictures he was considering, and pondered them endlessly. Year after year, he went to Europe and trudged the galleries. He was eternally asking questions of anyone whose opinion he valued about the pictures he thought he might buy. 'Why is this picture so good?' he would ask. 'Why is it better than the picture by the same artist that Soandso has? What makes it worth so much? I'm told it's been repainted. Which part has been repainted? Has that cloud in the upper lefthand corner been repainted or is that the original cloud? What about that flying angel in the upper righthand corner? Has she been repainted? With all that repainting, should I pay so much?' The interrogation went on continuously, not only in galleries but in his apartment, on walks, and on boats. Duveen put up with that. He also put up with Kress's exceptionally wary nature. One day, to allay any suspicion in Kress's mind that Mellon, though no longer on the scene, was *still* No. 1 to him, Duveen said to him, '*You* have the mountains. Mellon has the peaks.' Duveen might just as easily have said to Mellon, had Mellon been alive, 'Kress has the mountains. *You* have the peaks.' Duveen was the master of the reversible compliment.

Duveen was subjected to his severest strain by Kress when, during the Christmas season of 1938, Kress did violence to one of Duveen's cherished principles. Duveen, a pasha furiously jealous of his pictures, refused ever to unveil them publicly; no Duveen was ever

Samuel H. Kress, Duveen's biggest client

visible in the Duveen windows at the Ministry of Marine during his lifetime, even though, as has been seen, it was a copy of a wing of a building designed by Jacques-Ange Gabriel, the illustrious architect who served Louis XV. If you wanted to see a Duveen, you couldn't do it just by strolling up Fifth Avenue; you had to penetrate the recesses of the harem, and this took some doing. On his walks along the streets of New York – and especially along Fifty-seventh Street – Duveen was always on the look-out for a non-Duveen he could denounce as a fake. As he was walking down Fifth Avenue one day, his eye was caught, at the corner of Thirty-ninth Street, by a picture in a window. He stopped to stare at it incredulously. He felt no impulse to denounce. The picture was a Duveen. It was one of the greatest and most costly – both in price and in emotional tribulation – of all Duveens. It was, in fact, 'The Adoration of the Shepherds', which Berenson had said was the earliest known Titian but which Duveen had sold to Kress as a Giorgione. This picture had cost Duveen his friendship and his valuable business relationship with Berenson. He had persuaded Kress that by buying it he could take a short cut to immortality and a fast sprint to pre-eminence in the National Gallery, out-distancing his late rival Mellon. This gift to the National Gallery was still a closely kept secret. And here it was, the lovely thing, quite naked, in the window of a building whose architect not only was not French but was, as far as Duveen was concerned, non-existent. It was staring at Duveen from behind the plate-glass window of Kress's five-and-ten, set there to lure the Christmas trade, an effulgent replacement for hair-nets, pin-cushions and soap dishes.

Duveen had to swallow this humiliation, as he had had to swallow so much else in his dealing with Kress. Nevertheless, when, towards the end of his life, he summarized his accomplishments, he said, 'I thought that in the Mellon business I had reached the limit of good fortune. The Kress business has made my cup run over.' In terms of sheer quantity, Kress was the biggest customer of Duveen's entire career, even though everything he bought was bought, in a fierce cataract of purchases, in the last two years of Duveen's life. Before Duveen died, he had got him well started towards a neck-and-neck position alongside Mellon in the National Gallery, and had let him become, indeed, No. 1.

The purchase by Kress of part of the collection of the banker Henry Goldman, of Goldman, Sachs, offers a compact illustration of how these men, who were acknowledged to be among the shrewdest financial manipulators in the history of the world and who were so parsimonious by instinct, let down their guards in their dealings with Duveen. At seventy-nine, when he was blind, Goldman decided to sell his pictures. He sent for a paid adviser of Kress's and asked whether Kress wanted to buy them. Kress's adviser said that he might, but that he never did things in a hurry. 'He'll have to do this in a hurry,' said Goldman. 'It's got to be decided this afternoon.' The adviser went to Kress and told him that Goldman wanted to sell his pictures. 'Is he broke?' Kress asked, that being the only situation in which he thought it justifiable to sell a picture. Kress was told that the offer had nothing to do with insolvency. 'Hold Goldman off,' said Kress, on general principles. Kress's adviser urged him strongly to buy the collection, and to start negotiations at once. 'Hold him off,' Kress repeated. By the time the adviser got to a telephone to try to hold Goldman off it was too late. Duveen had bought the pictures back. When this information was relayed to Kress, the effect was electric. A collection that belonged to Duveen was not a collection that belonged to Goldman, even when it was the same collection. He asked his friend to arrange for him to see the pictures. The adviser promised to do so but begged Kress to be careful about one of them, which had been so restored that he didn't think it was worth anything even if it was authentic, and it might not be. The showing took place in Kress's apartment. Duveen paraded the procession of Goldman's masterpieces, holding out until the end the picture Kress had been warned against. In his enthusiasm for it, the current of Duveen's customary vivacity whirled into panegyric. Of this painting, he related that when he had originally showed it to Goldman (who had probably been sprayed with a strong panegyric himself), Goldman had experienced, merely from being near it, a kind of religious ecstasy. When at last he had bought it, when it was actually in his apartment, his excitement at the thought of his permanent proximity to this masterpiece had been so great that he couldn't sleep. Kress, who already had insomnia, was not impressed. He asked abruptly, 'What makes it so wonderful?' At this rude query, Duveen was stuck; he was so used to having his assertions accepted that all he could do was reiterate that the picture was, beyond human expression, wonderful. Kress repeated his query: 'What makes it so wonderful?' Duveen gave another evasive answer, and there the matter rested while Kress and his adviser went for a walk to hash things over. In the conversation that followed, Kress reversed his attitude. 'Why do you say that it's not wonderful?' he demanded. The adviser gave his reason: whatever the painting might have been once, it was now largely the work of a restorer. But Kress, sceptical in the presence of Duveen, proved himself a true believer in the presence of his adviser, who, by virtue of being a paid adviser, was automatically in a position to be contradicted. Once a collector had set his heart on a picture, it irritated him to have his professional adviser discourage him. In this instance, Kress brought up a heavy battery of argument. 'After all,' he said, by way of conclusion, 'Goldman *did* own the picture and Duveen *did* buy it. Duveen *has* it!' Kress bought the picture and all the others. Had he bought the pictures directly from Goldman, he would have saved millions. But then he wouldn't have had the warm feeling of owning a lot of Duveens.

In the long line of Duveen's clients, beginning early with Morgan, Altman, and Collis and H. E. Huntington and their successive wife, Arabella, and ending grandly with

Mellon and Kress, Goldman occupied a special position. He filled in a stage wait between the exit of the former group and the entrance of the latter. After Goldman's retirement from banking, he and Duveen often met for lunch at the St Regis. The two men were inveterate gossips. 'What's new on the Rialto?' Goldman would ask Duveen, and Duveen would tell him. Goldman was hungry to hear everything about Duveen's activities: what had Duveen bought, and to whom was he selling it, and for how much? Goldman was entranced with Duveen's stories of his coups; alongside Duveen's great clients, he modestly regarded himself as a minor one, and he delightedly absorbed the detailed stories of how Duveen played the big fish and netted them. He was like a small-town merchant who enjoys hearing how the town's richest and most inaccessible citizen has, by adroit strategy, been made to sign up. Every particular of these manoeuvres interested Goldman vastly.

Goldman's blindness had developed gradually, in his later years. It is an instance of Duveen's capacity for disinterested friendship that after Goldman was totally blind and was no longer buying pictures, Duveen continued to see him constantly and supplied him with news of that Rialto that for him, as for the great collector tycoons of the time, held his deepest desires and was the true centre of his being. One Christmas, Duveen gave him two Holbein miniatures that the old collector had long loved. This gift brought Goldman enormous joy, even though he could not see it. Duveen's frequent visits meant much to Goldman in his last days. He would ask, when Duveen was late, 'Isn't Joe coming?' But Joe always did come. Sometimes he expounded on the beauty of the two Holbeins with as much enthusiasm as if he were selling them, and the old gentleman revelled in his unseen vision.

Many of the major Duveen clients became either totally blind or very nearly so, among them not only Goldman but Altman, Arabella Huntington, and Kress. The fact that for them the pictures he sold them were invisible or almost invisible did not in the least deter them from buying. An art critic, returning from Washington, where he had just inspected the Kress pictures in the National Gallery, sat by their donor's bedside and praised him for contributing to the nation a beauty he could no longer see. Kress's face lit up with pleasure, perhaps from his memory of a time when he had beheld the beauty. Another collector, less well known but equally picture-haunted, was, like Kress, bedridden for some time. He was blind and nearly deaf, and paralysed. His only way of acknowledging even the presence of a rare visitor was to move his bandaged arm in a slight, semi-circular gesture. Once, one of these visitors, sitting by his bedside, looked round the room and noticed that the pictures in it had been changed since his last visit. He remarked upon this, saying that the new pictures were lovely and that the room looked much better with them. In acknowledgment of this compliment, the sick man moved his arm so violently that the nurse became frightened and asked the visitor to leave the room at once.

Philosophers interested in the Duveen Era have engaged in a good deal of subtle speculation on one point, and it is still a tantalizing mystery: how did it come about that the great money men of that era gradually came to accept Duveen's simple, unworldly view that art was more important than money? One theory is that Duveen had inculcated into them the idea that art was priceless and that when you pay for the infinite with the finite, you are indeed getting a bargain. Perhaps it was for this reason that they felt better when they paid a lot. It gave them the assurance of acquiring genuineness, rarity, uniqueness. A lesser dealer had a Rossellino bust for which he had paid twenty-two thousand dollars. Joseph E. Widener went in to look at it. The dealer needed money and offered it for twenty-five thousand, thinking to tempt Widener into a quick purchase. The moderateness of the price was fatal. 'Find me a better one,' said Widener. Duveen would have asked a quarter of a million, and got it. The same thing happened with the same bust, when the dealer showed it to Mackay. 'Find me a better one,' said Mackay. Of one of the most wary and haggling and penny-pinching of his clients, who in his dealings with Duveen penny-pinched himself out of a great many millions of dollars, it has been remarked that only Duveen could have inflated such caution to such abandon. 'Oh, well,' an intimate of this man has said, 'he liked to deal with Duveen because Duveen was at the top. It was like tootling around in a custom-built Rolls-Royce.' Duveen's clients preferred to pay huge sums, and Duveen made them happy. A dealer offered a room to Hearst for fifty thousand dollars; Hearst spurned it. Duveen offered it to him later for two hundred thousand and he bought it with gratitude. A man called up a New York dealer one day and asked him if he wanted to buy a rug. The 'rug' turned out to be a fine Boucher tapestry. The dealer paid a rug price for it and then offered it to Michael Dreicer, the jeweller, for fifteen thousand dollars. Dreicer, who had once sold a clock for sixty thousand dollars and was accustomed to selling necklaces for a hundred thousand, was suspicious of anything you could get for a mere fifteen thousand. 'Get me something better,' he said. The New York dealer sold the Boucher to a Paris dealer, who eventually sold it to Dreicer, when the latter was abroad, for seventy thousand dollars. After Dreicer brought it back, the first dealer pointed out to him that it was the same tapestry he himself had offered him for fifteen thousand. Dreicer was a little bewildered at the coincidence, and a little ashamed. 'In Paris, you go crazy,' he said lamely. Duveen gave his clients a perpetual sense of being in Paris. In his dealings with them, he inspired them with a feeling of release; they could throw their customary business practices to the four winds and go on a kind of jag of prodigality; and in good company; they could go haywire about beauty. He substituted the liberation of reckless spending for the austerities of hoarding. The inherited Puritanism of many of these men made them feel guilty about ordinary spending, but spending for art could be rationalized morally.

The millionaires of the Duveen Era were all dressed up, but they really had nowhere to go. Duveen supplied a favoured few of them with a destination. The private lives of these sad tycoons were often bitter; their children and their family life disappointed them. The fathers had too much to give; the returns were often in inverse ratio to the size of the gifts. They knew that they were ruining their children and yet they didn't know how to stop it. Their children made disastrous marriages, got killed in racing cars, had to pay blackmail to avoid scandal. But with the works of art it was different. They asked for nothing. They were rewarding. They shed their radiance, and it was a lovely, soothing light. You could take them or leave them and when you had visitors you could bask in the admiration the pictures and sculptures excited which was directed towards you even more subtly than towards them, as if you yourself had gathered them and, even, created them. The works of art *became* their children. Towards the end of Joseph E. Widener's life, before his pictures, which he had presented to the National Gallery, were packed and sent off, he made the rounds and had a long, last look at each of them. He had arranged for them to have a good home and he knew that they would be well cared for, but now that they were about to leave him, he was like a father losing his children, and he wept.

But there was more to it than desolation at home, more than the privilege of expensiveness. The ambition of the Duveen millionaires to own famous works of art and to be associated in men's minds with the artists became the controlling obsession of their lives. Frick, Mellon, and Kress practically gave up their business careers to devote their energies to acquiring art. What was behind it? What were the ultimate reasons? Expensiveness helped, the desolation helped, just as acquisitiveness helped, the impulse for conspicuous consumption helped, the social *cachet* helped, the Medici complex helped, but in their consuming avidity there was something more: a hint of desperation, of loneliness, of futility, even of fear. Was it that these men, whose material conquests were unlimited, felt the need, as they grew older, to ally themselves with reputations that were solid and unassailable and, as far as the mind could project, eternal? The paintings in the National Gallery are Kresses and Mellons and Wideners, and before that many of them were Duveens, but if you trace them far enough back, they are Botticellis and Raphaels and Giottos and Fra Filippo Lippis. These old names had lasted a long time. It was reassuring.

The Duveen millionaires had varying degrees of knowledge about the artists with whom they bought partnerships. One of Duveen's clients fixed his partners in his mind by chronological association; of a painter whose dates were 1471–1528 he said with satisfaction, 'Well, then, he lived just about the time of the discovery of America,' and he felt that he had doubly acquired him – that he could write *him* off. They knew more or they knew less, but they must have realized that, no matter how many directorships they held, they would for ever be only the junior partners in their newly bought associations with these memorialized shadows. Perhaps they were content with the inferior position, content to let Raphael and Bellini and the others have the best of it. It was mainly the *for ever* that they were buying. And they had perhaps become uneasily aware of the fact that the reputations of their new partners were unambiguous in a way that their own were not, and perhaps they hoped that the mergers would be lustral. The painters might have been dissolute, but they had not been furtive; they might have been impecunious, but they had managed, by following their inner vision, to achieve spiritual solvency; they might have led degraded and obscure lives, but they had survived as proud giants. For their latter-day partners, things had begun to become uncomfortable. They were grilled about the machine-gunning of strikers; they were virulently caricatured as exploiters of the poor; they were asked sternly why they did not go and look at the misery that was grinding out their fortunes; the very possession of wealth was beginning to be regarded with suspicion; there had been a sudden shift from idolatry to bitter criticism. Their new partners had miraculously avoided all this; for their moral lapses the world had long since forgiven them. And, above all, they had got what they wanted; they had been themselves, they had enjoyed life, they had been gay. What the rich men had accumulated was slipping away from them. As they aged, as they felt futility and hostility closing in around them, they longed passionately for the happy company, in the even darker regions ahead, of these magical and secure and vivid shades.

Duveen's customers were harshly caricatured as exploiters of every sort; left John D. Rockefeller Sr; right William Randolph Hearst

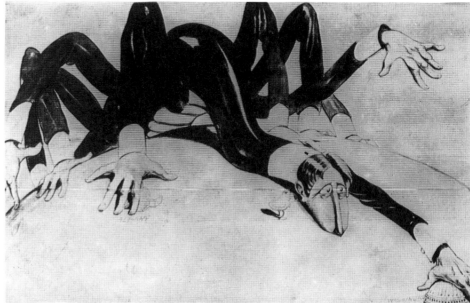

Everyone who saw Duveen in the last five years of his life spoke of his extraordinary equanimity in the face of his frightful affliction. Osbert Sitwell said that it was always Duveen's chief concern that everyone he came in contact with should have a good time. Both Berenson and Kenneth Clark said that he was one of the best story-tellers they ever met. All during his illness, Duveen kept up the amiability and the story-telling. He would never admit that he was more than mildly ill. Something of a gourmet, he would account for the fact that at this period he hardly ate anything by saying that the doctor had put him 'on a bit of a diet'. A chain smoker now forbidden to smoke, he worked out an ingenious device for keeping people from offering him cigarettes, which he would have to refuse; he had an imitation cigarette made of ivory, with an imitation light at the end of it made of phosphorus, and kept it constantly in his hand or between his lips, so that he would appear to be smoking. Although he needed daily medical attention, he pursued his ordinary activities as if he were only slightly indisposed. There was one exception. In the last years of his life, he was sued by the art collector and dealer Carl W. Hamilton, who had bought three pictures from him – a Fra Angelico 'Annunciation', for $50,000; a Fra Filippo Lippi 'Madonna and Child', for $50,000; and a Piero della Francesca 'Crucifixion', for $65,000. Hamilton decided to sell these pictures. He sold the Fra Angelico to Edsel Ford for $187,000. The two others were then put up at auction (the first art auction, as it happens, to be broadcast on the radio). The Fra Filippo Lippi

Caricatures of left to right *Andrew Mellon, Henry Ford, J. Pierpont Morgan Sr*

sold for $125,000, and Duveen bought the Piero della Francesca for $375,000, up to that time the highest price ever paid for a picture at an auction in America. Hamilton sued Duveen for two million dollars, on the ground that certain remarks Duveen made before the auction caused his pictures to be undervalued. Duveen hired John W. Davis to assist his regular counsel in his defence. As the pictures for which Hamilton had paid Duveen $165,000 had sold for more than half a million, Duveen's lawyers felt that this was a suit he couldn't possibly lose, yet Duveen, who throughout his life had had a zest for litigation, called them up from Nassau, where he had gone for a rest, and implored them not to go through with it. They implored him to go ahead, for they were sure of their ground. But he insisted, and they had to yield. Duveen was indeed desperately ill.

Unlike the death of many of his clients, Duveen's death was, in characteristic fashion, beautifully timed. When Neville Chamberlain returned from Munich, Duveen, believing that he actually had preserved peace in our time, acclaimed him as the greatest man in the world. Four months after Duveen's death, his country was at war. The holiday was over, but Duveen had lived to the last minute of it. In the years that followed, the outstanding collectors were Hitler and Göring, who never had to pay Duveen prices. The American collections went underground, against air raids that never came.

For Duveen to praise Chamberlain required a certain detachment, for the Prime Minister had caused him some of his most poignant grief. This resulted from Chamberlain's decision not to let him continue as a trustee of the London National Gallery. What precipitated this decision was an offer by Duveen to sell the Gallery the eight Sassetta panels that had formed the back of the altar of the Church of Saint Francis in Sanse-polcro, Italy, and that he had sold to and then bought back from Mackay. Some members of the board felt that Duveen should not be in the position of offering to the Gallery as a seller works that, representing the Gallery, he had to approve as a buyer. Chamberlain was persuaded that this was so. The dismissal hurt Duveen deeply. Then, in Duveen's last years, Kress couldn't make up his mind about a considerable quantity of merchandise he had on consignment. Kress was going through the old routine of having everything photo-graphed and asking questions. This, too, disturbed Duveen.

On 17 May 1939 Duveen sailed for what he called home. The day before Bache called on him. Afterwards, Bache said sadly, 'I'm afraid we'll never see Joe again.' That same day, Duveen telephoned one of his assistants at the Ministry of Marine and asked him to drive through Central Park with him. At Seventy-second Street, Duveen proposed that they get out of the car and walk, but after a few steps he had to sit down on a bench. He was mortally ill, and looked it. Nevertheless, he asked his associate to help him tackle a new and formidable project. The Widener Collection had been offered to the National Gallery in Washington, and it was Duveen's understanding that the Gallery was going to reject the donation. The Gallery, he had heard, was prepared to accept Widener's paintings and sculptures but did not want the tapestries, armour, and other miscellany, which it felt were outside the Gallery's scope. Widener wanted his immortality intact, and wouldn't agree to split up his collection. Duveen proposed to his associate that the firm buy the entire Widener Collection. He would sell the paintings and the sculptures to the National Gallery at the price he would pay Widener for everything. The rest of the collection, according to his scheme, would cost him nothing; whatever he could sell it for would be velvet. 'How much do you think it will take to swing this?' Duveen's associated asked. 'Twenty-five million dollars,' said Duveen calmly. He instructed his man to get going immediately and to send progress reports to him in London. He also reminded him to keep after Kress about the unsold pictures.

Eight days after Duveen sailed, he died, at Claridge's. His last words, addressed to his nurse, were 'Well, I fooled 'em for five years.' The funeral service was held in his gallery in Grafton Street. Duveen's last letter, written on shipboard in his own hand, arrived in New York the day after his death. It urged his associates to expedite the Widener deal – a deal that never was to be consummated, for the National Gallery decided to meet Widener's terms on the donation. Two years after Duveen died, Kress bought all the pictures that had been hanging fire. Duveen went right on selling.

The title-page of the catalogue
which Duveen Brothers produced as a tribute to
'the most spectacular art-dealer of all time'

DUVEEN PICTURES

IN

PUBLIC COLLECTIONS

OF

AMERICA

A Catalogue Raisonné with Three
Hundred Illustrations of Paintings
by the Great Masters, which
have passed through the
House of Duveen

THE WILLIAM BRADFORD PRESS
NEW YORK
1941

Catalogue of 500 masterpieces sold by Duveen

This catalogue, though compiled from a wide range of sources, could not be a definitive list of all the greatest works sold by Duveen. It does, however, give an indication of the scope and quality of the works he handled, and shows particularly how much many of the great American galleries are indebted to him.

Collections mentioned frequently are abbreviated thus :

Abdy	Sir Thomas Neville Abdy – Sir William Neville Abdy – Lady Neville Abdy, Newdigate, Dorking
Anhalt	Dukes of Anhalt, Schloss Dessau, Wörlitz
Altman	Benjamin Altman, New York
Ashburnham	Earl of Ashburnham, Battle, Sussex
Bache	Jules S. Bache, New York
Bardini	Stefano Bardini, Florence
Benson	Robert H. and Evelyn Benson, London
Berlin Museum	Kaiser-Friedrich Museum, Berlin, *later* Staatliche Museen der Stiftung Preussischer Kulturbesitz – Gemäldegalerie
Boymans-van Beuningen	*formerly* D. G. van Beuningen, Verhouten, *now* Museum Boymans-van Beuningen, Rotterdam
Butler	Charles Butler, London
Lady Carnarvon	Almina, Countess of Carnarvon, London and Newbury, Berks.
Donaldson	Sir George Donaldson, Hove, Sussex
Dreyfus	Gustave Dreyfus, Paris
Mrs Emery	Mrs Mary M. Emery, Cincinnati
Fairfax-Murray	Charles Fairfax-Murray, London
Fogg Art Museum	Fogg Art Museum, Harvard University, Cambridge, Mass.
Frick	Henry Clay Frick – The Frick Collection, New York
Goldman	Henry Goldman, New York
Gould	George J. Gould, Lakewood, New Jersey
Graham	William Graham, London
Grassi	Luigi Grassi, Florence and Rome
Hainauer	Oscar Hainauer, Berlin
Hamilton Palace	Dukes of Hamilton, Hamilton Palace, Scotland
C. W. Hamilton	Carl W. Hamilton, New York
Harkness	Edward S. Harkness, New York
Hearst	William Randolph Hearst, New York
A. M. Huntington	A. M. Huntington, New York
Mrs C. P. Huntington	Mrs Collis Potter Huntington, New York
HEH	H. E. Huntington – H. E. Huntington Library and Art Gallery, San Marino, California
Ingenheim	Count Gustav Adolf Wilhelm von Ingenheim and family, Schloss Reisewitz, Silesia; Ober-Rengersdorf, nr Dresden; and Munich
Mrs Jacobs	Mrs Henry Barton Jacobs, Baltimore, Ohio
Kahn	Otto H. Kahn, New York (Mogmar Art Foundation)
A. Kann	Alphonse Kann, Paris
E. Kann	Edouard Kann, Paris

M. Kann	Maurice Kann, Paris
R. Kann	Rodolphe Kann, Paris
Kress	Samuel H. Kress – The Kress Foundation, New York
Lazzaroni	Baron Michele Lazzaroni, Paris
Lehman	Lehman Collection, New York
Libbey	Edward Drummond Libbey, Toledo, Ohio
Mackay	Clarence H. Mackay, Harbor Hill, Roslyn, Long Island
Marlborough	Duke of Marlborough, Blenheim Palace
Mellon	Andrew W. Mellon, Washington D.C.
MMA	Metropolitan Museum of Art, New York
Michelham	Herbert Stern, 1st Baron Michelham – Lady Aimée Geraldine Michelham, Strawberry Hill, Twickenham
Morgan	J. Pierpont Morgan, New York
NGW	National Gallery of Art, Washington D.C.
Northbrook	Sir Thomas Baring, Baron Northbrook – Earl of Northbrook, Stratton, Micheldever, Hants.
Ouroussoff	Prince Léon Ouroussoff, Russian Ambassador, Vienna and Paris
Pembroke	Earls of Pembroke, Wilton House, Wilts.
Pfungst	Henry J. Pfungst, London
Piot	Eugène Piot, Paris
Pourtalès	Comtesse Hubert de Pourtalès, Paris
Pourtalès-Gorgier	Comte Charles de Pourtalès-Gorgier, Paris
Ringling	John and Mable Ringling Museum of Art, Sarasota, Florida
Rosenfeld	Ernst Rosenfeld, New York
A. de Rothschild	Baron Adolphe de Rothschild, Paris
A. C. de Rothschild	Baron Alfred Charles de Rothschild, London
M. de Rothschild	Baron Maurice de Rothschild, Paris
Salomon	William Salomon, New York
San Donato	Anatoli, Prince Demidoff, Palazzo San Donato, Florence
Schickler	Baron Arthur de Schickler, Martinvast, Normandy
Norton Simon	Norton Simon – The Norton Simon Foundation, Los Angeles
Spencer	Earls of Spencer, Althorp, Lincs.
Spilimbergo	Conte Niccolo d'Attimis Maniago, Spilimbergo, Lombardy
Spitzer	Frédéric Spitzer, Paris
Sulley	Arthur J. Sulley, London
Thyssen	Thyssen-Bornemisza Collection, Villa Favorita, Castagnola – Lugano
Timbal	Louis Charles Timbal, Paris
Toronto Art Gallery	Art Gallery of Ontario, Toronto
Weber	Consul Eduard F. Weber, Hamburg

Westminster   Dukes of Westminster, London
Widener   P. A. B. Widener – Joseph E. Widener, Lynnewood Hall, Elkins Park, Pa.
Willet   Henry Willet, Brighton

Wood   Mr and Mrs Frank P. Wood, Toronto
Wyndham   Earls of Egremont – Colonel Egremont Wyndham – Lord Leconfield, Petworth, Sussex

British School

Constable, John (1776–1837)
A View on the Stour, near Dedham. T. Horrocks Miller, Paulton-le-Fielde, Lancs. – HEH

Gainsborough, Thomas (1727–88)
Charles Frederick Abel. Queen Charlotte of England – Wyndham – Lord G... – Gould – HEH
Mrs Peter William Baker. Baker family, Dorset – Frick
Mrs Henry Beaufoy. Beaufoy family – Sir William Heathcote, Hants. – A. C. de Rothschild – Lady Carnarvon – HEH
Jonathan Buttall, 'The Blue Boy' (ILLUSTRATED). Buttall family, London – John Nesbitt, M.P. – John Hoppner, R.A. – Westminster – HEH
Queen Charlotte. Counts of Waldeck-Pyrmont, Schloss Arolsen – Leopold Hirsch – Bache – MMA
Anne, Duchess of Cumberland. Sitter – Lawley family (Lord Wenlock) – HEH
Georgiana, Duchess of Devonshire. Spencer – Mellon – NGW
Hon. Frances Duncombe. Mrs John Bowater – Rev. W. G. Sawyer – Henry Graves – Baron Lionel de Rothschild, London – Frick
Hon. Mrs Mary Fane. Hon. Henry Fane, Lincs. – Michel family, Devon – E. L. Raphael, London – HEH
Margaret and Mary Gainsborough. Sir Thomas Baring, London – Mr Bryant – J. W. Brett, London – Henry Wilkinson, London – Colette – Sir Edgar Vincent, Viscount d'Abernon – Art Museum, Worcester, Mass.
Edward, 2nd Viscount Ligonier; Penelope, Viscountess Ligonier. Rivers family – HEH
Mrs John Meares. Truman family, London – Henry Villebois I and II, London – A. C. de Rothschild – Lady Carnarvon – HEH
Juliana, Lady Petre. Petre family, Brentwood, Essex – HEH
Mrs Richard Brinsley Sheridan. Sheridan family, Bath – Rothschild family, Tring Park, Herts. – Mellon – NGW

Gainsborough (cont.)
Miss Catherine Elizabeth Tatton. Tatton family, Rothenfield, Sussex – Drake-Brockman family, Folkestone, Kent – Michelham – Mellon – NGW
The Cottage Door. Thomas Harvey, Norfolk – Mr Coppin, Norwich – Lord de Tabley, London – Westminster – HEH
Cottage Door with Children Playing. Earl of Mulgrave – Marquess of Normanby – Earl of Normanton – Mr and Mrs Charles Finn Williams, Cincinnati – Cincinnati Art Museum
The Harvest Waggon. Mrs Fitzherbert (gift of the Prince of Wales) – Hon. Mrs Dawson Damer – John Gibbons – Sir Lionel Phillips – Judge Elbert H. Gary, New York – Wood – Toronto Art Gallery
The Mall in St James's Park. George Frost – Samuel H. Kilderbee, Ipswich – Neeld family, Wilts. – Frick
Mountain Landscape with Peasants crossing a Bridge. Sir J. Leicester – Lady Lindsay – Lord d'Abernon – Mellon – NGW

Hoppner, John (1758–1810)
Lady Beauchamp, afterwards Marchioness of Hertford. J. C. F. Ramsden, Willinghurst – HEH
Mrs Belford and her son. J. F. M. Chabot, Wassenaar – HEH

Lawrence, Thomas (1769–1830)
'Little Red Riding Hood' (Miss Emily Anderson). Anderson family, Cromarty Bay – HEH
Emily and Laura Anne Calmady. Calmady family – C. P. Huntington – MMA
Lady Elizabeth Conyngham. Conyngham family, Co. Meath – E. T. Stotesbury – Calouste Gulbenkian Foundation, Lisbon
Hon. Mrs Cunliffe Offley. Lord Houghton – Marquess of Crewe – HEH
Elizabeth Farren, later Countess of Derby. 12th Earl of Derby – Earls of Wilton – Ludwig Neumann – Morgan – Harkness – MMA

Lawrence (cont.)
Miss Sarah Moulton-Barrett, 'Pinkie' (ILLUSTRATED). Moulton-Barrett family, Isle of Wight – Michelham – HEH
Lady Templetown and her son Henry. A. C. de Rothschild – Lady Carnarvon – Mellon – NGW
Mrs Thomson and her child (afterwards Lord Sydenham). G. P. Scrope, M.P. – E. T. Stotesbury – Oscar B. Cintas – Leger Galleries, London – USA Collection

Raeburn, Sir Henry (1756–1823)
Master William Blair. Home family, Wedderburn – HEH
William Scott-Elliot of Arkleton. Raeburn family, Edinburgh – Scott-Elliot family, Arkleton – Bache – MMA

Reynolds, Sir Joshua (1723–92)
Lady Sarah Bunbury Sacrificing to the Graces. Bunbury family, Barton Hall, London – Mrs W. W. Kimball – Art Institute of Chicago
Frances, Marchioness Camden. Earl of Lucan – Spencer – HEH
Diana, Viscountess Crosbie. Sitter's family – Tennant family (Baron Glenconner of the Glen) – HEH
Lady Betty Delmé and her children. Delmé family, Hants. – Morgan – Mrs H. L. Satterlee, New York – Mellon – NGW
Georgiana, Duchess of Devonshire. Spencer – HEH
Jane, Countess of Harrington (when Miss Fleming). Earls of Harrington, Elvaston Castle, Derby – HEH
Lady Caroline Howard. Howard family (Earl of Carlisle), Castle Howard – Mellon – NGW
Mrs Edwin Lascelles (formerly Lady Fleming, afterwards Lady Harewood). Sitter – Countess of Harrington, Elvaston Castle, Derby – HEH
Miss Theresa Parker. Parker family (Earl of Morley), Devon – HEH

Reynolds (cont.)
Mrs Siddons as the Tragic Muse (ILLUS-
TRATED). Sir Joshua Reynolds – Charles-
Alexandre de Calonne – William Smith,
Norwich – George Watson Taylor, London
– Westminster – HEH
Lavinia, Countess Spencer (considered by the
museum a studio repetition). Henrietta,
Countess of Bessborough – Ponsonby family
– Earl of Bessborough – HEH
*Lavinia, Countess Spencer, and her son Viscount
Althorp* (ILLUSTRATED). Spencer –
HEH
Lady Elizabeth Taylor. Taylor family – M.
Kann – Frick

Reynolds (cont.)
The Young Fortune Teller. Marlborough –
Baron Glenconner of the Glen – HEH

Romney, George (1734–1802)
*Mrs Penelope Lee Acton; Mrs Susannah Lee
Acton.* Sitters' family, Suffolk – Baron de
Saumarez, London – HEH
The Beckford Children. William Beckford,
Fonthill – Hamilton Palace – HEH
Mrs Bryan Cooke. Cooke and Davies-Cooke
families – Bache – MMA
Mrs Davenport (ILLUSTRATED). Daven-
port and Bromley-Davenport families,
Cheshire – Mellon – NGW

Romney (cont.)
Emma, Lady Hamilton in a Straw Hat. Artist –
John Crawford – Tankerville Chamber-
layne, Winchester – A. C. de Rothschild –
Lady Carnarvon – HEH
Charlotte, Lady Milnes. Milnes family – Earl
of Crewe – Frick
*Caroline, Viscountess Clifden and her sister
Lady Elizabeth Spencer.* Marlborough –
Henry, 4th Viscount Clifden – HEH

Turner, J. M. W. (1775–1851)
The Grand Canal, Venice: Shylock. John
Ruskin – Ralph Brocklebank, Cheshire –
HEH

French School

Boucher, François (1703–70)
*The Arts and Sciences: Poetry and Music,
Comedy and Tragedy, Painting and Sculpture,
Singing and Dancing, Architecture and Chemistry,
Astronomy and Hydraulics, Fowling and Horti-
culture, Fishing and Hunting* (8 panels painted
probably for the Château de Crécy). Mar-
quise de Pompadour(?) – Duc de Pen-
thièvre (?) – Pembroke – Alexander Barker,
London – M. Kann – Frick
*The Four Seasons: The Charms of Spring,
The Pleasures of Summer, The Delights of
Autumn, The Amusements of Winter* (4 panels).
Marquise de Pompadour – Marquis de
Marigny – M. Beaujon, Paris – Mme
Munroe Ridgway, Paris – Edward R.
and Virginia Bacon, New York – Frick

Burgundian School (late 15th cent.)
*Claude de Toulongeon and his Patron Saint,
Claude (?).* Hainauer – Art Museum, Wor-
cester, Mass.
*Guillemette de Vergy and her Patron Saint,
Elizabeth of Hungary(?).* Hainauer – Museum
of Art, Rhode Island School of Design,
Providence – Art Museum, Worcester

Fragonard, Jean-Honoré (1732–1806)
*The Progress of Love: The Pursuit, The Decla-
ration of Love or the Love Letters, The Meeting or
Storming the Citadel, The Lover Crowned;*

The Progress of Love (cont.)
*Hollyhocks (4 panels), The Reverie or Expecta-
tion, Love the Sentinel, Love the Jester, Love
pursuing a Dove, Love Triumphant, Love the
Avenger* (4 original panels with 10 panels to
complete the decorative scheme). Mme du
Barry, Louveciennes – J.-H. Fragonard,
Paris and Grasse – A. Maubert, Grasse –
Malvilan, Grasse – Morgan – Frick
The Love Letter. Baron Feuillet de Conches –
Mme Jäger-Schmidt – Ernest Cronier,
Paris – Joseph Bardac – Bache – MMA
*Catherine-Rosalie Gérard, called Mlle Duthé;
Marie-Madeleine Guimard.* Baronne Natha-
niel de Rothschild – Baron Arthur de Roths-
child – F. Wallis – John W. Simpson, New
York – Thyssen

Greuze, Jean-Baptiste (1725–1805)
*Portrait of the Bookseller Babuti, the artist's
father-in-law.* Mrs Lyne-Stephens, London
– R. Kann – Roussel – D. David-Weill,
Paris – Pierre David-Weill, Paris

Attr. Jacques de Lajoue (1687–1761)
*Screen: Mother Nursing her Child; Shep-
herdess; Shepherdess Asleep; Youth with a
Spade; Girl with a Spear; The Shepherd's
Song; Girl with Cupid* (7 decorative panels).
Mme du Sommerard, Paris – Morgan –
Frick

Lancret, Nicolas (1690–1743)
Portraits of La Famille de Bourbon-Conti.
Bourbon-Conti family – Krannert Art
Museum, University of Illinois, Champaign

Nattier, Jean-Marc (1685–1766)
*Portrait of Mme La Comtesse de Brac as
Aurora.* L. Goldschmidt, Paris – Comtesse
André de Pastre, Paris – Norton Simon

Pater, Jean-Baptiste (1695–1736)
Procession of Italian Comedians. Pembroke –
Frick
The Village Orchestra. Pembroke – Frick
The Fair at Bezons. A. C. de Rothschild –
Lady Carnarvon – Bache – MMA

Perroneau, Jean-Baptiste (1715–83)
Girl with a Kitten. Lady Dorothy Nevill –
National Gallery, London (presented by
Duveen)

Watteau, Jean Antoine (1684–1721)
The French Comedians. Jean de Julienne,
Paris – Count von Rothenburg – Frederick
the Great and Prussian Royal Collection –
Bache – MMA
Minuet in a Pavilion. Frederick the Great and
Prussian Royal Collection – Louis D.
Beaumont, Cap d'Antibes – Cleveland
Museum of Art

Early Flemish School

Bouts, Dirk (*c.* 1415–75)
The Madonna and Child. Gabriel J. P. Weyer, Cologne – Royal Museum, Sigmaringen – Bache – MMA
Moses before the Burning Bush. T. Lloyd Roberts, London – Willet – R. Kann – John G. Johnson Art Collection, Philadelphia

Christus, Petrus (d. 1472/3)
The Nativity. Prince Manuel Yturbe, Madrid – Duchess of Parcent, Madrid – Mellon – NGW

David, Gerard (*c.* 1460–1523)
Two Wings of a Triptych: *Jesus Falls beneath His Cross; The Resurrection; Reverse: The Annunciation.* Ashburnham – Willet – R. Kann – Lehman
Rest on the Flight into Egypt. Frank Stoop – Bache – MMA
The Nativity with Donors and Patron Saints (triptych). Ramon F. Urrutia, Madrid – Bache – MMA

David (cont.)
Rest on the Flight into Egypt. R. Kann – Mellon – NGW

Franco-Flemish School (early 15th cent.) (attr. Pisanello by Duveen)
Profile Portrait of a Lady, *c.* 1410–20 (ILLUSTRATED). Lord Stafford – James Gurney, London – Marquis de Villeroy, Paris – Mackay – Mellon – NGW

Massys, Quentin (1465/6–1530)
The Adoration of the Magi. H. R. Hughes, North Wales – R. Kann – MMA

Memling, Hans (*c.* 1440–94)
The Madonna and Child with Angels. Anhalt – Mellon – NGW
The Madonna and Child. René della Faille de Waerloos, Antwerp – Caspar Bourgeois, Cologne – Richard von Kaufmann, Berlin – Bache – MMA
The Annunciation. Ashburnham – R. Kann – Morgan – MMA

Patinir, Joachim (*fl.* 1515–24)
St Jerome. R. Kann – Henry Oppenheimer – National Gallery, London
Landscape with St Jerome. J. K. Huysmans – Mlle Og – Musée du Louvre, Paris (presented by Duveen)

Weyden, Rogier van der (1399/1400–64)
The Madonna and Child. Willet – R. Kann – Mrs C. P. Huntington – HEH
Christ Appearing to His Mother. Chapel Royal, Granada Cathedral – Dukes of Osuña, Madrid – Michael Dreicer, New York – MMA
Christ Appearing to His Mother. Madrazo family, Madrid – Mellon – NGW
Portrait of a Young Man (called Jehan de Gros). Dr de Meyer, Bruges – R. Kann – Martin A. Ryerson, Chicago – Art Institute of Chicago
Man in a Turban. Private Collection in Holland – Bache – MMA
Portrait of a Lady. (ILLUSTRATED). Anhalt – Mellon – NGW

Later Flemish and Dutch Schools

Brouwer, Adriaen (1605/6–38)
A Young Woman Seated (Pigritia – Laziness). R. Kann – Alte Pinakothek, Munich – Private Collection, Paris
The Brawl. Baron De Beurnonville, Paris – Alexis Febvre, Paris – R. Kann – Michael Friedsam, New York – MMA

Cuyp, Aelbert (1620–91)
The River Maas at Dordrecht. English Collectors – Earl of Brownlow, Berkhamstead, Herts. – Mellon – NGW
Young Herdsmen with Cows. R. Kann – Altman – MMA

Dyck, Anthony van (1599–1641)
Queen Henrietta Maria and her Dwarf (ILLUSTRATED). Earls of Bradford – Earl of Mountrath – Earl of Dorchester – Earl of Portarlington – Northbrook – Hearst – Kress – NGW

Dyck (cont.)
Queen Henrietta Maria. Lord Ailesbury, Savernake, Wilts. – Rosenfeld – Fine Arts Gallery, San Diego, Calif.
The Marchesa Balbi. Balbi family, Genoa – Baron Heath – Holford family, London – Mellon – NGW
The Marchesa Durazzo. Marchese Gropallo, Genoa – R. Kann – Altman – MMA
Frederick Henry, Prince of Orange. Anhalt – Mrs Jacobs – Museum of Art, Baltimore
Robert Rich, Earl of Warwick. Marquess of Breadalbane and family – Bache – MMA
General Ambrogio Spinola, Duke of San Severino. Lord Radstock, London – W. H. Wayne, London – Rev. D. R. Wayne – R. Kann – Morgan – Sterling and Francine Clark Art Institute, Williamstown, Mass.
Self Portrait as a Young Man. Earl of Arlington – Dukes of Grafton, Euston Hall, Suffolk – Bache – MMA

Dyck (cont.)
Lucas van Uffel. Dukes of Sutherland, London – Altman – MMA
Daedalus and Icarus. Spencer – Wood – Toronto Art Gallery

Fyt, Jan (1611–61)
Still Life with Dead Birds. R. Kann – Berlin Museum
Peacocks and Rabbits in a Park. Duchesse de Polignac, Paris – R. Kann – Mrs J. E. Parkinson – Sotheby's, 3 December 1969

Hals, Frans (1581/5–1666)
Claes Duyst van Voorhout. Wyndham – Bache – MMA
Isaak Abrahamszoon Massa. Spencer – Wood – Toronto Art Gallery
Paulus Verschuur. Adolf Joseph Bösch, Vienna – Mrs C. P. Huntington – A. M. Huntington – MMA

Hals (cont.)
Dorothea Berck, wife of Joseph Coymans. Coymans family, Haarlem – Mrs Woollaston, London – R. Kann – Mrs C. P. Huntington – A. M. Huntington – Mrs Jacobs – Museum of Art, Baltimore
Gentleman of the Coymans Family (called Balthasar Coymans) (ILLUSTRATED). Coymans family, Haarlem – Mrs Woollaston, London – R. Kann – Mrs C. P. Huntington – A. M. Huntington – Mellon – N G W
The Merry Lute-Player. Count Bonde, Stockholm – Jules Porgès, Paris – Baron Ferdinand de Rothschild, Waddesdon Manor – Veil-Picard family – John R. Thompson, Chicago – Private Collection, England
Portrait of an Elderly Man. Lord Arundell, Wardour Castle – M. Kann – Frick
Portrait of a Man, 1652-4. Spencer – Frick
Portrait of a Woman. J. Bernard – De Vries – D. P. Sellar – Charles Schiff – C. T. Yerkes, Chicago – Frick
Portrait of an Elderly Lady, 1633. Amsterdam collectors – Comtesse de la Rupelle, Paris – Dr James Simon, Berlin – Mellon – N G W
Portrait of a Woman, 1634. Count André Mniszechof, Paris – August de Ridder – Jacob Epstein, Baltimore – Museum of Art, Baltimore

Hobbema, Meindert (1638-1709)
Entrance to a Village. Thomas Emmerson – John Lucy, Charlecote Park – Baron Lionel de Rothschild, London – R. Kann – Altman – M M A

Hooch, Pieter de (1629-after 1684)
A Dutch Courtyard (ILLUSTRATED). Dutch collectors – Baron Lionel de Rothschild, London – A. C. de Rothschild – Lady Carnarvon – Mellon – N G W
Interior with a Young Couple. R. Kann – Altman – M M A

Maes, Nicolaes (1632-93)
Young Girl Peeling Apples. Ralph Bernal – M. Zachary – John Walter, Bearwood – R. Kann – Altman – M M A

Metsu, Gabriel (1629-67)
Visit to the Nursery. Dutch collectors – Duc de Morny, Paris – R. Kann – Morgan – M M A
The Intruder. English collectors – Baron Verstolk van Soelen, The Hague – Northbrook – Mellon – N G W

Mor, Anthonis (1519-76)
Portrait of a Gentleman. Philip II of Spain – Sir Peter Lely – Thomas Betterton – Spencer – Mellon – N G W

Potter, Paulus (1625-54)
A Farrier's Shop. J.-Ph. de Monté, Rotterdam – L. J. Nieuwenhuys, London – Comte de Perrégaux, Paris – Mme Autran, Marseilles – R. Kann – Widener – N G W

Rembrandt Harmensz van Rijn (1606-69)
Titus, the Artist's Son, 1660. Duke of Rutland – James Stillman family, New York – Mrs Jacobs – Museum of Art, Baltimore
Flora. Spencer – Mrs C. P. Huntington A. M. Huntington – M M A
Hendrickje Stoffels. Marquesa de la Cenia, Madrid – R. Kann – Mrs C. P. Huntington – A. M. Huntington – M M A
Aristotle Contemplating the Bust of Homer (ILLUSTRATED). Sir Abraham Hume, Bart – Lord Brownlow – R. Kann – Mrs C. P. Huntington – A. M. Huntington – Alfred W. Erickson, New York – M M A
Christ with a Pilgrim's Staff. Sir C. Bethel Codrington, Bart, London – L. J. Nieuwenhuys, London – Baron von Mecklenburg, Paris – Count Eduard Raczynski Rogolin, Poland – Bache – M M A
Christ and the Woman of Samaria at the Well. J. Blackwood, London – Van Mulden, Brussels – Fry family, Bristol – R. Kann – Berlin Museum
The Standard-Bearer. Sir Joshua Reynolds – Earl of Warwick – Gould – Bache – M M A
Toilet of Bathsheba. Baron Steengracht, The Hague – Altman – M M A
Young Man Seated at a Table (ILLUSTRATED). Count Gustave Sparre, Stockholm – Count de la Gardie, Helsingborg – Count de Geer, Stockholm – Count Wachtmeister, Vanas, Sweden – Mellon – N G W
Youth with a Black Cap, 1666. Wyndham – William Rockhill Nelson Gallery of Art, Kansas City
Lady with a Pink; Man with a Magnifying Glass. Count Ferdinand d'Oultremont, Brussels – R. Kann – M. Kann – E. Kann – Altman – M M A
Old Lady with a Book. Amsterdam Collectors – Paris Collectors – John Alnutt, London – F. Nieuwenhuys, Brussels – Louis Lebeuf de Montergermont, Paris – Prince Louis de Broglie, Paris – Mellon – N G W

Rubens, Peter Paul (1577-1640)
The Four Evangelists; The Fathers of the Church; The Israelites Gathering Manna in the Desert; Abraham Receiving Bread and Wine from Melchizedek. Spanish Royal Collections – M. Bourke – Westminster – Ringling
Martyrdom of St Lieven (sketch). Prosper Crabbe, Brussels – R. Kann – Baron Reitzes, Vienna – Stephen von Auspitz, Vienna – Boymans-van Beuningen

Rubens (cont.)
Atalanta and Meleager. Marlborough – Hon. George Cavendish-Bentinck, Corfe Castle, Dorset – R. Kann – Goldman – M M A

Ruisdael, Jacob van (1628/9-82)
Quay at Amsterdam. Baron de Beurnonville, Paris – M. Kann – Frick
The Bleaching Grounds of Overveen, near Haarlem. Evrard Rhoné – Isaac Pereire – Marquis de Blaisel – Max Kann – San Donato – R. Kann – William Berg – Leonard Koetser Gallery, London – English Private Collection
Windmill beside a River. Comte de Vence – R. Kann – Berlin Museum
Wheatfields. Comte de Colbert La Place – M. Kann – Altman – M M A

Steen, Jan (1626-79)
The Wrath of Ahasuerus. R. Pickfatt, Amsterdam – Col. Hankey, Beaulieu, Hants. – R. Kann – Barber Institute of Fine Art, Birmingham
Self Portrait with Lute. Sir J. Young, London – Amsterdam Collectors – Baron Verstolk van Soelen, The Hague – Northbrook – Thyssen

Ter Borch, Gerard (1617-81)
The Suitor's Visit. Duc de Morny, Paris – Marqués de Salamanca, Madrid – A. de Rothschild – M. de Rothschild – Mellon – N G W
Curiosity (ILLUSTRATED). Gaillard de Gagny – Lalive de Jully – Marquis de Removille, Paris – Randon de Boisset – M. Robit – Duchesse de Berry – Baron von Mecklenburgh – San Donato – Baron Achille Seillière, Paris – Princesse de Sagan, Paris – Baronne Mathilde de Rothschild, Frankfurt-am-Main – Baron Goldschmidt de Rothschild, Frankfurt-am-Main – Bache – M M A
The Toilet. Blondel de Gagny – Dulac, Paris – Le Brun, Paris – Villiers – Lapeyrière, Paris – Patureau – Vicomte Du Bus de Gisignies, Brussels – Goldschmidt – R. Kann – Morgan – M M A

Vermeer, Jan (1632-75)
Girl Asleep. Artist's Collection – John W. Wilson, Paris – R. Kann – Altman – M M A
The Lacemaker. Harold R. Wright, Bremen – Mellon – N G W
The Smiling Girl (ILLUSTRATED). Walter Kurt Rohde, Berlin – Mellon – N G W

Wouwerman, Philips (1619-68)
Winter. San Donato – R. Kann – Berlin Museum

German School

Dürer, Albrecht (1471–1528)
The Virgin and Child with St Anne (ILLUS-TRATED). Nuremberg Collectors – Maximilian I, Elector of Bavaria – Royal Gallery, Schleissheim – J. O. Entres, Munich – Marshal de Kuriss, Odessa – Altman – MMA

Hans Holbein the Younger (1497/8–1543)
Edward VI when Prince of Wales (ILLUS-TRATED). Viscount Lee of Fareham, Richmond – Bache – MMA

Holbein (cont.)
Dirk Berck of Cologne. Wyndham – Bache – MMA
Margaret Wyatt, Lady Lee. Major Charles Palmer, Windsor – Altman – MMA
Elizabeth Jenks, Lady Rich. Croft family – Moseley family, Salop. – Altman – MMA
A Member of the Wedigh Family. Counts Schönborn, Vienna – Frank D. Stout, Chicago – Harkness – MMA
Portrait of a Man. Arthur W. Sachs – Bache – MMA

Holbein (cont.)
A Lady of the Court of Henry VIII. Stanislas Poniatowski, King of Poland – Joseph Poniatowski, Leipzig – Count Casimir Rzewuski – Ludovica Countess Rzewuski – Counts Lanckoronski, Vienna – Bache – MMA

Strigel, Bernardin (c. 1460–1528)
St Mary Cleophas and Her Family. R. Kann – Bromberg, Hamburg – Dr Emden, Hamburg – Kress – NGW

Italian School

Allegretto Nuzi, (doc. 1346–73) and Master of the Fabriano Altarpiece
The Madonna and Child Enthroned. Lord Glanusk, Brecknocks. – Mellon – NGW

Andrea del Castagno (c. 1421–57)
Portrait of a Gentleman. Barone Cerbone del Nero, Florence – Marchese Torrigiani, Florence – R. Kann – Morgan – Mellon – NGW

Andrea del Sarto (1486–1530)
Madonna and Child with the Infant St John. George Watson Taylor, London – Princess Woronzow, Florence – Benson – Hearst – Kress – Joe and Emily Lowe Art Gallery, University of Miami, Florida

Fra Angelico da Fiesole (c. 1400–55)
The Annunciation. Hamilton Palace – John Edward Taylor, London – C. W. Hamilton – Edsel Ford, Detroit

Attr. Fra Angelico
The Entombment. Medici family(?) – Bardini – Grassi – Goldman – Kress – NGW

Antonello da Messina (c. 1430–79)
Madonna and Child. Graham – Benson – Mackay – Mellon – NGW
Portrait of a Young Man. Doge Alvise Mocenigo IV, Venice – Prince Giovanelli, Venice – Mellon – NGW

Antoniazzo Romano (doc. 1460–1508)
Madonna and Child with Cherubs. Butler – Benson – L. Henkel-Haass, Detroit – Norton Simon – Los Angeles County Museum of Art

Barna da Siena (14th cent.)
Christ Carrying the Cross. Lord Leighton, London – Benson – Miss Helen C. Frick – Frick

Bartolomeo Veneto (doc. 1502–30)
Portrait of a Gentleman. Castello Sforzesco, Milan – Milan Collectors – Goldman – Kress – NGW
Portrait of a Youth. Lazzaroni – James Parmelee, Washington D.C. – Cleveland Museum of Art

Bellini, Giovanni (?1430–1516)
The Madonna and Child. Lazzaroni – HEH
The Madonna and Child with St Peter and St Clare. Walter Wysard, Bucks. – John R. Thompson, Chicago – Kress – NGW
The Madonna and Child. Prince Potenziani, Rieti – Lehman
St Jerome Reading (ILLUSTRATED). Lord Monson, Surrey – Butler – Benson – Mackay – Kress – NGW
Portrait of a Condottiere (called Bartolommeo Colleoni). Dr Pellegrini, Venice – Sir Abraham Hume – Viscount Alford – Earls of Brownlow, Herts. – Kress – NGW

Bellini (cont.)
Portrait of a Young Man in Red. Andrea Vendramin, Venice – Ingenheim – Mellon – NGW

Bellini, Giovanni, and Assistant
Madonna and Child in a Landscape. Otto Wesendonk, Berlin – Kress – NGW
Madonna and Child with Saints. Wynn Ellis, M.P., London – Graham – Benson – Bache – MMA

Attr. Jacopo Bellini (c. 1400–70/1)
Profile Portrait of a Boy. Otto Mündler, Paris – Dreyfus – Kress – NGW

Benvenuto di Giovanni (1436–1517)
The Madonna and Child. Pope Pius II – Maurice Chabrière-Arlès, Lyons – Ernest Odiot, Paris – Lehman
The Madonna and Child with Two Angels. Pietro Giomarelli, Siena – Ashburnham – Detroit Institute of Arts

Biagio d'Antonio da Firenze (active 1476–1504)
(attr. by Duveen to Giovanni Battista Utili)
The Adoration of the Child with Saints and Donors. Church of San Michele, Faenza – Marchese Filippo Hercolani, Bologna – Rev. William Stogdon, Harrow – C. W. Hamilton – Kress – Philbrook Art Center, Tulsa, Oklahoma

Bissolo, Francesco (*fl.*1492–1554)
The Annunciation. Manfrini Gallery – Benson – Norton Simon – Los Angeles County Museum of Art

The 'Pseudo Boccaccino' (Giovanni Agostino da Lodi, 16th cent.)
Pan and Syrinx. Benson – Thyssen

Boltraffio, Giovanni Antonio (1467–1516)
Portrait of a Girl Crowned with Flowers. Ferencz Szarvady, Budapest – Dreyfus – Kress – North Carolina Museum of Art, Raleigh

Bonfigli, Benedetto (*c.*1420–96)
Madonna and Child. Lazzaroni – Kress – El Paso Museum of Art, Texas

Bonifazio di Pitati (1487–1553)
Allegory of Dawn (The Chariot of the Day); *Allegory of Twilight (The Chariot of the Night)*; *Allegory of Summer (Ceres)*. Palazzo Giustiniani-Calerghi, Padua – Benson – Ringling

Botticelli, Sandro (1445–1510)
The Madonna and Child. Corsini family, Florence – Mellon – N G W
Head of the Risen Christ. Emile Gavet, Paris – Mrs Oliver H. P. Belmont, Newport, R.I. – Dr. W. R. Valentiner, Detroit – Detroit Institute of Arts
The Last Communion of St Jerome. Florentine Collectors – Altman – M M A
Portrait of Giuliano de' Medici. Count Procolo Isolani, Bologna – Kahn – Thyssen – Countess Batthyany, Castagnola – ?
Portrait of a Youth (ILLUSTRATED). Pourtalès-Gorgier – Schickler – Pourtalès – Mackay – Mellon – N G W

Attr. Botticelli
Madonna and Child with Angels. Mrs Nicholas F. Brady, Manhasset, L.I., N.Y. – Mr William J. Babington Macaulay – Kress – N G W
The Nativity. Abdy – Prideaux – Marczell von Nemes, Budapest – M. Broux-Gilbert, Paris – Berlin Museum – Kress – Museum of Art, Columbia, South Carolina

Follower of Botticelli
The Coronation of the Virgin. Sir Edward C. Burne-Jones, Bart, London – Prince Max von Lichnowsky, Kuchelna, Austria – Bache – M M A

Botticini, Francesco di Giovanni (1446–97)
Madonna and Child. Palazzo Panciatichi, Florence – Benson – Hearst – Cincinnati Art Museum

Bronzino, Angelo (1503–72)
Cosimo I de' Medici, Duke of Tuscany. Hainauer – Libbey – Museum of Art, Toledo, Ohio

Bulgarini, Bartolommeo (*fl.*1343–68)
(attr. by Duveen to 'Ugolino Lorenzetti')
Nativity (ILLUSTRATED). M. Bonnal, Nice – Giuseppe Grassi, Rome – Goldman – Fogg Art Museum

Carpaccio, Vittore (*c.*1465–1526)
The Virgin Reading. Marquess of Exeter, Burghley House – Benson – Kress – N G W

Cima da Conegliano (*c.*1459–*c.*1517)
Madonna and Child with St Francis and St Clare. Baron de Beurnonville, Paris – Hainauer – Frau Julie Hainauer – George and Florence Blumenthal, New York – M M A

Cimabue (*c.*1250–after 1300)
Triptych: Christ between St Peter and St James Major. French Collectors – Mellon – N G W

Correggio (Antonio Allegri, *c.*1489–1534)
Christ Taking Leave of His Mother. Rossi family, Milan(?) – Prof. Parlatore, Florence – Fairfax-Murray – Benson – National Gallery, London (presented by Duveen)

Cossa, Francesco del (*c.*1436–78)
St Florian and St Lucy; two panels from the Griffoni altarpiece. Church of S. Petronio, Bologna – Conte U. Beni, Gubbio – Joseph Spiridon, Paris – Kress – N G W

Credi, Lorenzo di (*c.*1456/60–1537)
The Ascension of St Louis. Conte di Corbelli, Florence – Caspar Bourgeois, Cologne – Weber – Charles Davis, London – H E H
Portrait of a Lady. Pucci family, Florence – Mellon – Richard de Wolfe Brixey, New York – M M A

Studio of Credi, Lorenzo di
The Madonna and Child with Angels. Rev. W. G. Beardmore, London – Sir George Elliott, Bart, Norfolk – Stanley Mortimer, New York – Princeton University

Crivelli, Carlo (1430/5–?1495)
Madonna and Child (ILLUSTRATED). Pier Giovanni Lenti, Ascoli Piceno – Walter Jones, Clytha, North Wales – Northbrook – Bache – M M A
Madonna and Child. Cardinal Joseph Fesch, Rome – G. H. Morland, London – Graham – Benson – Alfred W. Erickson, New York – Parke-Bernet Sale, November 1961

Crivelli (cont.)
Madonna and Child. Eugen Miller von Aichholz, Vienna – Camillo Castiglione, Vienna – E. ten Cate, Enschede – Kress – N G W
Madonna and Child. Lazzaroni – Lehman

Daddi, Bernardo (14th cent.)
St Paul with Twelve Adorers. Monastery of San Felice, Florence – Comm. Elia Volpi, Florence – Mellon – N G W

Daddi, Bernardo and Assistant
Madonna and Child with Saints and Angels (ILLUSTRATED). Capt. Stirling, Renfrewshire – G. C. Somervell, Edinburgh – Butler – H. C. S. Somerset, Reigate – Goldman – Kress – William Rockhill Nelson Gallery of Art, Kansas City

Danti, Vincenzo (1530–76)
The Descent from the Cross. Bardini – Hainauer – Widener – N G W

Domenico di Bartolo (active 1400–45)
Madonna and Child Enthroned with St Peter and St Paul. Ashburnham – Kress – N G W

Domenico Veneziano (d.1461)
Madonna and Child. Edgeworth family, Longford – Kress – N G W
Portrait of Matteo Olivieri. Bardini – Mellon – N G W

Dosso Dossi (active 1512–42)
Circe and her Lovers in a Landscape. Graham – Benson – Kress – N G W

Duccio di Buoninsegna (*c.*1255–before 1319)
Four Scenes from the Life of Christ. Duomo of Siena and Sienese Collectors – Fairfax-Murray – Benson; sold separately by Duveen: *The Calling of the Apostles Peter and Andrew.* Mackay – Kress – N G W; *Christ and the Woman of Samaria.* John D. Rockefeller Jr, New York – ?; *The Raising of Lazarus.* John D. Rockefeller Jr, New York – Private Collection, New York; *The Temptation of Christ.* Frick
The Nativity, with the Prophets Isaiah and Ezekiel. Private collection, Florence – Berlin Museum – Mellon – N G W

Fei, Paolo di Giovanni (doc.1372–1410)
The Madonna Enthroned. Grassi – Mrs A. E. Goodhart, New York – Lehman

Fiorenzo di Lorenzo (*c.*1445–1525)
The Madonna and Child with St Jerome. Bacchettoni family, San Gemini, Italy – Mrs W. Scott Fitz, Boston – Museum of Fine Arts, Boston

Francesco di Giorgio (1439–1501)
God the Father surrounded by Angels and Cherubim. A. Kann – Lehman – Kress – N G W

Francia, Francesco (c.1450/3–1517)
The Virgin and Child with the Infant St John and an Angel. Pourtalès – Mackay – Messrs French and Co., New York, 1963
Federigo Gonzaga (ILLUSTRATED). Isabella d'Este, Mantua – Gianfrancesco Zaninello, Ferrara – Prince Jerome Bonaparte – Leatham family, Cirencester – Altman – M M A

Gaddi, Agnolo (c.1345–96)
The Madonna Enthroned with Angels (attr. by Duveen to Gherardo Starnina). Ashburnham – Mellon – N G W
The Marriage of the Virgin. Bohn – Benson – Fogg Art Museum

Gentile da Fabriano (c.1370–1427)
Madonna and Child. Alexander Barker, London – E. J. Sartoris, Paris – Goldman – Kress – N G W

Ghirlandaio, Domenico (1449–94)
Francesco Sassetti and his Son Teodoro (?) (ILLUSTRATED). Graham – Benson – Bache – M M A
Portrait of Giovanni Tornabuoni. Tornabuoni and Pandolfini families – Mme de Sagan, Paris – Willet – R. Kann – Morgan – Thyssen
Portrait of a Young Florentine Nobleman. Frizzoni, Bergamo – Hainauer – Schlichting, Paris – Musée du Louvre, Paris

Attr. Giampetrino (Giovanni Pedrini, 15th–16th cents)
Madonna and Child with St John the Baptist. Butler – Benson – Kress – Seattle Art Museum, Washington

Giolfino, Niccolo (1476–1555)
The Sacrifice of Iphigenia. Butler – Benson – N. S. Trivas, Berlin – R. Wheatland Collection, Boston

Giorgione (Giorgio da Castelfranco, c.1477–1510)
The Holy Family. James II of England (?) – Allard van Everdingen (?) – French private collection, Brighton – Willet – Benson – Kress – N G W
The Adoration of the Shepherds (ILLUSTRATED). Cardinal Joseph Fesch, Rome – Claudius Tarral, Paris – Wentworth Beaumont family (Lord Allendale), Northumberland – Kress – N G W

Giotto di Bondone (?1267–1336/7)
Madonna and Child (ILLUSTRATED). Eugène Max, Paris – Goldman – Kress – N G W

Giovanni di Paolo (?1403–83)
The Annunciation and Expulsion from Paradise. Sir William J. Farrer, Westminster – Sir J. Charles Robinson, London – Fairfax-Murray – Benson – Kress – N G W
The Adoration of the Magi. Lord Northwick, Cheltenham – W. Fuller-Marland, Essex – Dr Eduard Simon, Berlin – Mellon – N G W
St Catherine of Siena. Ouroussoff – Fogg Art Museum (presented by Duveen)

Girolamo di Benvenuto (15th–16th cents)
Portrait of a Young Woman. Cav. Antonio Piccolomini, Siena – Signora Ciaccheri, Siena – George Salting, London – Arthur Sanderson, Edinburgh – Benson – Kress – N G W

Gozzoli, Benozzo (1420–97)
St Ursula with Angels and Donor. Dukes of Saxe-Meiningen, Thuringia – Kress – N G W
Miracle of St Zenobius. R. Kann – Berlin Museum

Jacometto Veneziano (d. 1472)
Portrait of a Young Man. Schickler – Pourtalès – Salomon – Bache – M M A

Jacopo del Conte (1510–98)
Portrait of the Papal Notary F. de Pisia. Sir W. Drake – Benson – Fitzwilliam Museum, Cambridge

Attr. Leonardo da Vinci (1452–1519)
Madonna and Child with a Pomegranate. John Warkins Brett, London – Timbal – Dreyfus – Kress – N G W

Studio of Leonardo da Vinci
Portrait of a Young Lady. Conte di Castel-Pizzuto, Milan – Cesare Canessa, Naples – Salomon – Kress – N G W

Lippi, Filippino (c.1457–1504)
The Adoration of the Child. Dukes of Saxe-Meiningen, Thuringia – Mellon – N G W
The Adoration of the Child. Timbal – Dreyfus – Libbey – Museum of Art, Toledo, Ohio
The Madonna and Child. Strozzi family, Florence – Marcello Masserenti, Florence – Prof. Götz Martius, Kiel – Bache – M M A
Pietà. Benson – Frederick Housman, New York – Frederick Montis, New York – Kress – N G W

Lippi, Filippino (cont.)
The Coronation of the Virgin. Marquess of Lothian, Newbattle Abbey, Scotland – Kress – N G W

Lippi, Fra Filippo (c.1406–69)
Madonna and Child (ILLUSTRATED). Edward Solly, London – King Frederick William III of Prussia – Berlin Museum – Kress – N G W
The Madonna and Child with Two Angels. Zanoli and Clavé von Bonhaben families, Cologne – Dr Ludwig Mond, London – Dr Adolph Schaeffer, Frankfurt-am-Main – Bache – M M A
Triptych: St Lawrence Enthroned with Saints and Donors. Cav. Messer Alessandro Alessandri – parish church of Villa Alessandri, Vincigliata – Palazzo Alessandri, Borgo degli Albizzi, Florence – Morgan – M M A (Rogers Fund)
The Annunciation. Palazzo della Signoria, Florence (?) – Dr Achillito Chiesa, Milan – Percy S. Strause, New York – Kress – N G W

Follower of Fra Filippo Lippi
Madonna and Child Enthroned. Edmond Foulc, Paris – Rosenfeld – Kress – New Orleans Museum of Art

Luini, Bernadino (c.1480/90–1532)
The Adoration of the Child. Maestri family, Milan – Conte Giovan Battista Lucini, Milan and Como – Butler – Benson – Kress – N G W
The Madonna and Child with St Catherine of Alexandria. Pope Pius VI – Gen. Sir Robert Browne-Clayton, Bart – Richard C. Browne – Mrs Emery – Cincinnati Art Museum
Portrait of a Lady. F. R. Leyland, London – Fairfax-Murray – Benson – Mellon – N G W
Frescoes: Procris' Prayer to Diana; Cephalus Hiding the Jewels; The Misfortunes of Cephalus; The Despair of Cephalus; The Death of Procris; Cephalus and the Nymphs; The Temple of Diana; Procris and the Unicorn. Casa Rabia, Milan – Michele Cavaleri, Milan – Enrico Cernuschi, Paris – R. Kann – Kress – N G W

Mainardi, Sebastiano (?1460–1513)
Portrait of a Young Man; Portrait of a Young Lady. Marchesi Gherardi, Florence – William Drury Lowe, Locko Park – Mrs C. P. Huntington – H E H

Mantegna, Andrea (?1431–1506)
The Holy Family with St Mary Magdalen. Pietro d'Aiuti, Munich and Naples – Weber – Altman – M M A

Mantegna (cont.)
The Adoration of the Shepherds. Estense family, Ferrara – Aldobrandini and Borghese families, Rome – Alexander Day, London – Knight family, Ludlow, Salop. – Mackay – MMA
Judith and Holofernes (ILLUSTRATED). Lorenzo de' Medici, Florence – King Charles I of England – Pembroke – Widener – NGW
St Jerome in the Wilderness. Sulley – Kahn – Mellon – NGW
Esther and Mordecai. Duke of Buccleuch, London – Mrs Emery – Cincinnati Art Museum
Madonna and Child. James Hugh Smith Barry, Cheshire – Lord Barrymore, Cheshire – Kress – NGW

Masaccio (1401–?1428)
Profile Portrait of a Young Man. Chevalier Artaud de Montor, Paris – Mellon – NGW

Attr. Masaccio
The Madonna of Humility. Princesse de Croy-Dullman, Gmünden – Carl, Count Lonyay, Vienna – Mellon – NGW

Masolino da Panicale (1383–1440/7)
The Annunciation. Earls of Wemyss, Gosford House, Scotland – Goldman – Mellon – NGW
The Archangel Gabriel; The Virgin Annunciate. Ingenheim – Kress – NGW

Master of the Barberini Panels (c.1445–75)
The Annunciation. Strozzi family, Florence – Timbal – Dreyfus – Kress – NGW

Master of the Blessed Clare (mid-14th cent.)
(attr. by Duveen to Giovanni Baronzio da Rimini)
The Adoration of the Magi. Monastero degli Angeli, Rimini – G. A. Hoskins – Kahn – Kress – Joe and Emily Lowe Art Gallery, University of Miami, Florida

Master of the Castello Nativity (15th cent.)
(attr. by Duveen to Domenico Veneziano)
Profile Portrait of a Lady (ILLUSTRATED). Holford family – Bache – MMA

Master of the Life of St John the Baptist (active mid-14th cent.)
Madonna and Child with Angels. Ouroussoff – Kahn – Kress – NGW

Master of the Ovile Madonna ('Ugolino Lorenzetti', 14th cent.)
(attr. by Duveen to Pietro Lorenzetti)
St Catherine of Alexandria. Monastery of San

St Catherine of Alexandria (cont.)
Cerbone, Lucca – Giulio Sterbini, Rome – Ringling, Munich – Godefroy Brauer, Nice – Kress – NGW

Master of San Miniato (14th cent.)
(attr. by Duveen to Filippo Lippi)
Madonna and Child. Butler – Hainauer – Frau Julie Hainauer – George and Florence Blumenthal, New York – MMA

Master of Santo Spirito (early 16th cent.)
Madonna and Child (attr. by Duveen to Cosimo Rosselli). James Stirling Dyce, Edinburgh – Donaldson – James G. Mann, Castle Craig, Scotland – Leonard Davis – Kress – Museum of Art, Birmingham, Alabama
Portrait of a Youth (attr. by Duveen to Pintoricchio). Herr Onnes van Nijenrode, Holland – Rosenfeld – Kress – NGW

Matteo di Giovanni (c.1435–c.1495)
The Madonna and Child with Angels. Ashburnham – Mellon – NGW
Madonna and Child with Saints and Angels. Ashburnham – Mackay – Kress – NGW

Memmi, Lippo (doc.1317–46)
The Madonna and Child with Saints and Angels. Martin T. Smith and family, London – Richard Norton, Boston – C. W. Hamilton – Maitland F. Griggs, New York – MMA
Madonna and Child with Donor. Benson – Mellon – NGW
St John the Baptist (attr. by Duveen to Simone Martini) (ILLUSTRATED). Count Oriola – Jacques Goudstikker, Amsterdam – Kress – NGW

Montagna, Bartolomeo (c.1450–1523)
A Young Woman as St Justina of Padua. Graham – Hainauer – Frau Julie Hainauer – Altman – MMA

Moroni, Giovanni Battista (c.1525–78)
'Titian's Schoolmaster'. Borghese Gallery, Rome – Duc d'Orléans, Paris – Duke of Sutherland, London – Widener – NGW

Nardo di Cione (d.1365/6)
Madonna and Child with St Peter and St John the Evangelist. Ingenheim – Goldman – Kress – NGW

Neroccio de' Landi (1447–1500)
Madonna and Child with St Jerome and St Mary Magdalen. Dukes of Saxe-Meiningen, Thuringia – Kress – MMA
The Madonna and Child with St Mary Magdalen and St Sebastian. Ouroussoff – Lehman

Neroccio de' Landi and Master of the Griselda Legend
Claudia Quinta, Roman Heroine. Timbal – Dreyfus – Mellon – NGW

Niccolò di Ser Sozzo Tegliacci (fl.1334–63)
(attr. by Duveen to Luca di Tommè)
Madonna and Child with Angels. Schickler – Pourtalès – Kress – University of Arizona, Tucson

Perugino (Pietro di Cristoforo di Vannucci, c.1450–1523)
Madonna and Child. Marchesi di Villafranca, Madrid (?) – Marqués de la Romana, Madrid – Marqués de Villamayor, Madrid – Mackay – Kress – NGW

Pesellino (Francesco di Stefano, 1422–57)
Madonna and Christ with St John the Baptist and Two Angels. Graham – Hainauer – Hoe – H. I. Pratt, New York – Museum of Art, Toledo, Ohio
Madonna and Child with St Jerome and St John the Baptist (attr. by Duveen to Filippo Lippi). Private collection, Florence – Hainauer – John G. Johnson Art Collection, Philadelphia
Panel of an Altarpiece: St Zeno and St Jerome. Kaiser Wilhelm II of Germany – Berlin Museum – National Gallery, London (presented by Duveen)

Follower of Pesellino
Madonna and Child with Angels. Giuseppe Toscanelli, Pisa – Dreyfus – Godfrey Locker-Lampson, London – Kress – Berea College, Study Collection, Kentucky

Pier Francesco Fiorentino (fl. c.1470–1500)
(attr. by Duveen to Baldovinetti)
Madonna and Child. Arnoldo Corsi, Florence – Salomon – Mackay – Kress – NGW

Piero di Cosimo (1462–1521)
The Adoration of the Child. Lady of the Guiducci family (according to tradition, a gift of Lorenzo de' Medici), Florence – Metzger collection, Florence – Alexander Barker, London – George Edmund Street, London – Arthur E. Street, London – Museum of Art, Toledo, Ohio
The Visitation with St Nicholas and St Anthony Abbot. Gino Capponi Chapel, Santo Spirito, Florence – Marchese Capponi, Legnajo, Florence – Hon. Mrs Frederick West, Chirk Castle, Denbighs. – Lord Lascelles, Hants. – Kress – NGW
Mythological Scene: The Findings of Vulcan on Lemnos. Graham – Benson – Wadsworth Atheneum, Hartford, Conn.

Piero della Francesca (c.1420–92)
The Crucifixion. Doria family, Milan –
Marco Antonio Colonna, Rome – C. W.
Hamilton – John D. Rockefeller Jr, New
York – Frick

Polidoro da Lanciano (1514/15–65)
*The Virgin and Child with St Catherine and
St Michael.* Wimpole – Benson – Boymans-
van Beuningen

Pollaiuolo, Piero (1443–96)
A Woman in Green and Crimson. Bardini –
Ernest Odiot, Paris – Hainauer – Isabella
Stewart Gardner Museum, Boston

Raffaellino del Garbo (1466–?1524)
*Madonna and Child, with the Infant St John and
Two Angels.* Lord Crawford – Graham –
Benson – Hearst – Col. H. Stewart, Dallas –
McCann – Christie's Sale, 23 June 1967
The Miracle of St Gregory. Church of S.
Spirito, Florence – Palazzo Antinori, Flor-
ence – Giovanni Gagliardi, Florence – S.
Woodburn – Sir John Ramsden, Bart –
Benson – Ringling

Raphael Sanzio (1483–1520)
The Small 'Cowper' Madonna (ILLUS-
TRATED). Private collection, Urbino –
Lord Cowper – Lord Lucas – Lady
Desborough, Panshanger, Herts. – Widener
– NGW
The Niccolini-Cowper Madonna. Marchesi
Niccolini, Florence – Lord Cowper – Lord
Lucas – Lady Desborough, Panshanger,
Herts. – Mellon – NGW
The Agony in the Garden. The Nuns of St
Anthony, Perugia – Queen Christina of
Sweden – Cardinal Azzolini – Don Livio
Odescalchi – the Regent, Duc d'Orléans –
Lord Eldin, Edinburgh – Samuel Rogers,
London – Baroness Burdett-Coutts, London
– Mackay – MMA
Bindo Altoviti. Altoviti family, Rome and
Florence – Johann Georg von Dillis –
Crown Prince Ludwig of Bavaria – Alte
Pinakothek, Munich – Kress – NGW

Copy after Raphael
Giuliano de' Medici, Duke of Nemours (ILLUS-
TRATED). Gaetano Capponi, Florence –
Baldovinetti family – Prof. Brini, Florence

Giuliano de' Medici (cont.)
– the Grand Duchess Marie of Russia –
Prince Sciarra-Colonna, Paris – Oscar
Huldschinsky, Berlin – Bache – MMA

Roberti, Ercole de' (1451/6–96)
Giovanni II Bentivoglio; Ginevra Bentivoglio.
Timbal – Dreyfus – Kress – NGW

Rosselli, Cosimo (1439–1507)
The Madonna and Child with Saints. Victor de
Cock, Paris – Frederick Lewisohn, New
York – Kress – Philbrook Art Center, Tulsa,
Oklahoma

Sassetta (Stefano di Giovanni ?1392–1450)
The Procession to Calvary. W. E. Erle-Drax,
Wye, Kent – C. W. Hamilton – Detroit
Institute of Arts
St Anthony in the Wilderness. Ouroussoff –
Lehman

Sassetta and Assistant
The Meeting of St Anthony and St Paul
(ILLUSTRATED). Granville Edward Har-
court Vernon, Notts. – Lord Allendale,
Northumberland – Kress – NGW

Sebastiano del Piombo (c.1485–1547)
Anton Francesco degli Albizzi. British Collectors – Benson – Kress – Houston Museum
of Fine Arts, Texas

Signorelli, Luca (1445/50–1532)
Madonna and Child. Tommasi family, Cor-
tona – Benson – Bache – MMA

Tintoretto (Jacopo Robusti, ?1518/19–94)
Portrait of a Venetian Senator. Dukes of Aber-
corn – George Eastman, Rochester, N.Y. –
Memorial Art Gallery, University of
Rochester, N.Y.

Circle of Tintoretto
Portrait of a Venetian Procurator. Dukes of
Abercorn – Frick

Titian (Tiziano Vecellio, 1488/90–1571)
The Madonna and Child. Jean de Julienne,
Paris – Earls of Exeter – Benson – Mellon –
Bache – MMA
Filippo Archinto, Archbishop of Milan – Archin-
to family, Milan – Altman – MMA

Titian (cont.)
Emilia di Spilimbergo; Irene di Spilimbergo.
Spilimbergo – Widener – NGW
Portrait of a Venetian Gentleman. Robert P.
Nichols, London – Graham – Henry
Doetsch, London – Lord Rochdale, Lancs.
· – Goldman – Kress – NGW
Portrait of a Man (attr. by Duveen to Gior-
gione). Grimani family, Venice – Walter
Savage Landor, Florence – Comtesse de
Turenne, Florence – Altman – MMA
Venus and the Lute Player. Prince Pio di
Savoia, Rome – Earls of Leicester – MMA
Venus and Adonis. Barbarigo Palace, Venice –
Lord Bristol – Lord Sutherland – Spencer –
Widener – NGW
Portrait of a Lady (called by Duveen Giulia
di Gonzaga Colonna). Wilbraham family,
Cheshire – Kress – NGW

Follower of Titian
Allegory (?Alfonso d'Este and Laura Dianti).
Conti Benacosi, Ferrara – Conte Leopoldo
Cicognani, Venice – Lord Charles William
Stewart – Pourtalès-Gorgier – Lazzaroni –
Goldman – Kress – NGW

Tura, Cosimo (1430–95)
The Flight into Egypt. Graham – Benson –
Bache – MMA
Portrait of a Ferrarese Nobleman. William
Drury Lowe, Locko Park, Derbyshire –
Altman – MMA

Attr. Cosimo Tura
Portrait of a Man. Matthieson Gallery, Berlin
– Kress – NGW

Workshop of Andrea del Verrocchio (1435–
88)
The Madonna and Child. Rev. W. Davenport-
Bromley, Derbys. – Sir Walter R. Farquhar,
London – Butler – Altman – MMA

Vivarini, Alvise (c.1445–1503/5)
(attr. by Duveen to Giovanni Bellini)
Portrait of a Senator. Comtesse de Béarn,
Paris – Kress – NGW

Byzantine School (13th cent.)
The Madonna and Child Enthroned. Convent in
Calahorra, Spain – Mellon – NGW

Spanish School

Goya, Francisco de (1746–1828)
Portrait of Señora Sabasa García. Don José Juan Herrero, Madrid – Berlin Collectors – Mellon – N G W
Don Manuel Osorio de Zuñiga (ILLUSTRATED). Sitter's family – Mme Henri Bernstein, Paris – Bache – M M A
Portrait of the Famous Toreador Pedro Romero. Infante Don Sebastian, Pau – Viuda de Vera, Seville – Lafitte, Madrid – R. Kann – HEH
Portrait of a Lady in Black Holding a Fan (Marquesa de Fontana). Marqués de Fontana, Madrid – Joslyn Art Museum, Omaha, Nebraska

Murillo, Bartolomé Esteban (1618–82)
The Holy Family with St John. Admiral Sir Eliab Harvey, M.P., Chigwell, Essex – English Collectors – Alfred Beit, London – M. Kann – Sir Ernest Cassel, London –

The Holy Family with St John (cont.)
Mrs Herbert Asquith, London – Aaron and Nettie G. Naumburg, New York – Fogg Art Museum

Velásquez, Diego Rodríguez de Silva y (1599–1660)
Philip IV of Spain, c.1623. Doña Antonia de Ypeñarrieta – Corral family, Zaraus – Duchess of Villahermosa, Madrid – Duke of Luna, Madrid – Altman – M M A
Philip IV of Spain, c.1650–55. Maréchal-Général Nicolas Soult, Duc de Dalmatie, and his heirs – Mrs Emery – Cincinnati Art Museum
The Infanta Maria Theresa (ILLUSTRATED). Philippe Ledieu, Paris – Col. H. Payne, New York – Harry Payne Bingham, New York – Bache – M M A
Count-Duke Olivares. Altamira Gallery, Madrid – Col. Hugh D. Baillie, London –

Count-Duke Olivares (cont.)
Charles Scarisbrick, Lanes. – Holford family, London – Mrs C. P. Huntington – The Hispanic Society of America, New York
Count-Duke Olivares. Doña Antonia de Ypeñarrieta – Corral family, Zaraus – Duchess of Villahermosa, Madrid – Duke of Luna, Madrid – London Collector – Museu de Arte, São Paulo, Brazil
Self Portrait. Royal House of Hanover – Bache – M M A
Man with a Wine Glass. Sir G. Prior Goldney, Bart, Chippenham, Wilts. – Libbey – Museum of Art, Toledo, Ohio
Portrait of a Young Man. Harrach family, Vienna – Mellon – N G W
Portrait of a Young Girl. Sir William Knighton, London – Arthur Sanderson, Edinburgh – R. Kann – Mrs C. P. Huntington – A. M. Huntington – The Hispanic Society of America, New York

Sculpture

Amadeo, Giovanni (c.1447–1522)
Gian Galeazzo Sforza, 6th Duke of Milan; Lodovico Sforza, 7th Duke of Milan. Sir John Robinson, London – Timbal – Dreyfus – Mellon – N G W
Filippo Maria Visconti, 3rd Duke of Milan. Emile Signol, Paris – Dreyfus – Kress – N G W

Bandini, Giovanni (c.1540–98)
Adonis. Morgan – Frick

After Bellano, Bartolomeo (c.1434–96/7)
David with the Head of Goliath. Saracini family, Siena – Chigi-Saracini family, Siena – Count Piccolomini della Triana, Siena – Godefroi Brauer, Nice – Bache – M M A

Benedetto da Maiano (1442–97)
The Madonna and Child. Max Lyon, Paris – Kress – N G W
A Florentine Statesman. Ginori family, Florence – Liechtenstein Gallery, Vienna – Mackay – Kress – N G W

Attr. Benedetto da Maiano
The Virgin Annunciate (ILLUSTRATED). Spinelli family, Borgo San Sepolcro – Altman – M M A

Bertoldo di Giovanni (?1420–91)
Heraldic Wild Man. Collection in Pisa – Charles Loeser, Florence – Morgan – Frick

Boizot, Louis-Simon (18th cent.)
Peter Adolph Hall. Hall family – Marquis de la Grange – Lowengard, Paris – Frick

Brandani, Federico (1522/5–75)
Antonio Galli. Baron Achille Seillière, Château de Mello, Oise – A. de Rothschild – M. de Rothschild, Paris – Frick

Caffieri, Jean-Jacques (1725–92)
Portrait of a Young Girl. Marquise de Trétaignes – Gould – HEH

Camelio (c.1455/60–1537)
A Faun playing the Flute. Morgan – Frick

Cattaneo, Danese (1509–73)
Bust of a Jurist. Mme Louis Stern, Paris – Frick

Cellini, Benvenuto (1500–71)
Virtue Overcoming Vice. John Edward Taylor, London – Widener – N G W

Civitali, Matteo (1436–1501)
St Sebastian. Piot – Timbal – Dreyfus – Kress – N G W

Clodion (Claude Michel, 1738–1814)
Woman playing with a Child. Ernest W. Beckett – Morgan – HEH

Desiderio da Settignano (c.1430–64)
The Madonna and Child. Timbal – Dreyfus – Mellon – N G W
The Infant Christ. Oratory of S. Francesco dei Vanchetoni, Florence – Kress – N G W
The Young Christ with St John the Baptist (ILLUSTRATED). Timbal – Dreyfus – Mellon – N G W

Desiderio da Settignano (cont.)
Bust of a Boy. Piot – Paul van Cuyck, Paris – Timbal – Dreyfus – Mellon – N G W
St Cecilia. Palazzo Brunaccini-Compagni, Florence – Gallerie Lombardi, Florence – Samuel Woodburn, London – Earls of Wemyss, Edinburgh – Museum of Art, Toledo, Ohio
Marietta Strozzi. Strozzi family, Florence – G. Magherini Graziani, Città di Castello – Grassi – Widener – N G W
Bust of a Lady. Alessandro Castellani, Rome – Schickler – Pourtalès – Mackay– Kress – N G W

After Desiderio da Settignano
The Young St John the Baptist. Martelli family, Florence – M. Kann – E. Kann – Altman – M M A

Donatello (?1386–1466)
The Madonna and Child. Conte Giacomo Michelozzi, Tavernelle, Florence – Goldman – Mellon – N G W
St John the Baptist. Emile Gavet, Paris – William K. Vanderbilt, Newport, R.I. – Mrs Oliver H. P. Belmont, Newport, R.I. – Kress – N G W
St John the Baptist (ILLUSTRATED). Piot – Timbal – Dreyfus – Mellon – N G W
Cupid. Westminster – Widener – N G W

Florentine School (15th cent.)
The Madonna and Child. Church of S. Spirito, Florence – Dr Eduard Simon, Berlin – Mackay – Kress – N G W
The Singing Boy. Piot – Timbal – Dreyfus – Cleveland Museum of Art

Francesco da Sant'Agata (16th cent.)
Hercules Strangling Antaeus. Mme Louis Stern, Paris – Widener – N G W

French School (17th cent.)
Hercules and Hydra. Spitzer – Hainauer – Frick
Bust of Louis XIV (attr. by Duveeen to G. L. Bernini). Philippe, duc d'Orléans, Château de Saint-Cloud – E. Williamson, Paris – Sir Stuart Samuel, Bart, London – Gould – Kress – N G W

Attr. Gerhard, Hubert (c.1545–1620)
Triton and Nereid. Charles Mannheim, Paris – Morgan – Frick

Giovanni Bologna (1529–1608)
Nessus and Dejanira. Marlborough – Morgan – HEH
Hercules and the Boar of Erymanthus. Donaldson – Widener – N G W

Gras, Caspar (1590–1674)
Infant Faun. Sir Henry Hope Edwardes, Bart, Ashbourne, Derbyshire – Morgan – Frick

Grupello, Gabriel (1644–1730)
Eve. Spitzer – Hainauer – Morgan – Frick

Houdon, Jean-Antoine (1741–1828)
Sabine Houdon aged 10 months. Mlle S. Houdon (Mme Henri Duval), Paris – Henri Perron, Paris – Jacques Doucet, Paris – Judge Elbert H. Gary, New York – Harkness – M M A
Sabine Houdon. Miallet, Paris – Altman – M M A
Sabine Houdon. Claudine Rochette – Raoul Perrin – Gould – HEH
Giuseppe Balsamo, Conte di Cagliostro. Sir Richard Wallace – Sir John Murray Scott, Paris – Kress – N G W
Portrait of a Lady. Marquis Auguste du Blaixel – A. de Rothschild – M. de Rothschild – HEH
Diana Huntress (bronze). Girardot de Marigny – Comte Aguado – Lord Hertford – Sir Richard Wallace – Sir John Murray Scott, Paris – Charles T. Yerkes, Chicago – Eduardo Guinle, Rio de Janeiro – HEH
Diana Huntress (terracotta). Cardinal Joseph Fesch(?), Rome – Henry de Montault, Paris – Susse – Victorien Sardou and Mme Sardou – Frick
The Bather. Duc de Chartres – Lord Hertford – Sir Richard Wallace – Sir John Murray Scott, Paris – Altman – M M A

Jonghelinck, Jacques (1530–1606)
The Duke of Alba. Dukes of Alba, Madrid – Maréchal Ney – Maréchal Vicomte de Reille and family – Frick

Laurana, Francesco da (c.1420–1503)
Beatrice of Aragon. Dreyfus – John D. Rockefeller Jr, New York – Frick
A Princess of the House of Aragon. Alessandro Castellani, Rome – Bardini – Thomas Fortune Ryan, New York – Mellon – N G W
Bust of a Lady (called Ippolita Maria Sforza, Duchess of Aragon). Louis Hercule de Ricard – Mme de Narbonne-Lara – Marquise de Mailly-Nesle, Paris – Frick

Lemoyne, Jean-Louis (1665–1755)
Garden Vase. R. Kann – Frick

Leoni, Leone (1509–90)
Giovanni Capponi. Hainauer – Kress – N G W

Lombardo, Pietro (c.1435–1515)
A Singing Angel. Max Chabrière-Arlès, Lyons – Mackay – Kress – N G W

School of Lombardo, Tullio (c.1455–1532)
Apollo, Defender of Delphi. Ferencz-Aurel von Pulszky, Budapest – George von Rath, Budapest – Morgan – HEH

Attr. Lorenzi, Battista (c.1527–94)
Triton Blowing Trumpet. Earl of Bessborough, London – Morgan – Frick

Maderno, Stefano (c.1576–1636)
Hercules and Antaeus. Cunard family, London – HEH

Mino da Fiesole (1429–84)
The Madonna and Child. Timbal – Dreyfus – Mellon – N G W
The Virgin Annunciate. De Sani family, Siena – Conte Antonio Palmieri-Nuti, Siena – Mackay – Kress – N G W
The Youthful St John. Conte Rasponi Spinelli, Florence – Raoul Heilbronner, Paris – Altman – M M A
Charity and Faith. Timbal – Dreyfus – Mackay – Mellon – N G W
Cardinal Guillaume d'Estouteville. Hainauer – Altman – M M A
Astorgio Manfredi II of Faenza. Timbal – Schickler – Pourtalès – Widener – N G W

Attr. Multscher, Hans (c.1400–67)
Reliquary Bust of a Female Saint. Church of Zamosc – Morgan – Frick

Nuremberg School (early 16th cent.)
Paris. Charles Mannheim, Paris – Morgan – Frick
Satyr Mother with Child. Pfungst – Morgan – Frick

Paduan School (early 16th cent.)
Cantering Horse. Baron A. C. de Casson, Chertsey, Surrey – Morgan – Frick

Pajou, Augustin (1730–1809)
Marie-Adélaïde Hall. Hall family – Marquis de la Grange – Lowengard, Paris – Frick

Pigalle, Jean-Baptiste (1714–85)
Child with Bird and Apple; Child with Birdcage. R. Kann – Morgan – Mrs C. P. Huntington – HEH

Pollaiuolo, Antonio (1431/2–98)
Hercules. Marchese Niccolini, Florence – Bardini – Morgan – Frick

Riccio, Andrea (1470–1532)
Naked Youth with Raised Left Arm. Morgan – Frick
Satyr with Inkstand and Candlestick. Morgan – Frick

Riccio (cont.)
Triton and Nereid. Spitzer – Morgan – Frick
Lamp. Petrus Campesius, Padua – Giacinto Fagnani, Padua – Girolamo Santasofia, Padua – Morgan – Frick

Attr. Riccio
Naked Female Figure. Comte Jacques de Bryas, Paris – Morgan – Frick

Workshop of Riccio
Atlas Supporting the Globe of Heaven. Spitzer – John Edward Taylor, London – Frick
Warrior on a Horse. Emile Gavet, Paris – Martin Heckscher, Vienna – Caspar Jongens, Cologne – Charles Stein, Paris – Morgan – Frick

Robbia, Andrea della (1435–1525)
The Adoration of the Child. Timbal – Dreyfus – Mellon – N G W

Studio of Andrea della Robbia
The Madonna and Child with Cherubim. M. de Nolivos, Paris – Dreyfus – Mellon – N G W
The Madonna and Child with God the Father and Cherubim. Timbal – Dreyfus – Mellon – N G W

Robbia, Luca della (1399/1400–82)
The Madonna and Child. Marchese Viviani della Robbia, Piazza d'Azeglio, Florence – San Donato – Theodore Finet, Brussels – Mme Paul Finet, Paris – Museum of Art, Toledo, Ohio
The Madonna and Child (ILLUSTRATED). Widener – N G W

Robbia, Luca della (cont.)
The Madonna and Child. Marchese Viviani della Robbia, Florence – Conte Lionello de' Nobili, Florence – Altman – M M A

Rossellino, Antonio (1427–79)
The Madonna and Child. Conte Cosimo Alessandri, Florence – Hainauer – Museum of Art, Toledo, Ohio
The Madonna and Child. Conte Cosimo Alessandri, Florence – Hainauer – Altman – M M A
The Madonna and Child. Granby family – Mackay – Kress – N G W
The Young St John. Church of S. Francesco dei Vanchetoni, Florence – Kress – N G W

San Gallo, Francesco da (1494–1576)
St John Baptizing. Bardini – Hainauer – Morgan – Frick

Sansovino, Jacopo (1486–1570)
Bacchus and a Young Faun. Duke Antonio Litta, Visconte Arese, Milan – Napoleon Bonaparte – French National Collections – Prince Napoleon, Palais Royal, Paris – Marquis de Ganay, Paris – Mellon – N G W
Venus Anadyomene. Duke Antonio Litta, Visconte Arese, Milan – Napoleon Bonaparte – French National Collections – Prince Napoleon, Palais Royal, Paris – Sir George Faudel-Phillips, Bart, London – Gould – Mellon – N G W

Severo da Ravenna (late 15th cent.)
Neptune on a Sea-Monster. Spitzer – Hainauer – Morgan – Frick

Severo da Ravenna (cont.)
Queen Tomyris with the Head of Cyrus. Chigi-Saracini family, Siena – A. Kann – Morgan – Frick

Solari, Cristoforo (c.1460–1527)
The Man of Sorrows. Timbal – Dreyfus – Kress – N G W

Soldani, Massimiliano (1658–1740)
Virtue Triumphant over Vice. Charles Mannheim, Paris – Morgan – Frick

Vecchietta (Lorenzo di Pietro, c.1412–80)
The Resurrection. Prince Chigi, Rome – R. Kann – Morgan – Frick

Verrocchio, Andrea del (1435–88)
A Putto Poised on a Globe. Timbal – Dreyfus – Mellon – N G W
Lorenzo de' Medici, 'The Magnificent' (ILLUSTRATED). Prof. Emilio Santarelli, Florence – Edward Nicholls Denny, London – Lord Taunton, Somerset – Stanley family, Somerset – Mackay – Kress – N G W
Giuliano de' Medici. Piot – Timbal – Dreyfus – Mellon – N G W

Vittoria, Alessandro (1525–1608)
Jacopo Contarini. Mackay – Kress – N G W

Attr. Vries, Adriaen de (c.1546–1626)
The Flying Mercury. Acciaiuoli family, Florence – Comte Alexandre Sergeievitch de Stroganoff, Rome – Donaldson – Mrs C. P. Huntington – Mellon – N G W
Nessus and Dejanira. Paris Collector – Frick

Some of Duveen's Donations to the Tate Gallery, London

Burne-Jones, Sir Edward, Bart (1833–98)
Head of Miss M. Benson
Medusa
The Pilgrim
Andromeda

Cézanne, Paul (1839–1906)
The Bathers

Cotman, John Sell (1782–1842)
Crowland Abbey

Gauguin, Paul (1848–1903)
Faa Iheihe

Hogarth, William (1697–1764)
The Graham Children

John, Augustus (1878–1961)
Madame Suggia

Lavery, Sir John (1856–1941)
The Golf Course, North Berwick

Mestrovic, Ivan (1883–1962)
Girl with a Guitar

Sargent, John Singer (1856–1925)
Ellen Terry as Lady Macbeth

Spencer, Sir Stanley (1891–1959)
The Resurrection, Cookham

Steer, Philip Wilson (1860–1942)
Farmyard

Acknowledgments for Illustrations

The producers of this book wish to express their thanks to all those who are indicated in the list below; in particular, thanks are given to the Hon. Mrs Burns for her kind assistance, to John Curtis, to Peter Mitchell, and to the staffs of the Metropolitan Museum of Art, New York, and the National Gallery of Art, Washington, whose great help and efficiency have, to a large extent, made this book possible.

The producers of the book also wish to explain why no French paintings are included. The best Duveen paintings from France were those sold to Frick. Unfortunately, the Frick Collection has not given permission for any of its paintings to be reproduced here.

The primary sources of some of the illustrations in this book have proved obscure. Every effort has been made to trace these; in one or two cases where it has not been possible, the producers wish to apologize if the acknowledgment proves to be inadequate. In no case is such inadequacy intentional, and if any owner of copyright who has remained untraced will kindly communicate with the producers, a reasonable fee will be paid, and the required acknowledgment made in future editions of the book.

Abbreviations used:
HEH: Henry E. Huntington Library and Art Gallery, San Marino, California; HTRC: Hans Tasiemka Research Club, London; ILN: *The Illustrated London News*; MMA: The Metropolitan Museum of Art, New York; NGW: National Gallery of Art, Washington, D.C.; RT: Radio Times Hulton Picture Library, London; UPI: United Press International, London

Page

8 Topix

17 MMA, The Jules S. Bache Collection, 1949

18 NGW, Andrew Mellon Collection

20 (*Left*) from *Mr Five Per Cent: The Biography of Calouste Gulbenkian* by Ralph Hewins, Hutchinson and Co. (Publishers) Ltd, 1957. HTRC
(*Right*) RT

21 (*Left and Right*) NGW

23 HTRC

24 UPI

25 ILN, 1933

27 NGW, Samuel H. Kress Collection

28 NGW, Andrew Mellon Collection

29 NGW, Andrew Mellon Collection

30 NGW, Andrew Mellon Collection

35 (*Left*) The Trustees of the Pierpont Morgan Library, New York
(*Right*) HTRC

36 Cunard Line

39 HEH

40 NGW, Andrew Mellon Collection

44 Museum of the City of New York

46 From *The Rise of the House of Duveen* by J. H. Duveen, Longmans, Green and Co. Ltd, 1957

47 HTRC

49 MMA, Bequest of Benjamin Altman, 1913

50 MMA, Bequest of Benjamin Altman, 1913

51 MMA, Bequest of Benjamin Altman, 1913

52 NGW, Widener Collection

54 ILN, 1935

55 HTRC

57 The Tate Gallery, London

59 HTRC

61 NGW, Widener Collection

62 NGW, Widener Collection

63 By kind permission of Frank Herman

70 HTRC

72 HTRC

74 Christie, Manson & Woods, Executors of the late Mrs Anna Thompson Dodge. Photo: A. C. Cooper

79 NGW, Samuel H. Kress Collection

80 MMA, The Jules S. Bache Collection, 1949

82 (*Left*) RT
(*Right*) HTRC

89 MMA, The Jules S Bache Collection, 1949

90 NGW, Samuel H. Kress Collection

91 MMA, The Jules S. Bache Collection, 1949

92 MMA, The Jules S. Bache Collection, 1949

96 (*Left*) RT
(*Right*) Photo: Sir Cecil Beaton

101 NGW, Andrew Mellon Collection

102 MMA, The Jules S. Bache Collection, 1949

105 (*Left*) Isabella Stewart Gardner Museum, Boston
(*Right*) The Tate Gallery, London

106 ILN, 1929

108 ILN, 1929

112 Photo: Sir Cecil Beaton

114 HTRC

116 (*Left*) Isabella Stewart Gardner Museum, Boston
(*Right*) HTRC

119 Courtesy of the Fogg Art Museum, Harvard University. Gift – Henry Goldman and Friends of the Fogg Art Museum

120 MMA, The Jules S. Bache Collection 1949

123 HTRC

129 NGW, Samuel H. Kress Collection

130-1 NGW, Samuel H. Kress Collection

132 MMA, The Jules S. Bache Collection, 1949

134 NGW, Samuel H. Kress Collection

141 HEH

142 HEH

145 UPI

148 HEH

149 HEH

153 ILN, 1925

159 HEH

160 NGW, Andrew Mellon Collection

162 UPI

163 UPI

164 Christie, Manson & Woods, Executors of the late Mrs Anna Thompson Dodge. Photo: A. C. Cooper

165 Philadelphia Museum of Art. Bequest of Eleanore Elkins Rice

166 ILN, 1933

170 RT

172 UPI

173 (Left and Right) HTRC

175 UPI

177 NGW, Andrew Mellon Collection

178 NGW, Andrew Mellon Collection

183 UPI

187 NGW, Samuel H. Kress Collection

188 NGW, Samuel H. Kress Collection

189 NGW, Samuel H. Kress Collection

190 NGW, Samuel H. Kress Collection

193 RT

204 Painting by Leopold Seyffert. NGW, Samuel H. Kress Collection

210 (Left) HTRC
(Right) RT

211 (Left) HTRC
(Centre and Right) HTRC

Index

The numbers in italics refer to illustrations.

Abrahams, Montague *46*
Agnew, Thomas, and Sons 10, 59, 161
Allen, Frederick Lewis 12, 32, 184
Allen, John H. 99, 104, 105
Allendale, Viscount *128*, 136, 137
Allom, Sir Charles 42, 166, 167, 181
Almanach de Gotha 82
Althorp 152, 154
Altman, Benjamin 11, 47, 48, 53, 64, 70, 71–3, 75, 99, 134, 161, 171, 173, 206, 207
Altman Collection 48, *48*, 73, 137
Alunno di Benozzo 117
Alunno di Domenico 117, 118, 121
Amico di Sandro 118, 121
Angelico, Fra:
  'Annunciation' 211
Aquitania 146, 147, 148
Art News 114, 176
Avignon school 180

Bache, Jules 9, 10, 12, 35, 83, 93, 94, 95, *96*, 110, 113, 134, 172, 173, 180, 181, 186, 201, 212
Bache Catalogue 84
Bache Collection *16, 81, 88, 103, 121, 133*, 181
Bagatelle 166
Barbizon school 32, 87, 158
Barnett, Rosetta, Lady (Joseph Joel) Duveen 46, 47, 55
Bartolommeo di Giovanni 118
Bath, William Pulteney, 1st Earl of 155
Beaconsfield, Benjamin Disraeli, Earl of 22, 25
Beauvais tapestry 167
Before the Bombardment (O. Sitwell) 35
Belasco, David 137
Bellini, Giovanni 146, 210:
  'Il Cristo Morto Sorretto da Angeli' 123
  'Il Salvatore Benedicente' 124
  'Madonna' (Berenson) *123*
  'St Jerome Reading' *191*
Bellini Exhibition, Venice 121–4
Benedetto da Maiano:
  'The Virgin Annunciate' *48*
Benson Collection *16*, 25, 100, *191*
Berengaria 36
Berenson, Bernard *26*, 82, 87, *88*, 107, 110, *112*, 113–40, *114, 123*, 162, 163, 205, 210
Berenson, Mrs Bernard 128
Berkman, Alexander 163
Berlin, Isaiah 140
Berlin, Kaiser-Friedrich-Museum 59, *186*, 196
Bernstein, Henri 94

Berry, Duchesse de *81*
Beruete y Moret, Aureliano de 161
Bessborough, Vere Brabazon Ponsonby, 9th Earl of 154, 155
Big Four, The (Lewis) 143
Bingham, Harry Payne *88*, 110
Birley, Oswald *148, 149*
Black, William Harman 107
Bocher, Ferdinand 115, 116
Bode, Wilhelm von 59, *59*, 60, 64, 104, *198*
Boggis, Bertram 9, 10, 34, 93, 127, 137
Bonheur, Rosa 32
Boston 47, 48, 53
Botticelli, Sandro 99, 118, 135, 179, 209:
  'The Adoration of the Magi' 191
  'Portrait of a Youth' *26*
Boucher, F. 76, 208
Bouguereau, A. W. 32, 33
Bowles, A. E. 133
Bowra, Sir Maurice 106
Boyer, Charles 94
Braque, Georges 94
Brighton College 55
British Red Cross 105
Brooks, Phillips 122
Bruell, Max 100, 103, 104, 105
Buckner, Emory R. 19
Bulgarini, Bartolommeo:
  'Nativity' *118*

Carlsbad 158, 161
Carnarvon, Countess of *176*
Carnegie, Andrew 75, 88
Carnegie Institute, Pittsburgh 183
Carrère and Hastings 42, 164
Carstairs, Charles 43
Carter, Morris 115
Cassel, Sir Ernest 56
Catalogue of Early Italian Paintings 63
Catalogues prepared by Duveen 83–4
Catena 138
Catherine the Great, Empress of Russia 196
Central Pacific Railroad 143, 146
Chamberlain, Neville 24, 212
Charles I, King of England *60*, 82
Charles X, King of France 167
Charles of London 64
Chatsworth 38
Chinese porcelain 48, 55, 56, 84
Christie's 26, 31, 156
Clark, Kenneth, Lord Clark 113, 140, 193, 211
Clodion 167
Cochran, Alexander Smith 179–80

Collection of Paintings, Sculptures etc. of Samuel H. Kress, The 83
Contini, Count Alessandro 95, 110
Conway, Sir Martin *108*
Coolidge, Calvin 184, 197
Corot, J. B. Camille 32
Cortesi, Salvatore 184
Cortissoz, Royal 137
Cosway, Richard *54*
Crivelli:
  'Madonna and Child' *133*
Crocker, Charles 144, 146
Crosse, Lawrence *54*

D'Abernon, Edgar Vincent, 1st Viscount 22, *23*, 24, *24*, 105
Daddi, Bernardo:
  'Madonna and Child with Saints and Angels' *186*
Davis, John W. 212
Dearborn 174, 176
Debrett's Peerage, Baronetage etc. 82
Delft pottery 45, 46, 47
Demidoff, Prince Anatole *81*
Desiderio da Settignano 13:
  'The Young Christ with St John the Baptist' *100*
Detroit 33
Devonshire, Duke of 38
Dijon 180, 181
Dodge, Anna Thompson (Mrs Horace E.) 75, 113, 164, *164*, 181
Donatello 11, 13, 179:
  'St John the Baptist' *31*, 38
Douglas, Captain R. Langton *108*, 138
Drawings of the Florentine Painters, The (Berenson) 116
Dreicer, Michael 208
Dresden 122
Dreyfus Collection 12, 13, *31*, 83, 100, *100*, 110–11, 201
Du Barry, Mme 82, 164, *166*
Duccio di Buoninsegna 196
Dürer, Albrecht 34, 181, 196:
  'The Virgin and Child with St Anne' *48*
Duveen, Anette *46*
Duveen, Benjamin (brother) 55, 64, 66
Duveen, Charles (brother) 55, 64
Duveen, Dora (Uncle Henry's wife) 65
Duveen, Dorothy (daughter) 66, 133
Duveen, Edward Joseph (brother) 55, 64
Duveen, Elsie (Lady Duveen) 65, 66, *66*, 78, 81
Duveen, Ernest (brother) 55, 64, 66

Duveen, Henry (Uncle Henry) 45, *46*, 47–8, 53, 56, 57, 58, 59, *63*, 64, 65, 66, 68, 69, 70, 71, 73, 85, 98, 99, 100, 158, 171
Duveen, Henry (brother) 55
Duveen, John (brother) 55, 64
Duveen, Joseph, Lord: appearance *8*, *23*, *25*, 37, *46*, *108*, *193*; as benefactor 104–5, 180; on Board of National Gallery 23–4; business relationship with his family 64–5; debut as art dealer 60; generosity to household staffs, deck stewards etc. 179, 180; fatal illness and death 77, 171, 211, 212–13; fondness for the theatre 41; as interior decorator and furnisher of houses 42, 163–8; library 38; knighthood and peerage 24, 37–8, 57. *See also* Lawsuits
Duveen, Joseph and Eva (grandparents) 45
Duveen, Sir Joseph Joel (father) 45, *46*, 47, 53, 55–7, *57*, 59, 64
Duveen, Louis (brother) 55, 64–5, 66
Duveen Brothers gallery, New York 9, 10, 12, 14–15, *14*, 36, *44*, 45, 57, 58–9, 64, 66, 78, 98, 111, 127, 135, 145, 152, 174, 179, *213*; contents of basement 87. *See also* Ministry of Marine
Duveen's gallery, London 9, 12, 64, 66, 98, 126, 145, 213; Paris 9, 64, 66, 98, 145, 161
Dwight, H. G. 176, 183

Edward VII, King 56, 98
El Greco 169
El Mirasol, Palm Beach 77
Emery, Mary M. 161
Esher, Reginald Baliol Brett, 2nd Viscount 56
Este, Isabella d' 115, 126
Etruria 58

Farquhar, Lord 98
Fenway Court, Boston 115
Ffoulke Collection 71
Fiesole 139
Finley, David E. 191
Florence 115, 139, 140
Ford, Edsel 33, 95, *175*, 211
Ford, Henry 174–6, *175*, *211*
Fragonard, J.-H. 76, 164, 165, 166, 167, 181
Francia, F.:
'Federigo Gonzaga' *48*
Francis I, King of France 31, 82
Franco-Flemish school *26*
Frankfurter, Alfred M. 32, 114
French and Co. 146
Frick, Henry Clay 11, 38, 42–3, 64, 75, 76, 85, 88, 95, 103, 125, 127, 134, 158, 161, *162*, 162–3, 167, 168, 169, 171, 172, 173, 180, 185, 201, 209
Frick Collection, The 125, 167, 176
Frick's house (now The Frick Collection), New York 42, *163*, 164–7, 168, 181; Boucher Room 42, 76, 167; Fragonard Room 42, 76, 164, 166–7, 168, 181; Oval Room 168

Friedländer, Dr M. J. *59*
Friedsam, Michael 48
Fromentin, Eugène 32
Fry, Roger *108*

Gabriel, Jacques-Ange 14–15, 205
Gainsborough, Thomas 12, 15, 151, 169:
'The Blue Boy' 26, 125, 147–8, 150, 151, 152, *158*
'The Cottage Door' 147, 150
'Georgiana, Duchess of Devonshire' *153*
'Harvest Wagon' 111
'Mall in St James's Park' 43
'Mrs Peter Baker' 167
'Portrait of Mrs Elliott' 87
'Portrait of Mrs Lowndes-Stone' 15
Galerie des Glaces, La (Bernstein) 94
Gardner, Isabella Stewart (Mrs Jack) 71, 115, 116, *116*, 126, 137
Gary, Elbert H. 95, 111, 173
Gary Collection 168–9
Genauer, Emily 82–3
George V, King 23, 42, 57, 58, 166
Ghirlandaio 118:
'Francesco Sassetti and his Son Teodoro' *16*
Gilmore, Myron P. 139, 140
Giorgione 137, 138, 139:
'The Adoration of the Shepherds' *128*, 136–8, 205
Giotto 209:
'Madonna and Child' *186*
Giotto school 86
Girolamo da Cremona 110
Goldman, Henry 95, 173, *186*, 201, 205–6, 207
Göring, Hermann 212
Gould, George J. 47, *47*, 69, 70, 99
Gould, Marjorie 47
Goya 169:
'Don Manuel Osorio de Zuñiga' 93, *93*
Grand Tour 31
Graves, Algernon 157
Greene, Belle da Costa 35, *35*, 103
Grundy, Sydney 41
Guaranty Trust 99
Gulbenkian, Calouste S. 15–16, 20, *20*, 22

Hahn, Andrée Ledoux (Mrs Harry J.) 106–9, *106*
Hainauer Collection 60, 64, 104, 126
Hals, Frans 85, 86, 146:
'Balthasar Coymans' *161*
'Portrait of a Man' *153*, 167
Hamilton, Carl W. 211–12
Harbor Hill, Roslyn 88
Harding, Warren G. 183, 184, 197
Harkness, Edward S. 169
Harrison, Benjamin 163
Harvey, George 185
Hastings, Thomas *163*, 164, 165, 166, 167, 181

Hauser, Professor 59
Hearst, William Randolph 75, 78, *78*, 81, *82*, 95, 113, 181, 201, 208, *210*
Hearst, Mrs W. R. 77–8, 81, 82, *82*
Hendy, Sir Philip 137
Henner, J. J. 32
Henschel, Charles R. 110
Herald Tribune 25, 83
Hitler, Adolf 196, 212
Hogan, Frank J. 193, *193*, 195
Hogarth, William:
'The Graham Children' 151
Holbein, Hans 196, 207:
'Edward VI' *103*
'Mrs Pemberton' *54*
Holmes, Burton 202
Holmes, Sir Charles J. *108*, 150, 154, 155
Homestead Strike 163
Hooch, Pieter de:
'A Dutch Courtyard' *176*
Hoover, Herbert C. 197
Hopkins, Mark 184
Hoppner, John:
'Lady Louisa Manners' 60
Hoskins, John *54*
Houdon, J. A. 167–8, *169*, 203
House of Lords 37, 38
Hull 46, 47, 53
Humphrey, Ozias 157
Huntington, Arabella 22, 113, 143–50, *148*, 155, 206, 207
Huntington, Collis Potter 22, 47, 99, 143, 144, 145, *145*, 146, 173, 184, 206
Huntington, H. E. 22, 26, 31, 64, 75, 83, 93, 109, 125, 134, 143, 146, 147, *149*, 152, 154, 155–7, 171, 172, 173, *186*, 206
Huntington Collection *38*, *140*, *143*, 150, 152, 154, *158*, 161

Italian Painters of the Renaissance (Berenson) 117, 125
Iveagh, Edward Guinness, Lord 58–9

Jackson, Robert H. 193, 194, 195
James, William 114
Jefferson, Thomas 168
Johnson, John G. 86
Jones, Chauncey 69

Kann (Maurice) Collection 60, 64, 104
Kann (Rodolphe) Collection 60, 64, 104, *161*, 201
Kansas City, Nelson Gallery of Art 126
Kelly, Sir Gerald 75
Kenwood House 59
Kirstein, Lincoln 31
Kismet 9
Knoblock, Edward 9
Knoedler's 26, 31, 43, 87, 110, 158, 161, 162, 169, 174, 176, *186*, 191, 195
Kresge, S. S. 202

Kress, Rush 202
Kress, Samuel H. 11, 75, 83–4, 88, 93, 95, 128, 133, 138, 172, 173, 182, 198, 201–6, *204*, 207, 209, 212, 213
Kress Collection *26*, *32*, *83*, *88*, 98, 111, *128*, *186*, *191*

Lamérie, Paul de 42
Lanman, Charles Rockwell 115
Lasker, Albert D. 95
Laurana, Francesco da 167
Lavery, Lady 95, *96*
Lavery, Sir John 95, *105*
Lawrence, Sir Thomas 15, 109, 149:
'Pinkie' 26, 31, *38*, *41*
Lawsuits 10, 16, 65, 136; 'La Belle Ferronnière' case 106–9; Carl W. Hamilton case 211–12; Mellon tax case 192–5; Reynolds' 'Lavinia' case 154–5; 'Romney's Mrs Siddons and Miss Kemble' 156–7; smuggling case 66, 68–71; Youssoupoff/Widener case 16, 19–22
Lee, Vernon 138
Left Hand, Right Hand! (O. Sitwell) 34–5, 150
Lehman, Philip 173
Lehman, Robert 173
Leningrad, Hermitage 163, 186, 191, 196
Leonardo da Vinci 31, 161, 167, *194*:
'La Belle Ferronnière' 106, 107, *108*
'Benois Madonna' 161–2
'Mona Lisa' 106
Lewis, Isaac 65
Lewis, Oscar 143, 144, 146
Levy, L. S. *108*
Lippi, Filippino 118
Lippi, Filippo 196, 209:
'Madonna and Child' *186*, 211
Loeb, William, Jr 66
London 10, 53; British Museum 37, 154, Elgin Marbles gallery 105, *105*, 181; Claridge's 22, 97, 179, 182, 185, 213; Dulwich Museum 161; Leicester Galleries 34; National Gallery 24, 105, 113, 137, 150, 151, 154, 183, 198, 212; National Portrait Gallery 155; Tate Gallery *23*, 25, 105, *105*; Wallace Collection 25. *See also* Duveen's gallery
Long Island 76
Lords of Creation, The (F. L. Allen) 32
Lorenzetti, Pietro *118*
'Lorenzetti, Ugolino' *118*
Lurfrose *108*
Lusitania 68
Lynnewood Hall 22

McCall, George H. 83, 84
MacDonald, Ramsay 23, 24, 42, 113
McEldowney 99
Mackay, Clarence H. 88, 99, 113, 173, 208, 212
Mackay Collection *26*, *191*

Malvilan 165
Mantegna, Andrea 110, 126:
'Judith and Holofernes' *60*
Marie-Antoinette, Queen 166; style 167
Martini, Simone 26
Mary, Queen *23*, 57, 179
Masaccio 127
Master of the Castello Nativity 117:
'Profile Portrait of a Lady' *121*
Master of San Miniato 117
Maubert, Alexandre 164
Mayfair and Montmartre (Cochran revue) 151
Medici, Lorenzo de' *60*, 76, *88*
Meissonier, E. 32
Mellon, Andrew 9, 11, 22–3, 25, 26, 31, 34, 42, 43, 75, 77, 94, 95, 99, 100, 105, 111, 113, 126, 133, 135, 136, 137, 138, 144, *170*, 172, 173, 174, 176, 182, 183–4, *183*, 185, 186, 191–201, *193*, 202, 203, 207, 209, *211*
Mellon Collection 19, *26*, *31*, *32*, *41*, 98, *100*, 111, *161*, *176*, *179*, 197, *198*
Mellon Trust 192
Memmi, Lippo:
'St John the Baptist' *26*
Meppel 45
Michelangelo 139, 194
Miller, Gilbert 94, 95
Miller, Mrs Gilbert 93, 94
Millet, J. F. 32
Ministry of Marine, Paris 14–15; Duveen's copy, New York *14*, 15, 26, 38, 65, 95, 181, 205, 212. *See also* Duveen Brothers gallery
Monet, Claude 85
Morgan, H. W. 11
Morgan, J. Pierpont, Sr 11, 12, *35*, 47, 53, 56, 58, 64, 69, 70, *70*, 71, *72*, 75, 76, 83, 94, 99, 103, 105, 156, 157, 165, 171, 173, 184, 201, *211*
Morgan, J. P., Jr *172*
Morgan Book of Watches, The (Williamson) 76
Morgan Collection 55, 84–5
Morris, William 56
Munich 135, 212; Alte Pinakothek 196

Neeld, Sir Audley Dallas 43
New Republic 31
New York 10, 25, 48, 53, 58, 65, 144, 151, 196; Metropolitan Museum *16*, 38, 48, 137, 138, 151–2, 182; Pierpont Morgan Library 35. *See also* Duveen Brothers gallery
Nicholas I, Tsar of Russia 197
Nicholas II, Tsar of Russia 57
Nicolle *108*
Norris, George 197
North Italian Painters of the Renaissance (Berenson) 107
Norton, Charles Eliot 114, 115

Oliver, Isaac *54*
Oxford University Press 83

Pair of Spectacles, A (Grundy) 41

Palma Vecchio 137
Paris 9, 10, 12, 26, 147, 161, 167; Louvre 106, 107, 124. *See also* Duveen's gallery *and* Ministry of Marine
Parr's Bank 98
Pater, J. B:
'Procession of Italian Comedians' 167
'Village Orchestra' 167
Pembroke, Earl of *60*
Perugino 194
Philadelphia Museum of Art 164
Picasso, Pablo 33
Pichetto, Stephen S. 181–2
Picture restoring 181–2
Piero della Francesca 71:
'Crucifixion' 211, 212
Pisanello 26
Pittsburgh 75, 99, 125, 176, 183, 185, 197; Carnegie Institute 183
Pompadour, Mme de 82, 167; Mrs A. T. Dodge as 75
Pope, John Russell 181, 197, 198
Pope-Hennessy, John 140
Porter, Cole 151
Proust, Marcel 113

Raphael 11, 105, 139, 179, 194, 196, 209, 210:
'Alba Madonna' 191
'Cowper Madonna' 26, *63*, 72, 73, 194
'Saint George and the Dragon' 191
Raphael (after):
'Giuliano de' Medici, Duke of Nemours' *88*
Reinhardt, Max 104
Rembrandt 16, 19, 22, 59, 76, 85, 86, 95, 96, 146, 168, 194:
'Aristotle Contemplating the Bust of Homer' *201*
'Portrait of a Gentleman with a Tall Hat and Gloves' 16, *21*
'Portrait of a Lady with an Ostrich-Feather Fan' 16, *21*
'Young Man Seated at a Table' *19*, 25
Removille, Marquis de *81*
Reynolds, Sir Joshua, P.R.A. 15, 86, 154:
'Frances, Marchioness Camden' 152
'Georgina, Duchess of Devonshire' 152, *153*
'Lavinia, Countess Spencer' (Bessborough Coll.) 154
'Lavinia, Countess Spencer' (Spencer Coll.) 152
'Lavinia, Countess Spencer and her Son, Viscount Althorp' *143*, 152, *153*
'Mrs Siddons as the Tragic Muse' *140*, 147, 148, 149, 150
Riccio, Andrea 38
Rice, Mrs A. Hamilton 164, *165*
Riesener, J. H. 167
Ringling, John W. 37

Robbia, Luca della:
  'Madonna and Child' *53*
Roberts, William 155, 156, 157
Rockefeller, John D., Sr 173, *173*, *210*
Rockefeller, John D., Jr 13–14, 75, 77, 81,
  85, 95, 104, 173, *173*, 181, 201
Romney, George 156, 157, 158:
  'Portrait of Mrs Davenport' 31, *41*
'Romney':
  picture of Mrs Siddons and Miss Kemble
  155–7
Roosevelt, F. D. 197
Rose Terrace, Detroit *164*
Rossellino 78, 208
Rothschild, Baroness Mathilde de *81*
Royal Academy 157
Rubens, Peter Paul 37, 71, 86
Ruskin, John 38

Salamon, Elsie *see* Duveen, Elsie, Lady
Samuels, Mitchell 146
San Francisco 143, 144
San Marino, Pasadena 31, 145, 150, 154,
  171
Sansepolcro 212
Santayana, George 114
Sarasota, Ringling museum 37
Sargent, J. S. *23*, *116*
Sassetta 117, 212
Sassetta and assistant:
  'The Meeting of St Anthony and St Paul'
  128
Sassoon, Sir Edward Albert 126
Sassoon, Lady 126
Sassoon, Sir Philip 126
Scarborough 35
Scott, Stevenson 156, 174
Scott and Fowles 156
Seligman 174
Sergent, Réné 15
Sèvres 42
Shaw, George Bernard 117
Shearn, Clarence J. 19, 20, 21
Sheridan, Mrs Richard Brinsley 76
Simon, Sir John 156, 157
Sitwell, Sir Osbert 34–5, 36, 150, 193, 211
Sketch for a Self-Portrait (Berenson) 116, 124,
  138–9
Smith, Logan Pearsall 114
Smithson, James 201
Sparrow, John 140
Spencer, George John, 2nd Earl 154
Spencer, Charles Robert, 6th Earl 152
Spencer Collection *143*, 152, *152*

Stanchfield, John B. 68
Stanchfield and Levy 68, 69
Stanford, Leland 146, 184
Stanford, Mrs Leland 126
Stark, Freya 122–3
Stern and Corbitt 66, 68
Sterne, Maurice 86
Stillman, James 185
Stones of Venice, The (Ruskin) 38
Stories of an Expert (Williamson) 158
Stotesbury, E. T. 75, 77, 104, 173
Stotesbury, Mrs E. T. 103, 109, 164
Strachey, Lytton 34–5
Sulley, Arthur J. 19, 20

Talleyrand, Marquis de 110
Tapestries 55, 56, 58, 69, 71, 88, 167
Tatti, I *112*, 114, *116*, 117, 121, 139–40
Teerlinc, Lavinia *54*
Tennessee marble 197–8
Ter Borch, Gerard:
  'Curiosity' *81*
Thompson, John R. 96–7
Tintoretto 86, 139
Titanic 100
Titian 11, 71, 75, 136, 137, 138, 139, 169,
  194, 205:
  'Venus with a Mirror' 191
Toy, Crawford Howell 115
Trevor-Roper, Hugh 140
Troyon, Constant 32:
  'Coming from the Market' 32
Trumbauer, Horace 15, 181
Turner, J. M. W. 71

Ugolino da Siena *118*
Unamuno 122
Unforgotten Years (L. Pearsall Smith) 114

Valentiner, W. R. 84, *193*
Van der Weyden, Rogier 146:
  'Portrait of a Lady' *179*
Van Dyck, Anthony 10, 76:
  'Daedalus and Icarus' *153*
  'Queen Henrietta Maria and her Dwarf'
  78, *78*, 81
  'Sir John Suckling' 167
Van Eyck, Jan 194:
  'The Annunciation' 191, 194
Velásquez, Diego 86, 146, 167, 169:
  'The Infanta Maria Theresa' *88*, 110
  'Philip IV of Spain' 125, 161
Veneziano, Domenico *121*, 128:
  'St John in the Desert' 128, *134*

Venice 121, 122
Venturi, Professor Adolfo *108*
Vermeer, Jan 169:
  'Mistress and Maid' 167
  'The Smiling Girl' *198*
Verrocchio 13:
  bust of Cardinal Riario 71
  'Lorenzo de' Medici' *88*
Vickers 156–7
Victoria, Queen 22
Vigée-Lebrun, Elizabeth:
  'Madame Du Barry' *166*
Vittel 9, 12

Wachtmeister, Count Carl 25
Wachtmeister Rembrandt *19*, 25
Waldegrave, Ladies Maria and Horatia 157
Walker, John 114, 125, 198
Walpole, Horace 157, 158
Walters, Henry 181
Ward, T. Humphrey 155, 156, 157
Washington, George 168
Washington, D.C. 195, 196; Corcoran
  Gallery 191, 192; National Gallery 22, 32,
  111, 114, 128, 138, 171, 172, 173, 181, 186,
  191, 195, 197–202, 205, 207, 209, 212–13;
  Smithsonian Institution 201
Wendell, Marrett 115
Westminster, Hugh Richard Arthur Gros-
  venor, 2nd Duke of 147, *158*
Westminster Abbey 56
Wharton, Edith 113
Whitmarsh Hall, Chestnut Hill 77
Whitney, William C. 58, 75
Widener, George 100
Widener, Joseph E. 11, 16, 19–22, 134, 173,
  201, 208, 209
Widener. P. A. B. 47, 70, 73, 75, 85, 95, 99,
  100, 135, 171, 173, 201
Widener Collection *21*, *53*, *60*, *63*, 212–13
Wildenstein, Felix 41, 174
Williams, Charles 161
Williamson, George C. 76, 157, 158
Wingwood House, Bar Harbor 77
Winkler, John Kennedy 83
Winoga, Chestnut Hill 77
Woolworth, F. W. 202
Worsham, A. D. 143

Yarrington, Arabella Duval *see* Hunting-
  ton, Arabella
Yerkes, Charles 32
Youssoupoff, Prince Felix 16, 19–22, *20*

Ziem, F. 32